THE
HUMAN
DRAMA

World History:
From 1900 to the Present

Donald James Johnson
and Jean Elliott Johnson

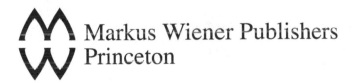 Markus Wiener Publishers
Princeton

For information, write to:
Markus Wiener Publishers
231 Nassau Street, Princeton, NJ 08542
www.markuswiener.com

Library of Congress Cataloging-in-Publication Data

LC Control No.: 00043628
LCCN Permalink: http://lccn.loc.gov/00043628
Type of Material: Book
Personal Name: Johnson, Jean, 1934–
Main Title: The human drama : world history / Jean Elliott Johnson
Donald James Johnson.
Contents: [4] From 1900 to the Present
Subjects: World history. Civilization — History.
LC Classification: D20
Published/Created: Princeton : Wiener, c2000–
Description: v. <3> : ill. ; 23 cm.
ISBN 978-1-55876-223-7 (Pbk. : alk. paper)
LOC Call Number: D20.J64 2000

Markus Wiener Publishers books are printed in the United States of America
on acid-free paper and meet the guidelines for permanence and durability
of the Committee on Production Guidelines for Book Longevity of the
Council on Library Resources.

THE HUMAN DRAMA

CONTENTS

ACT FOUR

The Cold War Era: Rebuilding and
Reordering the World, 1945–1960 109

We dedicate this volume to students everywhere who are studying world history and hope that their discovery of our common past will help motivate them to work to achieve stability, justice, and peace in our increasingly interdependent world.

ACKNOWLEDGEMENTS

Projects such as *The Human Drama* are made possible by the support, advice, and contributions of many. As in the earlier volumes in the series, we could not have completed this effort without the work of the many scholars and leaders of the world history movement who have contributed their vision of a history that actually includes the world. We continue to be indebted to the members of the World History Association whose continual search for new and exciting dimensions of world history has stimulated new approaches and helped make the latest research in the field available. We especially thank Jerry Bentley and the many contributors to the *Journal of World History* for their insightful and stimulating articles, many of which have shaped this volume of *The Human Drama*.

It is impossible for us to publicly thank all the teachers and colleagues who have shared their scholarship and insights and have read and critiqued *The Human Drama* and have used it in their classes. But we want to offer special thanks to the teachers who have encouraged us over the years, especially those who first adopted the series, and who urged us to write this final volume. David Burzillo and Ben Leeming of the Rivers School and Patience Berkman of the Newton Country Day School of the Sacred Heart were especially supportive in this regard. The encouragement of Susan Meeker and Joan Kenyon of Hunter College High School in New York, who used early versions of this volume before it was even published, motivated us to complete the series. Special thanks also go to Michele Forman, Middlebury Union High School in Vermont; Deborah Johnston, Lake Side School in Seattle, Washington; Lorne Swarthout, Berkeley Carroll School in New York City; Bram Hubbel, Friends Seminary in New York City; and Gwen Johnson, Scarsdale High School in New York. Each of them has continued to inspire and encourage us in countless ways.

We are especially indebted to Jennifer Laden-Murphy, District Supervisor for Secondary Social Studies, Harrison School District,

New York, and Robert Swacker, Dean at the Saint Ann's School in Brooklyn, New York, for their critical evaluation of this fourth volume of *The Human Drama*. Their diligent critiques and numerous suggestions significantly improved the work.

We especially are indebted to Markus Wiener for his continuing faith in *The Human Drama* and his willingness to publish all four volumes. We are also indebted to Janet Stern, our editor on this volume, and Susie Lorand, who is an amazing proofreader, fact checker, and editorial critic. Finally, we want to thank our daughter, Karen, for her ongoing encouragement and our sons Keith, for his expert technical support, and Mark, for the excellent maps and his aesthetic advice.

SETTING THE STAGE

This final volume of *The Human Drama* ushers in the twentieth century, the bloodiest in world history and arguably the century that saw more accelerated and profound changes than any previous era. The story begins with the growing number of European nation-states, in addition to Japan and the United States, competing for world power. The vicious competition among these nation-states as they form political alliances repeatedly threatens world peace. While the highly industrialized nations become increasingly more powerful, people living under the yoke of colonialism grow poorer and will attempt to strengthen their nationalist movements in an effort to rid their countries of foreign domination.

In the first half of the century new technology—both weapons of mass destruction and remarkable new medicines and inventions that help make life more enjoyable—will change the way we look at the world. New technologies, discoveries, and inventions will also challenge existing beliefs and values and usher in "an age of uncertainty." Capitalism, socialism, democracy, and fascism will compete for followers as democracy appears to be on the decline. At the same time, outbursts of popular unrest and violence, fueled as were the violent struggles recounted in the third volume by factors such as inequality, increasing colonization, rivalry among nation-states, and shifting alliances, will become more treacherous with the development of increasingly deadly weapons.

Beside examining how new nation-states compete for political power and prestige, we will consider how artists, writers, and theorists begin to offer challenging new ways of seeing, thinking, and believing, including concepts such as relativity and innovative interpretations of the human mind. Interest in human psychology and other social sciences will challenge earlier beliefs in progress and rationalism. During the same period, we will watch the world become involved in two great wars that set new records for death and destruction and result in the death of more civilians than combatants.

1

World War II will leave in its wake a period of reordering and reconstruction of the war-torn world, including the defeated Germany and Japan. Communist revolutions in the Soviet Union and China will challenge the world's democratic and capitalist societies. The United States and the Soviet Union will rise to the pinnacle of world power and enter into a forty-four year struggle called the "Cold War." This clash will involve two radically different ideologies: a democratic, free market system pitted against a socialist, totalitarian state. Each power will rely on a storehouse of nuclear weapons that can be delivered by rockets capable of destroying the other's major cities. The age of MAD (Mutually Assured Destruction) will bring with it an unsteady peace that allows Europe to recover and prosper.

Soon after World War II, millions of people throughout the colonized world will demand independence, and new nations will be formed out of the former colonized regions. This process, called *decolonization*, is the last major pattern in our consideration of the human drama, and it will result in a proliferation of new nations after 1945 that by 2010 will have numbered nearly two hundred.

We will continue to analyze the long-lasting legacy of the Industrial Revolution that resulted in the profound inequality between industrialized and nonindustrialized states which persists to our own time. We will also examine the various ways nations choose to modernize and compete in the emerging world system. Some will choose planned economies based on socialist and communist ideals; some will choose democracy and free market systems; others will combine features of both systems. With the collapse of the Soviet empire after 1989, as the United States emerged as the single most powerful nation, some of its leaders began to imagine the worldwide triumph of American democracy and free market capitalism.

Internally, nation-states will have to deal with an upsurge in identity politics as different racial, religious, ethnic, and language groups within their own societies strive for cultural autonomy and often threaten the authority of their governments. This search for identity can foster powerful religious zeal that sometimes expresses itself in violence and terrorist attacks.

By the beginning of the twenty-first century, globalization will have encircled the globe, making instant contact possible among most

of the world's people. We will analyze the process by which globalization brings a new prosperity to millions around the world but at the
same time fosters massive inequalities in other areas and fuels a
growing unrest among groups excluded from the new prosperity. We
will also explore how India and China have begun to move to the
forefront of a new global order, a place they had enjoyed before the
industrial age.

The new era of accelerated globalization offers powerful challenges to all of us, with its freer exchange of goods and instant communications. In this contemporary global age, you and your
classmates will have to compete with young people from around the
world, but you can also play a role in trying to achieve a more equi-
table and fair system for all the world's people.

History is created out of the everyday decisions and the actions of
billions of people just like you. The decisions you and your generation make will help shape not only the changes globalization will
bring but also the very direction human history will take in the future.
We sincerely hope that your study of world history will not only provide you with a deeper understanding of how things got the way they
are now but, more important, offer you insights and the courage to
creatively and compassionately face and shape the continuing drama
of human history.

ACT ONE

The World in Disorder, 1900–1940

The increasing power of nationalism that swept through both Europe and the colonial world in the nineteenth century brought unprecedented power and riches to some of the European nations as well as to the United States and Japan. These states were the main beneficiaries of the enormous increases in productivity and wealth brought about by industrialization and the machine age. The new wealth also fueled ever-expanding government bureaucracies that provided more and more benefits to the citizens in these societies, but at the same time the expanding national governments assumed more and more control over their citizens.

Nationalism also deepened. Success in building colonial empires brought with it international prestige and grudging respect for a nation's power. Those nations that were the chief beneficiaries of the industrial revolution and imperialism enjoyed unprecedented economic growth and prosperity. However, by the end of the nineteenth century, intensifying rivalries among these world powers led to a series of alliances that separated the industrial world into larger competitive groups that would prove nearly fatal to the world's nation-state system.

In the first quarter of the twentieth century, historians and other writers in the United States were beginning to use the term "the West." This term included many of the nations of Europe, plus the United States and other white settlements that were strong national states, highly industrialized, and were believed to share some common cultural traits, notably rationalism, republicanism, Christianity, and Enlightenment ideals. A key "Western" value was the belief in the superiority of its general culture and its right to control most of the people in the world.

Many colonized people thought this concept of the West was an arrogant excuse for colonialism. Outsiders also wondered how the West's common set of cultural values could lead to such bitter competition among its members. Many outside the West looked at the struggles in Europe and the United States during the age of intensive national rivalry as a "family struggle," or a European problem, rather than as World Wars. Interestingly, despite the bloody struggles within the West, the concept would only strengthen during the twentieth century.

SCENE ONE

TRAPPED IN ALLIANCES THAT LEAD TO WORLD WAR I

Setting the Stage

Competition among European nation-states, fueled by increasing national pride, pushed the European nation-states closer to armed conflict. To increase their security, several nations sought to create alliances with other states that guaranteed that if one of them was attacked, the others would immediately join the conflict. Great Britain tried to remain aloof from these foreign entanglements and instead maintain a balance of power among the various nations by backing one state and then another. But even Great Britain was drawn into the power struggles.

To add to the probability of armed conflict, many of the alliances the nations negotiated were secret. As a result, national leaders did not know who had joined their enemies and who was supporting their friends. By 1914, there were 20 nation-states in Europe and there was no higher authority to which a nation could take its grievances or ask for mediation, nor any formal institutions that could help solve disputes among the nations.

Industrialism added to the threat of war by providing increasingly deadly weapons and new forms of transportation and mass production that enabled rich nations to develop powerful armies and navies. At the same time, sophisticated financial institutions could arrange loans and other ways of financing wars. Without capital, there would have been no expansion of industry, and without industries, no nation-state could expect to be militarily successful no matter how brave its soldiers were. In order to maintain their military advantage, national governments borrowed huge sums of money to finance their military.

The modern national governments, using new banking systems, could rapidly redirect industrial output from peacetime consumer goods to wartime weapons. In addition, by 1900 the major European powers had some 4,500,000 soldiers ready to fight. These standing armies cost more than two billion dollars a year, an astronomical sum considering that the entire yearly budget of the United States at that time was about one billion dollars.

The Rocky Road to Conflict

With nationalism's growing importance, many minorities were living in nation-states that did not grant them full rights as citizens. Germany almost completely ignored the interests of its Polish and French citizens. Germany's effort to Germanize its diverse cultural groups antagonized those groups and created a counter-nationalism from within. As one Polish student said in a popular cartoon of the time, "If I say my prayers in German, my father beats me; if I say them in Polish, my teacher beats me; if I don't say them at all, my priest beats me."[1]

When Germany annexed the French provinces of Alsace-Lorraine in 1871, thousands of French fled from that area. Those who stayed faced German attempts to Germanize them. Speaking French was discouraged and German authorities censored French-language newspapers and magazines.

Russia also had problems with its minority populations. Following the German example of assimilation, the Russians required the Poles, Finns, and other non-Russian groups to speak Russian and give complete loyalty to their adopted nation. However, the minorities in both France and Russia clung to their languages and cultural heritages and continued to dream of independence.

In the Austro-Hungarian Empire, more than half the population was composed of Czechs, Slavs, Poles, Serbs, and Croats. The German Austrians and the Hungarian Magyars had made a deal in 1867 that each would dominate the many ethnic groups in their respective regions, but neither power was able to extinguish the fires of ethnic nationalism.

The many separate ethnic and religious groups in the Balkan states, which had broken away from the Ottoman Empire by 1900, soon posed a major challenge to the stability of Europe. These independent states, especially Serbia, tried to free their ethnic brothers and sisters who were still under Turkish rule. Serbian Slavs worked to form a pan-Slavic nation by uniting their fellow Slavs in Bosnia, Herzegovina, and Albania. Russia fully supported this pan-Slavic movement to gain close allies near the Black Sea, which it hoped would one day give it a warm-water route to the Mediterranean Sea. Russia's support of her "little Slavic Brothers" would soon lead to confrontation with the European powers.

By the 1800s, Jews in most European states had been accorded the same rights as other citizens. With these guaranteed rights and the increasingly cosmopolitan culture in the larger cities, large numbers of Jews became leaders in the arts, literature, music, and science. Some succeeded politically as well. Benjamin Disraeli, who was Jewish, served as the British prime minister several times during the reign of Queen Victoria.

But one of the tragic consequences of the increasing European nationalism was a virulent outbreak of anti-Semitism. Persecution of Jews in the late nineteenth century signaled a major change in European attitudes as anti-Semitism began to replace earlier cosmopolitanism. Instead of classifying Jews as one of the many ethnic groups, Europeans began to refer to Jews as a "race" of people. German political parties based solely on anti-Jewish propaganda attracted hundreds of thousands of votes. One successful German politician of the time preached, "The Jews are our calamity."[2]

French anti-Semitism boiled over in 1894 in the famous Dreyfus case. Alfred Dreyfus was the first Jewish officer to gain admission to the French general staff. But some of his aristocratic fellow soldiers falsely accused him of selling military secrets to France's enemies. In a show trial, Dreyfus was thrown out of the army and sent to Devil's Island, France's notorious prison. The shameful Dreyfus affair was enshrined in history when Émile Zola, one of France's greatest writers, sent a moving open letter, "J'accuse," to the French president in 1898. The president finally pardoned the innocent Dreyfus, but the memory of the affair lingered.

During the early years of the twentieth century, France had finally established what seemed to be a stable Third Republic. By 1914, France was rich and powerful, and, along with Great Britain, was one of Europe's leading democracies. Most French people had the right to vote, newspapers were free to print what they wanted, and a single set of laws was used to judge people. Despite an unwieldy proliferation of parties, prime ministers managed to form coalition governments and France looked forward to a glorious future as one of the world's major powers.

By 1914, the newly unified Germany had also gained prominence and stability. With a population of about 70 million, it was the largest state in Western Europe. Although liberal democracy had not found a hospitable home in Germany, the remarkable Chancellor Bismarck was leading a united and powerful nation. Prussia was the most powerful state in the new Germany and a succession of Hohenzollern kings were the heads of the German state. Supported by a mature industrial economy, Germany also maintained the largest and most efficient European army. Bismarck's major concern was protecting his fledgling state from a French effort to reacquire the territories it had lost in the 1871 Franco-Prussian War.

Bismarck's authoritarian nationalism tolerated no opposition. One of his most aggressive moves was against the Catholic Church, an institution he called the "black menace." The Church had won a large block of seats in the first Reichstag elections and those representatives worked to implement the Pope's goal of independence in matters such as opposing divorce, returning public education to the Church, and opposing "freedom of conscience." Bismarck vehemently opposed the Church on all these questions and also denounced its doctrine of "papal infallibility."

Under Bismarck's program against the Church, called the Civilization Struggle (*Kulturkampf*), the clergy was not to criticize the government and it was banned from teaching in the schools. Bismarck also expelled all Jesuits from Germany. He then had the Reichstag pass a series of laws that required all marriages to be civil ceremonies, ended government support for the Church and required all priests to study in state universities. The Pope immediately ordered all Catholics to disobey these laws. Bismarck responded by sending priests to prison, closing churches, and confiscating church property. In response, Catholics formed a Catholic Center Party that continued to gain voter support. Realizing the Church's power, Bismarck repealed most of the anti-Catholic laws and finally made peace with the Church.

Bismarck then set his sights on destroying the socialists, who he thought were another threat to German unity. The socialists had long opposed Bismarck's policies, especially his many wars. In an all-out attack on the Socialists in 1878, Bismarck closed 200 local socialist organizations, banned most socialist publications, and sent many socialist leaders to prison. He also clamped down on free speech and forbade public demonstrations. His goal of wiping away socialism also failed, but this time Bismarck had decided to co-opt much of the socialist program as his own.

Bismarck then sponsored very progressive legislation for workers, including insurance against illness, compensation for industrial accidents, and the first social security laws for retired workers in history. Despite these liberal welfare laws, his Social Democratic Party continued to grow.

In June, 1888, Kaiser Frederick was succeeded by his son William II. Unlike his father, who had left most of the governing to Chancellor Bismarck, the new kaiser was intent on ruling his country directly. He quickly fired Bismarck and took charge himself. William was well educated, curious, and ambitious. He employed all the symbols of German nationalism that would appeal to the German masses.

Germany in 1914 was a highly educated nation, with expansive industry, a sophisticated culture, and impressive military power, but its slow development of republican government had been crushed.

Turmoil in Russia

The flames that burst out in Russia in 1917 had been smoldering for many years. Under the oppressive rule of Czar Alexander III (1881–94), Russian peasants and workers had not achieved better working conditions nor a fair share of the economy. Instead, the czar had relied on his secret police to put down any potential opposition. Spies infiltrated many political organizations, radical professors were fired, freedom of the press was curtailed, and priests were encouraged to inform on church members. Most peasants thought the few reforms Alexander had instituted were inadequate. To make matters worse, in 1890 the peasants faced the worst famine in Russian history.

Alexander's policies also alienated the various minorities within the empire. His efforts to "Russify" all his subjects, including forcing everyone to accept the Russian Orthodox faith, caused Poles, Finns, and Ukrainians to resist. At a time when democratic ideology was spreading throughout Europe, Alexander still believed his authoritarian rule stood above any laws.

Nicholas II (1894–1917), Alexander III's successor, tried to follow his predecessor's policies, but he was a weak and indecisive leader who tended to react to events rather than shape them. As an ardent pan-Slavist, he was dedicated to supporting the interest of his fellow Slavs in the Balkans. However, he did further Russian industrialization and finance the building of railroads, including the famous Trans-Siberian Railroad, which in 1905 connected Moscow with the Pacific Ocean.

Labor unions were rapidly expanding in Russia, and Nicholas introduced labor reforms that limited working hours and provided modest insurance for workers. Despite the overwhelming peasant population, Russia was slowly becoming urbanized and industrialized. However, the czar's extremely heavy-handed dictatorial powers seriously impeded the normal growth of individual rights that had already taken place in most of Europe.

The frequent violent suppression of any threats to the czar's power motivated workers, peasants, and intellectuals to organize, often in secret. Members of a widespread coalition of small peasant-based reform groups became the "Social Revolutionaries." Throwing bombs was one of their chief methods of resistance.

For a brief time in 1898, two Marxist groups combined into the Russian Social Democratic Labor Party, but they soon split into two large factions. The liberal Mensheviks believed in basic democratic principles and that achieving a successful transition to socialism required mass democratic participation. They also wanted to include liberals and progressives in the revolutionary movement. The more radical group, the Bolsheviks, believed that a vanguard party composed of orthodox Marxists should act on behalf of the masses and lead a revolution. Vladimir Lenin (1870–1924) quickly became the leader of the Bolsheviks, and he was the chief architect of its strategy to gain control of Russia's whole revolutionary movement.

At the same time, another major political movement in Russia focused on the industrial workers. Also influenced by Marx, these revolutionaries believed that Russia had to move through feudalism and capitalism before it could achieve socialism.

Although the czar's authoritarian rule and general unrest continued to stimulate opposition, the Russo-Japanese War (1904) brought these radical groups together. The swift Japanese victory over Russian forces and the Japanese occupation of Russian land in Manchuria shocked the Russian people. How, many asked, could this small and insignificant Asian country so easily defeat their huge empire?

To pay for his disastrous war, the czar imposed higher taxes on the peasants. The ensuing critical shortages of food and basic commodities spurred even greater unrest. Reformers, including middle-class liberals who believed in a republican form of government, demanded the creation of a national assembly called the Duma. Many middle-class liberals joined the efforts to introduce a democratic government. However, the majority of Russians were unmoved by calls for either revolution or democracy.

Following its embarrassing loss to Japan in 1904, the next year Russians experienced a second shock. A peaceful march of factory workers and their wives and children approached the czar's Winter Palace in St. Petersburg, intent on giving the czar a petition of their grievances. The unarmed marchers were met with a hail of bullets that killed many of them. This event, known as "Bloody Sunday," mobilized the docile countryside into action. The czar fled from his palace, his legitimacy all but gone. Strikes and riots broke out all over the country and the peasants increased their occupation of large estates. The czar's modest attempts to grant some democratic reforms to address the myriad problems facing their country had completely failed, and the Bolsheviks chose to remain outside the parliamentary system.

Meanwhile, in St. Petersburg, a young Menshevik named Leon Trotsky (1877–1940) was organizing a council of workers known as a *soviet*. In October 1905, the czar agreed to form a Duma, but it was soon dominated by the conservative landholders, nobles, and other conservatives who formed a party called the Octoberists. The Duma was doomed from the beginning because the Social Revolutionaries and Social Democrats boycotted it. Soon after, the czar dissolved the Duma.

The efforts at reform and the continued agitations of many groups dragged on without resolution. Attempts to establish a republican constitutional democracy had failed. By 1916, these peasant groups were seizing lands from their landlords and setting up communal farms called *mirs* where land was held and worked in common. Following Marx's teaching, the Social Revolutionaries wanted to end private ownership of land and turn most of Russia's farmland into communal holdings.

By 1917 Russia had become partially industrialized and the professional class of writers, lawyers, doctors, teachers, and journalists had increased significantly. But the czars clung to their authoritarian style of government while the Russian peasants were growing poorer; most had no land of their own.

Is the World on the Brink of War?

If the European nation-states had been struggling to build "pure" nations, clearly, by 1914, the European empires were having far more trouble holding their pluralist communities together. The Ottoman Empire was slowly disintegrating. The emperor and his advisors could find no adequate way to address the militant nationalism that was fueling incipient revolts in its Balkan and North African provinces. They were having trouble just holding their empire together, often by sheer force. The Russian Duma also was not effective in dealing with these issues. The Austro-Hungarian Empire could not satisfy the nationalist movements within its borders. All three of these empires seemed to be waiting for the spark that would ignite their ethnic and class discontents into a raging fire.

After the 1848 revolutions that had swept Europe, many European nation-states had established constitutional governments with viable legislatures. Scandinavians had succeeded in establishing republican governments. Norway peacefully separated from Sweden in 1906 and created the most democratic monarchy in Europe. In Norway, women were given the right to vote, and all Norwegians had the same basic rights as those won in the American and French revolutions. Sweden and Denmark also formed democratic monarchies and the Social Democrats gained more power.

At the start of the twentieth century, Great Britain was still

Europe's most stable democracy. Its industrial might, vast colonial empire, and the world's largest and best-equipped navy made Britain the most powerful nation in the world. It generally did not join alliances with other powers. If threats appeared to upset the unstable balance of power in Europe, leaders used British power to restore the balance. This long period from 1815 to 1914 is often called the Pax Britannica. It ended in the frantic scramble for political and military superiority.

Although British power was impressive, it was being challenged from several directions. Russia posed serious threats to British interests in Afghanistan and the Balkans and was competing for control of the Bosporus—all of which potentially jeopardized England's lifelines to India. France rivaled Britain in Africa as the contest for colonies there continued. Facing these political realities, Great Britain attempted to forge closer relations with Germany. The Germans, concluding that the British overtures originated from Britain's weakness, rebuffed the offers.

Germany turned instead to Russia and Austria-Hungary and formed the Three Emperors' League in 1873. However, by 1878, Germany abandoned Russia, weakening the alliance. In 1882, Germany invited Italy to join it and Austria in the Triple Alliance, which called for these three nations to pledge their military support if any of them was attacked. For example, if the French made war against Germany or Italy, Austria would fight France.

In 1881, Bismarck was able to mollify Russia and renew the Three Emperors' League, giving Germany a strong hand to play in the competition for world power. But Germany's efforts to strengthen its power rang alarm bells in Britain. Realizing reluctantly that Germany was a real competitor, the British decided to end its centuries-old conflict with France. In 1902, it formed the Entente Cordiale, an alliance that included England, France, and Japan. In the meantime, Italy, uneasy about joining an alliance that included Austria (which held land that the Italians thought was rightfully their own), made overtures to Great Britain and France.

These two powerful alliances—the Entente Cordiale and the Triple Alliance—greatly enhanced the threat of a major war. Each challenged the others' interests to see how far they could go before evoking a response. At the same time, Germany worried that it was increasingly surrounded by hostile alliances and could not convince any major power except Austria to join its cause.

In 1905 France tried to expand its influence in Morocco. Germany, seizing the opportunity to weaken France, championed Moroccan independence. In the face of German support for Morocco, France ended its bid to extend its African empire. Italy finally joined England and France. Germany was left with only Austria as a reliable ally. With increasing paranoia, Germany faced an uncertain future.

The Balkans

The uneasy balance of power found its greatest challenge in the contest for influence in the newly formed Balkan states, most of which had been part of the Ottoman Empire. Germany and Austria were adamantly opposed to Russian expansion into that region and feared that a pan-Slavic movement would enhance Russian influence. Germany wanted to expand its economic influence in the Balkans; Austria feared that a Russian-backed alliance of Slavs would threaten its eastern borders.

Austria angered Serbia in 1908 by annexing Bosnia-Herzegovina. Austria had also promised Russia access to the Bosporus, but later went back on that bargain. So far, the Triple Alliance of Germany, Italy and Austria was coming out ahead. Russia had been greatly weakened by its defeat in the Russo-Japanese war, and England and France decided not to support the Russian and Serbian demands against Austria.

In 1912 the Balkan states joined in the Balkan Alliance, a third alliance led by Greece and Bulgaria that sought to dislodge the Ottoman Empire completely from the Balkans. Members of this alliance attacked the Ottomans in 1912, ending Ottoman control in the region. With new lands to fight over, Serbia moved to annex the newly freed Albania. Fearing Serbian expansion, Austria would not allow Serbia to take over Albania. This move, together with the demands for land of several other Balkan states, led to a second Balkan war. Finally, in 1913, Austria succeeded in undoing Serbia's occupation of Albania.

The Balkan anxieties intensified with the growing tensions

between Austria and Serbia. Austria was adamant about stopping Serbian advances and Serbia was equally determined to expand its influence among the Balkan Slavs. Groups of Serb zealots organized the Black Hand Society that wanted to unite all Serbs, using terrorist tactics if necessary. Germany, Austria's ally, then sided with Turkey and offered military assistance to quell the Balkan uprisings. France, fearing a growing German influence in the unstable region then joined with Russia to reduce Germany's influence in the Balkans.

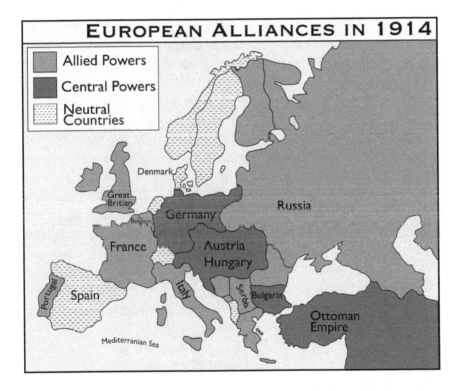

EUROPEAN ALLIANCES IN 1914

Allied Powers

Central Powers

Neutral Countries

Denmark

Great Britian

Belgium

Germany

Russia

France

Austria Hungary

Portugal

Spain

Italy

Serbia

Bulgaria

Ottoman Empire

Mediterranean Sea

With most of the European powers entangled in these two alliances—the Balkan Alliance and the Triple Alliance—even a small incident could spark an all-out war, if all countries honored their commitments. That fatal event came in Sarajevo on June 28, 1914, when a young, avid supporter of Greater Serbia shot and killed Archduke Ferdinand, the heir to the Austrian throne. War became more

probable when the German government offered unqualified support
for any action that Austria-Hungary might undertake against Serbia
following the assassination of Archduke Ferdinand.

Austria sent the Serbian government a list of harsh demands. It
ordered Serbia to stop all anti-Austrian activities and to remove all
military personnel involved in attacks on Austria. Serbia responded
immediately, but only accepted two of the demands. Germany,
Britain, Austria, and France all tried to calm the Serbian crisis and
avoid a general war, but by this time, diplomatic efforts were too little
and too late.

On July 27, 1914, Austria invaded Serbia. Germany was opposed
to this invasion, but while German diplomats were desperately trying
to convince Austria to avoid war, the Russian government called for a
mobilization for war. Concerned that Germany would face war with
both Russia and France, German officials decided to make a lightning
attack on France and then, after crushing France, to make a more pro-
tracted war against Russia.

When Germany declared war on both France and Russia in early
August, Britain was caught in a dilemma. Technically Great Britain
was not obligated to send military aid to either Russia or France or to
join the war on their behalf. However, when Germany notified Belgium that they would use it as a highway so the German armies could
invade France, Great Britain also declared war on Germany and Austria. The "Great War," the bloodiest and most costly war in human
history until that time, was underway. The next month Japan joined
the British, French, and Russian alliance and Turkey joined forces
with Germany.

The Great War

Europe's progress toward republican government and the economic
advances and creativity that had marked the nineteenth century came
to a sudden halt in 1914. This was a total war, fought on land, sea,
and, for the first time, in the air. It would involve armies and investments of money unequalled in history. Its participants would include
not just the armed forces but also civilians who would have to sacrifice their standards of living and help build munitions, ships, tanks,
and submarines. The war would bring unparalleled destruction and

death to millions of people. No wonder many Europeans believed it would be the war that would end all wars.

By 1914, both sides had access to new and more deadly weapons. The airplane, used for the first time, could drop explosives all along the enemy's lines. The British tank was a frightening new, seemingly impenetrable, vehicle. The wide use of submarines, especially by the Germans, meant no large ship was safe on the high seas. Newly designed machine guns could cut down charging infantrymen like reapers mowing wheat. Rapidly repeating rifles gave soldiers an effective killing weapon not known earlier. The number of combatant nations and the size of the armies and navies had grown dramatically as well.

Twenty-seven nations participated in World War I. The Central Powers that included Germany, Austria, Bulgaria, and Turkey brought 21 million men under arms. Italy did not honor its commitment to support Germany and waited until 1915 to join the Allies. The Allied forces, which included Great Britain, France, Russia, Japan, and ultimately the United States, raised an astounding 40 million troops, including 12 million Russians. Cannons that could fire missiles 75 miles, poison gas, and land mines were also used for the first time. New gasoline- and diesel-powered engines moved thousands of trucks, ambulances, airplanes, and dirigibles. The German generals and their highly disciplined armies gave the Central Powers a distinct advantage. However, the Allies had more troops, a greater manufacturing capacity, and more money.

At the beginning of the war, both sides thought they could make a fast major strike and quickly end the war. The Allies planned to send the Russians to attack Prussia and the French to attack Alsace, an area where many French lived. The Germans planned to attack France through Belgium with one army and send another to Alsace-Lorraine.

At first the German armies moved rapidly, almost reaching Paris by September. The German command then diverted troops to fight Russia, making a French counterattack possible. In the five-day battle at the Marne, each army tried to outflank the other until they had drawn a rough line from Switzerland to the English Channel. Since neither force was winning, both the French and German armies dug

Trench warfare, World War I

hundreds of miles of trenches in which their soldiers took cover. Occasionally they mounted a charge against the other entrenched forces, only to be thrown back to their respective trenches. Instead of the lightning-fast war both sides had envisioned, the troops spent years in the trenches, moving back and forth only a few miles.

On the Russian front, the German armies pounded the ill-equipped Russians and penetrated deep into Poland. Meanwhile, a Churchill-sponsored English plan to free the Dardanelles from Turkish control turned into a disaster. The Australian and New Zealand forces that landed at Gallipoli in April 1915 suffered enormous losses and the survivors were bogged down for months in a small area on the beaches until January 1916, when they finally surrendered.

In the summer of 1916, to end the stalemate on the Western front, the Germans tried to break through the French lines at Verdun, sending wave after wave of soldiers, but the French did not budge. By the time the Germans abandoned their Verdun offensive, 700,000 French and Germans soldiers had been either killed or wounded.

Encouraged by the French defense at Verdun, in July the British decided to climb out of their trenches and attack the German forces at the Somme River. Despite extraordinary losses, the British kept up their offensive until October, when slashing rains turned the battlefield into deep mud. At the Battle of the Somme, the British suffered 400,000, the French 200,000 casualties, and the Germans 500,000, all over a few square miles of land. After these two major offensives, both sides knew it would be almost impossible to penetrate their enemies' trench lines.

In 1916, the only real naval battle of the war gave the British navy command of the seas and enabled the British to tighten their blockade against Germany. By 1917, both sides were having trouble keeping up public support for the war in spite of vicious propaganda. Two cruel years of fighting had decided nothing. The Allied armies, especially the French, were at their breaking point. Large numbers of French soldiers began to desert and hundreds of thousands of troops had already been lost.

In three months during 1915, German submarines sank 470 British ships.[3] The British decided to blockade German ships but allow non-military shipping to continue. On May 7, 1915, the Lusitania, a British passenger ship sailing from the United States to England, was torpedoed off the Irish coast. Over a thousand passengers died as the ship sank, including 128 Americans.

While all this fighting was going on, the United States had claimed it was neutral. It demanded that the seas be open to all ships and free for trade with all sides. Officially just a bystander, President Wilson, a strong believer in the superiority of the Anglo-Saxon "race," believed the war was a contest for the future of Western civilization, and he was moving closer to joining the Allied side.

Although the Lusitania was almost certainly carrying ammunition and other military supplies for the English, Wilson used its sinking to incite American hostility against the Germans. Finally, on April 6, 1917, Wilson declared war against the Central Powers, claiming that the United States was entering the war in order to "make the world safe for democracy." The French and English troops enthusiastically welcomed the American forces.

In 1917, the war dramatically changed on another front. In November, Lenin and the Communists had staged a successful revolution in Russia. With this dramatic victory at home, Lenin withdrew Russian troops from the war and was willing to surrender 500,000 square miles of territory where 66 million Russians lived.

Facing what they saw as their last opportunity for victory, the Germans launched one more offensive against the very weary French army on the western front. But this time the British and French forces, augmented by fresh American troops, stopped the German advance. Heartened by this success, the Allied armies went on the offensive. On November 11, 1917, both sides declared an armistice and the "war to end all wars" was over.

THE VERSAILLES PEACE CONFERENCE AND POSTWAR EUROPE

Setting the Stage

Europe emerged from the Great War with a far different outlook than the relatively optimistic worldview with which it had entered this "war to end all wars," which had killed nine million and wounded another twenty-two million on the battlefields. Beyond military losses, approximately ten million civilians had also died. The war cost more money—$186 billion in direct costs and another $151 billion in indirect costs—than any previous war in history.[4] In the postwar atmosphere, many people in both the victorious and the defeated nations questioned the assumption of historic progress and the ability of humans to act rationally.

The world leaders who gathered in Versailles at the end of the Great War to begin the peace process faced numerous challenges. It soon became apparent that the leaders did not agree on what goals to pursue, what the appropriate punishments for Germany should be, or how to compensate the victorious nations for all their losses. Once the final treaty was signed, both the victorious and the defeated nations began the arduous task of rebuilding.

Debates over the Versailles Treaty

From the beginning of the negotiations, the United States, France, and Britain were far apart in how they wanted to deal with the defeated Germany. The U.S. President, Woodrow Wilson, came to the table with a set of principles that sought to guarantee a lasting peace. Britain and France came as exhausted victors demanding payment for their losses and punishment for the defeated Germans.

Wilson offered an idealistic set of principles called the "Fourteen Points." Among his "Points" were open diplomacy instead of secret alliances, free trade, reduction of armaments, and self-determination for colonial peoples and for people in Austria-Hungary, the Ottoman

Empire, and Poland. He also called for an international organization that would guarantee all nations' political independence and territorial integrity. The Germans welcomed Wilson's Fourteen Points; however, their idealism struck France and Great Britain not only as naïve, but as in no way compensating them for all the lives and money they had lost.

Wilson's main goal was the formation of a League of Nations, an international organization whose major objective would be to prevent future wars and ensure stability and peace. Even though they were not enthusiastic about the proposed League, the idea gained enough support from France and Britain to become a reality. The League had a general assembly where nations could discuss their differences and reach peaceful settlements. Member nations could impose sanctions on the nations they deemed aggressors and, as a last resort, they could use force to impose their decisions. Unfortunately, the League had no army to enforce its decisions and it required the cooperation of a majority of its members even to impose sanctions.

One of the most contentious issues the Versailles Peace Conference faced was whether to impose large indemnities on Germany. The victorious allies believed that Germany, having lost the war, must have been the most responsible for launching the conflict. Therefore, they reasoned, Germany should now pay the victors for some of the losses it had inflicted on them.

The secret treaties made during the war also complicated the peace process. England and France had promised Japan some land in China. Although Britain had promised the Arabs independence once the Ottomans were defeated, France and Britain had already agreed to share control of the newly freed Arabs. Further, Britain had promised the Jews a homeland in Palestine even though they had already assured the Palestinians that they would become independent. Wilson seemed baffled when these secret agreements were made public, even though most of these treaties had already been reported in American newspapers.

The Treaty of Versailles that was written and adopted by the Big Three nations called for the creation of the League of Nations that Wilson wanted. However, the rest of the treaty and the earlier secret treaties among the Europeans were far removed from the idealism of

Wilson's Fourteen Points. The boundaries of Germany were completely redrawn. The treaty took about 25,000 square miles of German land with about 6 million people and gave it to other nations.
The League was to administer Danzig as a free city. The League was
also to administer the coal-rich Saar Basin.

The most humiliating portion of the treaty for Germany was the
"War Guilt Clause." This clause forced Germany to accept complete
responsibility for initiating World War I. The Treaty also inflicted
severe punishment on Germany, setting the stage for renewed international tensions. As the English economist John Maynard Keynes
warned in 1919:

> The Treaty includes no provisions for the economic
> rehabilitation of Europe,—nothing to make the de-
> feated Central Empires into good neighbours, noth-
> ing to stabilize the new States of Europe, nothing to
> reclaim Russia; nor does it promote in any way a
> compact of economic solidarity among the Allies
> themselves; no arrangement was reached at Paris
> for restoring the disordered finances of France and
> Italy, or to adjust the systems of the Old World and
> the new.[5]

In addition, the treaty severely punished Germany by imposing reparations (payments for starting the war). Initially, France demanded
$200 billion in payments. Meanwhile, Germany would be required to
make annual payments to the victors that would total $5 billion by
1921. After much negotiation, the allies agreed on a final figure of
about $32 billion (roughly equivalent to $393.6 billion as of 2005).
Many economists thought this amount was far too much, and later
that year, it was reduced to about half that amount. This sum still
seemed outrageous to most German observers and would have
required Germany to make payments until 1984.

Besides cash payments, Germany was forced to give the allies all
its merchant ships that weighed more than 1,600 tons and half of
those weighing 1,000 to 1,600 tons. In addition, Germany was to
build the Allies a million tons of new shipping. Further, the Allies

could take large amounts of coal, machinery, tools, and other equipment from Germany. The German army would be reduced to only 100,000 men, its navy was to be drastically limited, and it was forbidden to have any war planes. Although the Kaiser, who had escaped to Holland, was allowed to stay in Holland, some 800 German officials were put on trial for alleged war atrocities.

This harsh treaty left Germany a crippled nation and radically reduced its military, economic, and international status. Rather than an armistice that would have given Germany the chance to recover and rebuild its economy, the defeated Germans went home bitter, perhaps to dream of revenge.

Western Society after World War I

Most of the people in the victorious nations could not immediately forget the ravages of war. Great Britain was willing to work for prosperity throughout Europe, but the other nations were not so forgiving. Italy was upset that even though it had joined the Allies, it was not given its share of the spoils. The United States adopted a decidedly isolationist policy and refused to join the League of Nations, even though it had been President Wilson's idea in the first place. France, believing the U.S. and Britain had reneged on their earlier promise to guarantee France's territorial integrity, sought new allies. Initially only Poland would join France in a mutual defense pact; later Romania and Yugoslavia also joined.

Germany was the most devastated of the war-torn nations. Besides losing millions of lives, at the war's end the German people were poverty-stricken and left with little food. This mighty European nation was now a second-class power that was to make impossible payments to the victors. In 1921, when Germany made a $250 million down payment on the reparation, its economy faced an economic crisis.

France was not much better off. Angered by the small effort Germany seemed to be making to pay its debts, France insisted that German workers in the Ruhr mines work for France. When these workers went on strike, France occupied the Ruhr and made it an independent "republic."

The loss of the Ruhr was not only a serious blow to Germany's pride, it also plunged the country into an even more severe recession.

Inflation reached ridiculous levels. In January 1923, it took 8,695 German marks to buy one American dollar. By the next November, it required 6,666,666,666,667 marks to equal a dollar.[6] By 1923, the former allies were angry with one another. Britain was furious at France for occupying the Ruhr and the United States had all but withdrawn from the international system altogether.

By 1925, the victorious allies, recognizing the futility of punishing Germany, ceased to demand reparations and began to try to patch up their many differences. France, Great Britain, and Italy agreed to respect the existing French-German and German-Belgian borders. These successful first steps led to a larger conference at Lacarno, Switzerland, in 1925 which included Germany.

The Lacarno Conference produced five Accords. The most important one promised that Germany, Great Britain, Belgium, France, and Italy would guarantee the existing frontiers along the Rhine. They also pledged that they would not go to war against one another. Following the Lacarno Accords, the major nations signed various treaties that were designed to end war as a legitimate means of settling disputes. Germany was also permitted to join the League of Nations. However, underneath the apparent agreements and the increasing prosperity, the traditional national rivalries continued unabated.

The Roaring Twenties in the West

During the 1920s, most of the industrialized nations retreated from active involvement in international affairs. Many people made a deliberate attempt to forget the tragedies World War I had caused and tried to find ways to enjoy life without worrying about world affairs. In both the United States and Europe, nightclubs flourished and alcohol flowed freely, perhaps in an effort to dull people's memories. John Maynard Keynes wrote, "Our power of feeling or caring beyond the immediate questions of our own material well-being is temporarily eclipsed. . . . We have been moved already beyond endurance, and need rest."[7] This period became known as the "Roaring Twenties."

After centuries of struggle, women in Great Britain and Germany won the right to vote in 1918 and in the United States in 1919. At the same time, many more women were joining the workforce, taking jobs such as clerks, secretaries and teachers.

Prior to World War I, a popular female symbol in the United States had been the Gibson Girl. She was pictured with long, upswept hair, dressed in a long skirt and a high-collared blouse. The 1920s produced the "flapper." One scholar explained, "In the 1920s, a new woman was born. She smoked, drank, danced, and voted. She cut her hair, wore make-up, and went to petting parties. She was giddy and took risks. She was a flapper."[8]

Although the flapper originated in Britain, she soon came to symbolize women in the United States and Europe as well. F. Scott Fitzgerald described her as "lovely, expensive, and about nineteen." In dance halls and living rooms, flappers danced the Charleston, the Black Bottom, the Shimmy, and the Tango.

The twenties were also known as the "Jazz Age," because of the popularity of African-American music that was not only played by African-Americans, but also attracted a large number of white musicians. When Louis Armstrong and many others moved from New Orleans to Chicago, they brought jazz with them. Armstrong, Jelly Roll Morton, and Duke Ellington were among the most popular jazz musicians. The phonograph record helped spread jazz and other popular music. Since the 1920s, jazz has become a worldwide and consistently popular music.

Class Discontents

One of the major difficulties the world faced after World War I was the fact that increasing industrialization was not bringing the workers the prosperity they believed was their due. Harsh working conditions, like those that Charles Dickens had described in his novels, were still common in crowded urban slums. The feeling of exploitation stimulated workers and farmers to organize on their own behalf.

Most political parties in Britain and the United States still believed that democracy was the best solution for the world's ills. In the late nineteenth century, reformers in both nations had worked to expand democratic participation to workers and farmers and, by 1919, to women as well. At the same time, the Social Gospel movement among Protestants and the Catholic Workers' movement brought the considerable moral authority of their churches to the cause of better treatment for workers. Even so, during the 1920s and 30s there were increasing challenges to the democratic governments in Great Britain, France, and the United States.

Both England and France had huge debts as a result of the war. France deflated its currency in an attempt to promote more exports. When this policy resulted in lowering workers' wages, the French government did little to help them. As a result, millions of French workers turned to socialism, and sharp class conflicts began to threaten the stability of its democratic government. Between 1919 and 1939, France suffered through forty changes of governments.

Great Britain also embraced a deflationary policy as a way to stimulate its exports, but this policy resulted in a nationwide general strike. Fearing a genuine worker revolt, many middle-class British subjects turned against labor. In spite of the stark class divisions this created, the British parliamentary system was sturdy enough to survive.

As one means of paying down the enormous war debts, nations imposed tariffs on imports. Even Great Britain, the chief supporter of free trade, imposed tariff barriers in 1930. The nations created from the former Austro-Hungarian Empire began to impose tariffs as well. As a result, world trade plunged and in 1929 the U.S. stock market crashed. Within a few years after the crash, world trade had diminished by more than 60 percent.

FUNDAMENTAL CHALLENGES TO THE CAPITALIST, DEMOCRATIC MODEL

Setting the Stage

At the beginning of the twentieth century, Russia, geographically the largest nation in the world, and China, the world's most populated nation, both faced growing unrest as peasants and workers rose in protest. These increasingly violent reactions broke out as the industrialized nations steadily increased their power. As millions of Russians and Chinese witnessed the growing gaps in wealth between their own societies and those of the Europeans, Americans, and Japanese, they sought leaders who could lead them out of poverty.

As these two giant nations both lagged far behind the industrial powers of the West, both Russia and China struggled to find ways to provide their massive peasant populations the basic necessities of life. Land reform was urgently needed. However, land reform alone was not enough to bring the two societies into the modern world. They would have to industrialize and find ways to balance the commitment to peasant concerns and, at the same time, find large amounts of capital to invest in building industries and financial institutions.

China, and to a lesser extent Russia, also faced the daunting problem of finding ways to secure their nations' sovereignty and eliminate foreign control of their lands and finances. These goals led to revolutionary movements that were highly nationalistic, especially in China. The combination of the intense desire for greater economic equality and intense nationalism proved to be the engines of their two great revolutions, both of which posed an enormous threat to Western-style republicanism.

Russians Create the USSR and Follow Communist Leaders

Russian participation in World War I was the last blow to Czarist totalitarianism. The Russian forces were ill equipped and poorly clothed and fed, and they suffered untold casualties. The mass desertion of Russian troops in 1917 was the beginning of a revolution that would radically change Russia.

In January 1917, strikers and demonstrators in major cities joined together to form the workers' and soldiers' soviets that Trotsky had been advocating. When the rebels demanded the czar resign, he and his advisors offered little resistance. Quickly leaders of the various soviets formed a provisional government, and soviets all over the country easily took control of local governments. The peasants demanded and seized land from the large estates, and the workers demanded a decent standard of living.

Lenin, who had remained outside the efforts at democratic reform, was in exile. He thought the war might be a catalyst for his taking over the various socialist and democratic movements. Lenin's party established a socialist government under Bolshevik control. His goal was to take over all the means of production and run the economy for everyone's benefit, especially the workers and peasants. In February 1917, Lenin and the soviets, with their 10,000 members, proclaimed the creation of the Union of Soviet Socialist Republics.

Eight months later, 200,000 people had joined Lenin's party. However, it had virtually no control over the hundreds of small soviets that were governing many towns and cities, or over the peasants who continued seizing land.

Lenin decided to make Petrograd, where a significant number of his party members lived, his power base. Instead of participating in the elections for the new Constituent Assembly, the Bolsheviks decided to break up the assembly when it met. Gradually the Bolsheviks formed an army and fought the White Russians, a confederacy of pro-Czarists, aristocrats, and foreign supporters from Europe and the United States.

The civil war between the Soviets and the White Russians lasted from 1917 until the Whites were all defeated in 1923. The Bolsheviks attracted 4 million to fight in their army. Even though France, Britain, Japan, and the United States raised armies to fight with the White Russians, the volunteer Soviet army of workers and peasants ultimately prevailed. The first successful Marxist socialist party in history now controlled Russia and renamed the country the Union of Soviet Socialist Republics.

While fighting the civil war, Lenin, in 1922, had introduced the New Economic Policy (NEP) that attempted to create a mixed economy of private enterprise and state controls. The NEP permitted shops and other small businesses to make a profit. The central government controlled banks, large industries, and international trade. Much of the land that peasants had confiscated from the aristocrats remained as private or cooperative land.

The impact of the Soviet Revolution around the world was sudden and profound. Millions of restless peasants in countries from Vietnam to Algeria were inspired by Lenin's example, and the Soviet Union became a model for nationalist movements throughout the colonial world. The European and American governments and their ruling elites feared their worst nightmares were coming true. European politicians began to label Russia's newly installed communist government "a specter haunting Europe." The growing power of Bolshevism and communism would eventually so frighten Europeans that many would opt for various types of authoritarian rule.

Stalin Takes Control

Lenin controlled the Soviet Union until 1924. When he died, Joseph Stalin (1879–1953) won the struggle for power and by 1927, he was Russia's most powerful leader. Stalin backed his policies with brutal force. He had almost absolute power to reshape Russian society and he purged those who opposed him, such as Leon Trotsky, who fled to Mexico and was assassinated there in 1940 by Stalin's agents. Stalin gained support by preaching that the capitalist imperialists were encircling the Soviet Union and the only way to repel this threat was for the Soviet Union to industrialize. He promised to narrow the gap between the industrialized economies and the Soviet Union within 10 years.

Ending Lenin's New Economic Policy, Stalin collectivized agriculture and nationalized industry. His efforts required a massive bureaucracy that included the KGB, a sophisticated secret police agency that spied on potential enemies and killed anyone suspected of disloyalty. The KGB also sent thousands of political prisoners to Siberian labor camps where many died premature deaths.

In the depths of the worldwide depression during the 1930s, Stalin introduced the Gosplan (State General Planning Commission) that

concentrated most re-
sources and manpower on
industrializing the econ-
omy. He focused on in-
dustrialization and the
collectivization of farm-
lands. His efforts to industrialize the Soviet Union
were largely successful,
but they resulted in great
suffering and loss of
human life.

The collectivization of
agriculture did not work
well, in part because the

Lenin and Stalin

government invested very little in modernizing farming. Moreover,
government food requisitioning intensified, especially in the main
grain-producing regions. Upon joining collective farms called
kolkhozes, peasants had to give up their own plots of land and other
property. Kolkhoz produce was sold to the state for the low price the
state had set. In many cases peasants bitterly opposed this process
and often slaughtered their animals rather than give them to these collective farms. By 1936, about 90% of Soviet agriculture was collectivized, but it led to a catastrophic drop in farming productivity.

During this process, the richer peasants, called *kulaks*, were
forcibly resettled to Siberia and the Russian Far North. In reality, just
about anyone who opposed collectivization was labeled a kulak.
Stalin's 1929 policy to liquidate kulaks as a class resulted in their
deportation to special settlements and forced labor camps and even
death.

During the effort at industrialization, the workers' standard of living decreased. They could be fired for missing a single day of work.
Later, they could be fired for being only twenty minutes late for
work. Workers were not allowed to quit their jobs, and any violation
of the rules meant they would lose their food ration cards and be
evicted from their apartments. Managers who did not enforce these
rules could be arrested and punished. Working conditions were harsh

and often hazardous. By some estimates, 127,000 workers died between 1928 and 1932. The use of forced labor was also common. In the construction of the industrial complexes, inmates of labor camps were used as expendable resources. It was also common for miners to work 16 to 18 hours a day.

The second five-year plan from 1933 to 1937 continued to emphasize industry at the expense of everything else. Coal and iron production continued to rise, and the manufacturing of weapons increased significantly. This diversion of investment into building industry, combined with the poor output from the collective farms, led to famines that took millions of lives.

In addition, the workers received few benefits from Stalin's policy of forced and rapid industrialization as most investment went into building heavy industry, especially a modern military. The industrial policy led to severe pollution that poisoned the air and water, leading to many outbreaks of diseases. Moreover, those who criticized his industrial and political policies were labeled traitors to the revolution and either shot or sent to brutal prison camps in Siberia. Communist Party leaders and the military were not immune to Stalin's purges. In the 1930s purges, half the Soviet officer corps were tried and executed.[9] The best estimate is that Stalin's policies led to some 5–6 million deaths.[10] In spite of Stalin's harsh policies and his killing of millions of his own mostly innocent people, the Soviet Union did industrialize and become a modern world power.

Employment rose from the expected total of 3.9 million per year by 1923 to an astounding 6.4 million in 1930. By 1937, the number reached about 7.9 million, and in 1940 it was 8.3 million. Between 1926 and 1939, the urban population increased by 30 million.[11]

To educate modern industrial workers, the Communist government opened a large number of schools. In 1927, 7.9 million students attended 118,558 schools. This number rose to 9.7 million students and 166,275 schools by 1933. In addition, 900 specialist departments and 566 institutions were built and functioning by 1933.[12]

The Soviet people also benefited from a type of social liberalization. Women were to be given equal education with men, and they had the same legal right to employment. In reality, these goals were not reached, but the efforts to achieve them and the statement of equality led to improvements in the socioeconomic status of women. Stalin's policies also granted the Soviet people universal access to health care that was a vast improvement over the health care system under the czars. Widespread immunization programs created the first generation free from the fear of typhus, cholera, and malaria. The incidence of these diseases dropped to record low numbers, increasing life spans by many years.

The Purge of 1937–38 had the effect of greatly slowing down production. During this period, Stalin demanded absolute loyalty and sought to eliminate dissidents from the entire Soviet Union. The secret police made up false charges against "traitors," many of whom were members of the Communist Party. Show trials were held where friends, colleagues, and neighbors of the accused were forced to give false testimony or face the purge themselves. Scholars estimate that about 500,000 were executed in 1937–39 and somewhere between 3 and 12 million were sent to labor camps.[13] As many as 20 million people were probably killed.[14]

The Kuomintang and the Communists Compete for Control of China

We have already considered how the British used opium as a way to get commercial privileges in China in the nineteenth century. Following the European-imposed trade treaties after the Opium Wars, the once rich and powerful Chinese Empire entered a period of decline. Humiliated by these unequal treaties, many Chinese intellectuals, military officers, and leaders called for thoroughgoing reforms of the millennia-old Confucian system. Arguments raged over how much China should copy Western ideas and institutions and how much of the Confucian tradition they should retain. During this turmoil, Hong Xiuquan (1814–64), a charismatic leader, launched a movement that led to the Taiping Rebellion, China's greatest upheaval during the nineteenth century.

Hong spent much of his young life studying for the Civil Service examinations. Because his family was poor, Hong had to end his formal studies and seek to educate himself. Although he passed the first level examination, he failed in his attempts to pass the highest level test.

After Hong had failed his civil service examination, he became interested in Christian teachings. He came to believe that he was the younger brother of Jesus whom God had sent to earth to reform China and rid it of foreign control. A new religious group called the God Worshipping Society soon formed around him. In 1851 Hong led the God Worshippers in a major rebellion and proclaimed a new Chinese dynasty he called Taiping Tianguo ("Heavenly Kingdom of Great Peace").

The Taiping Rebellion Ultimately Leads to Efforts for Reforms

Hong instituted strict rules. He prohibited prostitution, foot-binding, and slavery, as well as opium smoking, adultery, gambling, and the use of tobacco and alcohol. The God Worshippers held all their property in common, a practice that attracted thousands of peasants. He tried to simplify the Chinese language so average people could read it, and he promoted the equality of women. Hong called the ruling Manchus a foreign dynasty that should be overthrown. Soon his ragtag army of men and women numbered a million soldiers. But despite its initial successes, his God Worshippers' army was stricken with divisions; rivals fought for leadership, weakening its power.

The European colonial powers feared Hong's activities would weaken their influence and upset their commercial activities in China. They formed the "Ever-Victorious Army," trained it to use modern tactics, and defeated Hong's forces. In 1864 the ailing Hong committed suicide and so did about 100,000 of his followers, who expected to meet again in heaven. In spite of its disastrous results, the Taiping Rebellion weakened the Qing Dynasty and sowed the seeds for the Self-Strengthening movement and other major reforms that China undertook during the last decades of the nineteenth century.

The Empress Dowager, Cixi, served as China's de facto ruler from 1861 to 1908. She had become increasingly resistant to efforts to reform China, especially its military forces. In spite of her resistance, many Chinese leaders advocated adopting Western technology, especially its weapons, while retaining the Confucian values system. Initial attempts at reform through building arsenals and Western-style factories became a full-fledged movement in 1898, when young

Emperor Guangxu supported the "100 Days of Reform." These reforms culminated in China's Self-Strengthening movement. Although the Empress Dowager and her reactionary advisors did everything they could to scuttle the reforms, she did support the anti-foreign movement that culminated in the Boxer Rebellion in 1900.

The Boxers were a secret society called the Fists of Righteous Harmony, who practiced martial arts. They thought foreign bullets could not harm them. At first, their goal was to get rid of the ruling Manchus and throw all the foreigners out of China. But the violence that the Boxer-led movement directed against the foreigners, especially against the Christian missionaries, united the western powers against China. Britain, France, Germany, and the United States quickly suppressed the Boxers and then stationed soldiers in Beijing. To further disgrace China, the western nations demanded a huge indemnity.

This humiliating defeat motivated the Chinese leaders, including the young emperor, to take reform seriously. In 1905, the government ended the examination system that had been an important method for selecting government officials for two thousand years. European-style schools were established to teach "modern" subjects and 10,000 Chinese students were sent to study in Japan. The new exams asked students to explain things like the importance of railroads.

The Chinese revolted against the Manchu government in October 1911. As soldiers from all over China joined the revolution, it soon became clear that the Manchus had lost the Mandate of Heaven.

Sun Yat-Sen (1866–1925) was the most important early nationalist leader. He had visited western countries and was familiar with western writings. Convinced that gradual reforms were unworkable, Sun tried to involve the Chinese people in a social revolution and bring the lower classes and peasants into the nationalist struggle. Unlike the earlier reformers, Sun had no great love for the Confucian tradition or any strong loyalty to China's historic values. He was a pragmatist who was willing to try new ways.

Sun had spent many years organizing Chinese middle-class merchants in Southeast Asia and beyond. Many of them gave Sun significant financial support so he could spread his revolutionary ideas. He also found vigorous support among Chinese students in Japan, Chinese communities in the Americas and across Southeast Asia, and among feminist leaders such as Qin Jin (1877–1907), who had studied in Japan and founded a women's magazine.

Sun's revolution rested on his "Three Principles of the People": nationalism, republicanism, and the people's livelihood. Sun wanted to overthrow the Manchu rulers and establish a constitutional system under Han rule, and he wanted to insure that everyone, especially the peasants, received a living wage.

In March 1912, the Qing dynastic rule ended. In order to avoid a general civil war that would further undermine China's power, Sun agreed to appoint Yuan Shikai, northern China's major military leader, as president of the new Republic of China, even though Yuan was known to have been close to the Manchus. Sun's liberal constitution, which included a national assembly, was adopted. The Kuomintang, an umbrella party that included many businessmen and also military officers, won a majority.

Yuan wanted a strong China and he thought the Kuomintang was too liberal. Seizing absolute power, he ordered major Kuomintang leaders killed. He exiled many others, including Sun Yat-Sen, and co-opted many more by promising them personal rewards. Yuan then declared himself emperor and wiped away reforms the new Constitution had guaranteed, including the right for women to get an education, to vote, and to work for wages and salaries. What had been the large and prosperous Qing Empire began to collapse.

When Yuan died in 1916, regional warlords took control of large areas of China and the country was left without a legitimate central government. Tibet and Manchuria declared their independence. To make matters worse, Japanese forces were occupying Manchuria.

Chinese Leaders Compete for Control

Chiang Kai-shek, a brilliant military leader, took control of the Kuomintang after Sun's death. Most Kuomintang leaders were from Whampoa Military Academy, the leading military school in China, and Chiang Kai-Shek was the head of Whampoa. He also had married into the very rich Soong family, which had ties with the Luce family in the U.S. Lacking Sun's broad intellectual interests and political skills, Chiang relied almost entirely on the military to unite the country.

Under the Kuomintang, the peasants were suffering from both the ravages of civil war and mismanagement of the economy. Chiang did little to alleviate the famines and epidemics. Many poor peasants could not even afford to bury their dead parents and had to leave them to be devoured by birds and animals.

When the German concessions in China were turned over to Japan after World War I, the Chinese, who had supported the allies in the Great War, were understandably angry over the continued violation of their homeland. Their outrage burst out on May 4, 1919, when Chinese students and nationalist leaders staged massive demonstrations in many Chinese cities. Exploiting the nationalist spirit unleashed by the May 4th Movement, the communists promised to rid China of the colonial powers that had sucked the lifeblood from China. Students, who had traditionally remained aloof from the common people, found their voices in these demonstrations, and intellectuals also began to involve themselves in the rough and tumble of politics.

Among the bright young men and women whose lives were changed by the May 4th movement were Li Dazhao and Mao Zedong. Li, one of the few young peasants who had managed to get an education, was a college professor. Unlike Lenin and Marx, Li believed peasants were best equipped not only to lead a genuine Communist movement but to rise up against the bourgeois and industrialized west and create a new path for China.

Young Mao Zedong, a star student of Li, had worked hard to get a good understanding of both philosophy and history. The son of a well-to-do peasant who had witnessed poor peasants being exploited, he was drawn to the Communist ideology. Unlike other groups, the fledgling Communist Party had a clear message and coherent ideology. Its leaders could make even the most illiterate peasant understand their message; what was perhaps more important, they were examples of the ideology they preached, and they brought peasants into the political process.

Like many others, Mao thought the Marxist-Leninist model was China's best hope for a better future. Both Li and Mao believed merchants, bankers, and other commercial groups were parasites on society, a view that echoed traditional Confucian values. Unlike Sun Yat-Sen, these young Communists believed an authoritarian government would act on behalf of the common people who were not capable of making the right decisions.

By the 1920s, an increasing number of Marxist study groups across China were becoming active political parties. In the summer of 1921, these groups formed the Communist Party of China. Because initially it was so small, Chinese officials and American missionaries and businessmen in China hardly paid much attention to it or its leaders until the 1930s. By then, Japan was in control of many of China's coastal cities.

After forging alliances with the various warlords in the Canton region, Chiang tried to increase his hold over China by marching the Kuomintang troops north. Chiang's armies took Shanghai in 1927 and then Beijing. By 1929, the Kuomintang controlled most of coastal China.

Mao's Long March

Once he had consolidated his power, Chiang turned his attention to subduing the Communists. By crushing a worker uprising in Shanghai in 1927, he gained support from Europe and the U.S. With German help, Chiang attacked the Communist-controlled area in Kiangsi in southern China in 1934.

Although nearly surrounded, Mao led his army of 90,000 on the "Long March" to Yenan, out of reach of the Nationalist forces. In the grueling 370-day, 8,000-mile journey, almost ninety percent of the Communist forces died. But the legend of the Long March spread across the Chinese countryside. It established Mao's authority in the Chinese Communist Party and turned Mao, Zhou Enlai, and others who had survived the march into national heroes.

While Chiang and Mao continued to struggle for the hearts and minds of the Chinese people in the 1930s, Japan continued to gain control of large areas in northern China, and in 1934, the Japanese occupied Shanghai. The Communists and the Kuomintang created a temporary united front to fight the Japanese. However, Chiang seemed more intent on defeating his Communist rivals than on fighting the Japanese. At the same time the largely volunteer Communist Army offered strong and persistent opposition to Japanese incursions. In 1937, Mao's army numbered about 90,000, and by the end of World War II, as we will soon see, it had grown to nearly a million.

SUMMARY

With the rise of Western hypernationalism, a growing number of nation-states tried to find alternatives to all-out war. First they formed a series of alliances where several nations agreed to fight together. However, because the nations pursued their own national interests, these alliances were unstable and nations often ignored their promises to support their allies.

With two powerful groups of nations armed and ready to fight, a small spark in the unstable Balkan states set off a major war. It was by far the bloodiest, costliest, and most devastating war in world history up to this time. The United States' entry into the war tipped the balance against Germany, which was forced to sign an armistice agreement in 1918.

Had the United States not entered World War I, that long and tragic conflict might have ended in a virtual stalemate with Germany keeping most of its territory and not being forced to pay crippling reparations. But after the indisputable allied victory, England and France were in no mood to compromise. Instead, the victorious nations—France, Great Britain, and the United States—negotiated a harsh peace with Germany and the other "Central Powers," and the map of Europe was fundamentally changed.

By the 1930s most nations in Europe were under some form of dictatorship. From 1920 to the 1940s, dictators ruled most of the new states created by the Treaty of Versailles. Latin America was an especially fertile ground for military dictators because totalitarian leaders had been in power there since the 1820s.

A major development in this act was the emergence of the Soviet Union and China as Communist states. China, with over 500 million people, was the most populated nation in the world, while the Soviet Union controlled the most land mass and had a population of 185 million. As these two huge nations embarked on new ways to build stable states, other nations would watch carefully how these two powers acted.

ACT TWO

Colonial Nationalism, 1900–1945

Prior to World War II, most of the colonial powers were convinced that none of their colonies were ready for self-government. In fact, however, people in the colonies had been building national movements for a long time. This act examines how colonial subjects embraced nationalism and sought independence.

National leaders in the colonized areas focused on two major challenges. One was creating a sense of the uniqueness of their country. The colonies had already begun constructing narratives about their unique past as part of their resistance to foreign rule and economic exploitation. These narratives stressed their historic greatness and criticized European and American exploitation and racist attitudes.

It is helpful to keep in mind Benedict Anderson's concept of a nation-state as an "imagined community." Other historians have focused on how strong nation-states acquire their citizens' ultimate loyalty by replacing religion as the major source of identity.[1]

The second major challenge the national leaders faced was how to handle diverse cultural groups within their nation's boundaries. Each cultural, linguistic, and/or religious group had its own imagined past and worldview. The national leaders sought to reconcile these diverse narratives and beliefs into a coherent nationalist unity. The leaders were also planning ways to overthrow their foreign rulers and take control of their country.

Most of the nationalist movements relied on mass mobilization and used newspapers and magazines to get people involved. However, since many of the colonized people could not read, creative leaders had to find other ways to communicate with the majority of the people. In this effort, traditional symbols, often taken from local religious beliefs and practices, served to connect the more educated leaders with their total population. The support of overseas diaspora communities also played a role in independence movements. Local factors such as size, resources, religion, diversity, culture, and history shaped the various responses to colonialism, as did the nature of the colonial rulers.

The national leaders, even those in the same country, often disagreed on how to achieve their goals. Many urged their people to focus on their traditions and celebrate a "golden age" when their own culture was "superior" to the culture of their European rulers. Others wanted to abandon much of their traditional culture and adopt modern, Western forms of government. They also argued over whether they should emulate the colonialists' capitalist philosophy or adopt some form of Marxism in order to avoid the cruelties they associated with capitalism, which many saw as a tool of imperialism. Debates also raged on whether to work for national unity or partition their country along ethnic or religious lines.

Leaders in each area also debated the best methods for achieving their independence. Should they initiate violent resistance or wait for slow reforms to take root? Could enough people be mobilized to make boycotting Western products and breaking rules effective? Would nonviolent resistance achieve their goals?

As the various colonial nationalist movements developed, each one forged its own unique synthesis from the many cultural groups that formed its society. The successful nationalist movements managed to blend their rich historic traditions with the modern concept of the nation-state.

The various colonies had gotten a psychological boost at the Versailles Peace Conference at the end of World War I when the victorious allies talked publicly about building a new social order. However, the Western leaders refused to seat delegations from Vietnam, Korea, and other colonized areas, or to even listen to their concerns. Even though they were ignored by the Western powers, President Wilson's Fourteen Points—calling for freedom of the seas, open covenants, and reconfiguring national boundaries—offered the colonial nationalists inspiration and specific goals.

The nationalists were also encouraged by Wilson's plan for an international organization that would guarantee political independence and territorial integrity for all nations. The colonized people especially emphasized Wilson's commitment to the self-determination of people, even though he really meant self-determination for white Europeans only. Despite what Wilson meant, many colonized people around the world heard him publicly advocate a

> Free, open-minded, and absolutely impartial adjustment of all colonial claims, based upon a strict observance of the principle that in determining all such questions of sovereignty the interests of the population concerned must have equal weight with the equitable claims of the Government whose title is to be determined.[2]

Colonial reactions to Wilson's principles were electric and they energized the emerging nationalist movements. Once unleashed, the call for self-determination burned brighter over the next decades.

NATIONALIST MOVEMENTS IN ASIA

Setting the Stage

One of the major differences in the colonial movements stemmed from the type of colonial rule the European rulers had imposed. In the more sparsely settled colonial areas, the colonial masters sent a large number of white settlers to manage plantation agriculture and supervise the extraction of precious resources. This type of colony was common in Africa and the Americas. In Asia and other thickly settled colonies, the European colonial powers sent mostly administrators and armed forces and let local people manage much of the administrative work as well as run the factories, banks, and other institutions. With their large populations, most Asian colonies could easily provide the necessary labor.

Colonies also differed in how the colonial masters governed them. In places like India, Indonesia, and Vietnam, the European powers imposed a strict and well-organized government. In other colonies such as Egypt and Iraq, the colonizers relied more on governments they controlled indirectly. In China, the Europeans, Americans, and Japanese simply carved out "spheres of influence" as their way of establishing economic control.

Gandhi and the Nationalist Movement in India

The Indian nationalist movement was the first genuine challenge to colonial rule. The British had tried to present themselves as good, kind colonial rulers who would improve India by building an extensive railroad system, canals, irrigation systems, good harbors, public buildings, and even New Delhi, a new capital. They also claimed to have taught their colonial subjects democratic values in order eventually to leave them better off than they had found them. While some Indians agreed, most did not accept this view of British colonialism, and the facts told a different story.

The British had invested in India to enhance their own economic prosperity. British rule actually bankrupted this rich land and turned it into a "third world" economy. The economic exploitation, the decay of indigenous industries, high taxation, the drain of wealth to Britain, and a backward agrarian structure resulted in agricultural stagnation and the shocking exploitation of poor peasants by zamindars, landlords, moneylenders, merchants, and the state. British colonial policy gradually reduced the Indian people to extreme poverty and kept India's colonial economy at a very low level.

	India	China	Total Third World	Currently Developed Countries
1750	24.5	32.8	73.0	27.0
1800	19.7	33.3	67.7	32.3
1830	17.6	29.8	60.5	39.5
1860	8.6	19.7	36.6	63.4
1880	2.8	12.5	20.9	79.1
1900	1.7	6.2	11.0	89.0
1913	1.4	3.6	7.5	92.5
1928	1.9	3.4	7.2	92.8
1938	2.4	3.1	7.2	92.8
1953	1.7	2.3	6.5	93.5
1980	2.3	5.0	12.0	88.0

Industrial development (manufacturing output as percentage of the world's total)

Britain's economic policies had prohibited India's industrial development and stalled any real industrial transformation in the subcontinent. In 1750, India's manufacturing had constituted about 25 percent of the world's total. By 1950, after 200 years of British colonial rule, India's manufacturing was less than 3 percent of the world's total.

Among the most lethal consequences of British rule were the recurring cycles of famines, caused mainly by diverting rich agricultural land to growing commercial crops such as coffee, indigo, tea, and opium. It is true that natural forces, particularly uneven rainfall during the monsoons, exacerbated some of the famines, but by far the majority of famines during British rule resulted from British economic and administrative policies.

The first great famine that occurred under East India Company rule in Bengal killed a third of the population. One nineteenth-century British writer calculated that during the period 1854–1901 over 28,825,000 people died as a result of famines,[3] and during the famine in Bengal in 1943–44, at least three million Bengalis perished in a man-made famine in British-ruled India.[4]

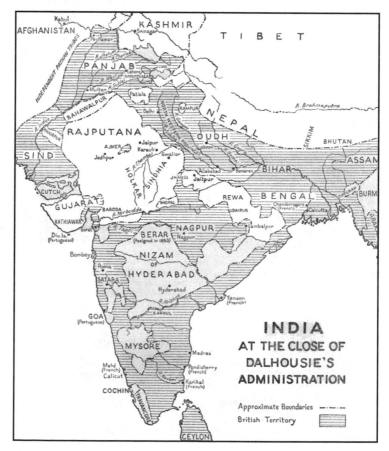

British India

Britain's control and exploitation of much of the subcontinent culminated in a major military uprising in 1857. As we have noted, the British called it a "Mutiny," but most contemporary Indians call it the "First War of Indian Independence." Although the uprising failed, it left an indelible mark on the British rulers. Rather than continuing their efforts to remake Indian society in their own image, the British Parliament ended the EIC's authority and eliminated the governor-general's position. In its place, it made India a part of the British Empire, under the control of a single Viceroy who was second only to Queen Victoria and British monarchs that succeeded her.

It is important to remember that the British did not directly govern the whole subcontinent. There were 562 independent Indian principalities that were indirectly controlled by Britain. Some of these "princely states" were as large as European countries, while some had only a few thousand people. The British supported the most reactionary rulers in these states who carried out few reforms. As a result, British rule in those areas after 1857 kept those states from modernizing.

The Indian response to British rule ran the spectrum from outright resistance and armed revolt to a keen desire to emulate British culture. Among those who resisted British colonialism, some espoused gradualism and the appeal to law and others demanded "freedom now" and championed aggressive opposition to colonial rule.

Although the civil service was theoretically open to Indians, each candidate had to pass the exam in England before he turned 19. The exam was about English literature, civil law, and history, so it's no surprise that few Indians qualified. Plus, few Indian families could afford to send their sons to England to take the exam.

In 1876, Surendranath Banerjea was the first Indian to pass the English Civil Service examination and be admitted to the Indian Civil Service. Banerjea and many young educated Indians hoped Indian nationalism would gradually result in an Indian government similar to Britain's constitutionalism. Toward that end, in 1885 they formed the Indian Nationalist Congress. This organization worked tirelessly to encourage Indians to subordinate their caste, language, region, and even their religious loyalties to the nation. In spite of its many achievements, the Indian National Congress was only composed of a few European-educated elite Indians who had little contact with village India.

Members of the lower castes challenged the goals of the Indian National Congress. They sought to break the dominance of the Brahmins and institutionalize equal opportunities for leadership positions from all castes and religious communities.

The fiery leader Bal Gangadhar Tilak (1844–1920) soon challenged this moderate approach to self-rule by espousing more radical opposition to British rule. To achieve this goal, which he called *swaraj* (self-rule), he skillfully combined Hindu images and practices with national independence goals. He encouraged Indians to wear hand-loomed clothing, pledge to boycott British goods, and participate in nationalistic projects. Tilak was not opposed to using violent means to achieve swaraj.

Other nationalist leaders campaigned for improved educational opportunities for Indians and the development of the civil skills that would make Indians ready for democracy. Gopal Krishna Gokhale (1866–1915), another major nationalist leader, counseled the gradual development of Indian independence through laws and rational arguments against the British. Gokhale also championed major reforms in Indian society.

Into the uncertainty about how India's future should develop came Mohandas Gandhi (1869–1948), a spindly lawyer with exciting new methods of political protest. While in South Africa, Gandhi had developed a philosophy of nonviolent resistance he called *satyagraha* (truth force). As Gandhi explained: "I thus began to call the Indian movement 'Satyagraha,' that is to say, the Force which is born of Truth and Love or non-violence."[5] This approach insisted that nationalist protesters should never resort to violence, even when they engaged in non-cooperation and civil disobedience campaigns.

Gandhi understood the oppressive conditions under which most Indians labored and the way colonialism had mired Indian villagers in grinding poverty. He realized that simply calling for India's independence was inadequate. Reform must start with personal discipline and responsibility. Gandhi was able to combine modern political objectives like representative government and belief in science with deeply held Hindu values.

Gandhi decided to live like most poor Indian villagers. He owned few possessions, ate only basic foods, and dressed as the poor

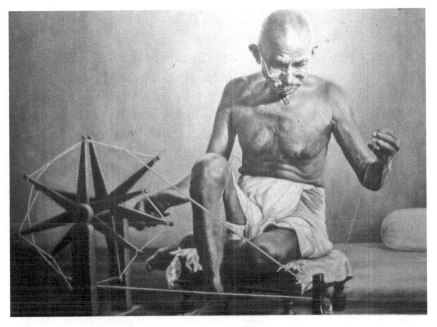

Gandhi spinning

dressed. Instead of advocating some abstract idea of parliamentary government, Gandhi called for Ram Raj, a return to the values of a mythic Hindu king who personified *dharma*—doing one's duty. Gandhi's nonviolent methods were accepted by millions as the best way to gain freedom. His strategies gave Indians from all castes, classes, and genders unique methods that everyone could employ. By 1917, Gandhi dominated the Indian nationalist movement.

While Hindus were attempting to apply religious values such as dharma to modern challenges, Indian Muslims were undertaking similar reforms. Syed Ahmad Khan (1817–1898) urged Muslims to return to the original teachings of purity and simplicity embodied in the Qur'an. He also championed English education and the pursuit of modern science. In 1864, he founded the Scientific Society, which translated western books into Urdu, a major Indian language, and published a liberal journal.

Faced with these movements, the British decided that dividing Hindus and Muslims was the way to weaken the independence movement. They began to support the Muslim League, hoping it would compete with the National Congress for the allegiance of Indian Muslims, thereby weakening both organizations.

During World War I, India contributed money, goods, and troops to the Allied cause. A million Indian soldiers fought with the allies, and perhaps 100,000 were killed. (In comparison, 116,000 Americans lost their lives.) Most Indian casualties occurred in the Ottoman Empire and in France. Further, taxes on Indians that were raised about 10 to 15 percent were used to support the Allied war effort.

The Amritsar Massacre on April 13, 1919, galvanized Indian public opinion against the British. Fearful of an Indian revolt, the British government had passed a law that gave it the right to detain suspected revolutionaries and to deny them normal legal protection. To protest this legislation, Gandhi invited Hindus and Muslims to participate in a nonviolent protest in Jallianwalla Bagh Park in Amritsar, the capital of the Punjab and a Sikh holy city.

In response, British troops opened fire on the crowd without giving them any warning or chance to disperse. Within fifteen minutes, at least eight hundred men, women, and children had been killed. The British troops then left without aiding the wounded or allowing other Indians to help them. Instead of censuring the troops for their actions, the British people gave General Dyer, the commanding officer, £10,000 in "appreciation for his heroic work at Jallianwalla Bagh."

After the massacre, Gandhi led a series of *hartals,* nonviolent, nationwide, day-long strikes that involved fasting and prayer. Soon after, he launched the non-cooperation movement. By 1921, students were leaving college, large groups were burning British-made cloth, merchants were closing their shops, and huge crowds were marching in many cities. Gandhi insisted that the protesters must be nonviolent. He urged them to "forget fear" and endure beatings and arrests without fighting back. When he learned that a mob had burned down a police station and killed twenty-three policemen, Gandhi temporarily called off the noncooperation movement until the people learned more self-discipline.

In an effort to promote self-help programs and to symbolize freedom from colonial economic exploitation, Gandhi also encouraged everyone to spin thread and then weave their own cloth. He also urged them to participate in social service programs for the poor, and even dig toilets, part of his continuing efforts to end India's historic system of untouchability. In 1930, the British put a tax on salt, a vital ingredient that even the poorest Indians used in cooking. Gandhi defied the law by organizing a 240-mile march to the ocean to make salt. Thousands of Indian men and women of all ages, castes, and social classes joined the march.

As soon as Gandhi picked up a lump of salt, he was arrested. The public was so incensed by his arrest that the British viceroy let Gandhi out of jail and invited him to London to talk with the leaders of the British government, including King George V. Churchill and many other British leaders were amazed that Gandhi dressed in a simple wrap-around piece of cloth when he appeared before the British monarch.

The British government did make concessions and grant some Indian representation in the state and central governments during the 1930s, but nothing it did could slow the momentum of the nationalist movement.

Colonial Exploitation in Indonesia and Vietnam

By 1800 the Dutch controlled the Indonesian islands and began instituting the Culture System. As a result, the Netherlands became a wealthy colonial power. By 1911, they had created the centralized state called Indonesia, which also included Bali and Aceh. The Dutch then transformed Sumatra, which had been covered with dense forests, into enormous tobacco and rubber plantations and encouraged Chinese farmers to go and work on the plantations. Before long, the Chinese dominated commerce there. When the Javanese unsuccessfully revolted against the Dutch in 1920, approximately 200,000 Javanese were killed. Adding to the exploitation, the Royal Dutch Shell Oil Company took control of the oil that was discovered there in the 1920s.

The Dutch provided a liberal Western education for a few members of the Indonesian elite and co-opted them as allies in the colonial system. However, they provided no education for the majority of the population. As a result, the Indonesian literacy rate was the lowest of any European colony in Asia. Most of the colonial subjects the Dutch controlled suffered from severe poverty.

Although the Dutch had created the Indonesian state, Indonesian nationalists in the twentieth century turned it into a nation. The first nationalist leaders were young, upper-class, Western-educated men and women. By 1910, their independence movement had attracted people from all walks of life. Indonesian newspapers and political parties had been formed. Nationalist leaders successfully waged strikes and the demand for independence was increasing. The movement included various political and economic ideas, and included many active communists.

The Dutch, determined to keep control of Indonesia, arrested thousands of Revolutionary party members, especially the Communists, and sentenced them to long jail terms. Undaunted, in 1928 the Indonesian National Youth Congress met in Batavia and raised a national flag, took a National Pledge for Indonesian independence, and sang nationalist songs. Sukarno (1901–1970) emerged as the most charismatic and outspoken leader of the Indonesian National Party (PNI) and called for a new republic that would include the Islands of Indonesia plus Malaysia and Northern Borneo.

Despite the growing nationalist movement, the Dutch were able, through force and by dividing the various religious, linguistic, and ideological groups, to hold on to their richest colony until the Japanese conquered the islands in 1942.

Nationalist resistance to French rule in Indochina, Dutch rule in Indonesia, and British control in Malaysia and Singapore increased during the interwar period but had limited success. In the 1930s, as Japanese power spread, many Southeast Asians thought that the Japanese might help them get free from European rule. However, because the Japanese armies acted in cruel and authoritarian ways and attempted to impose their own harsh rule, many of these colonized people turned against both the Japanese and their European colonial masters. The Japanese did leave one important legacy. During their rule in Indonesia they raised and trained young men to serve in the army; that army, in turn, successfully fought against the Dutch masters after the war.

In Vietnam, by 1850, the French colonialists had imposed a radical commercialization of farming. Growing commercial crops for export exposed the peasants to the capricious ups and downs of the world market. Although the French prospered, the Vietnamese peasants grew poorer. In 1900, the average rice consumption of Vietnamese peasants was 262 kilograms per person; by 1939, it had shrunk to 182 kilograms. An estimated 250 kilograms is necessary for survival.[6] The French also introduced many rubber plantations: over a thousand by World War II. Workers for these plantations were rounded up and taken by force.

By the twentieth century, the Vietnamese population had risen dramatically, but the people did not benefit from the commercial economy. Instead, they were offered little education or health care. Most peasants were poor, illiterate, and deeply in debt. Only the few that cooperated with the French could get rich, and no real middle class developed.

The introduction of a capitalist economy in Vietnam alienated the majority of peasants who simply wanted to grow food on their own land. The disgruntled peasants found their leader in Nguyễn Ái Quốc (1890–1969), also known as Ho Chih Minh, who was born in a farming village. Although Ho was drawn to communist ideology, he became a leader because the millions of Vietnamese peasants saw him

Ho Chih Minh and followers

as a champion of their efforts to restore their traditional peasant rights. Ho soon was leading the Vietminh, the nationalist organization. Although the Vietminh was peasant-based, it also attracted the educated middle class and the small but vocal group of urban workers.

Ho made a series of trips that took him around the world. In 1911, he visited France, and during 1912 and 1913 he worked in the United States as a pastry cook in Boston. Later Ho worked in England. In 1919, he attended the Versailles Peace Conference as an observer. He even rented a fancy suit so that he could meet President Wilson, but the president dismissed him without listening to what he had to say. While in France, Ho became one of the founders of the French Communist Party. Later he lived in the Soviet Union and China before returning to Vietnam. During World War II, Ho became the undisputed leader of the nationalist movement and an ardent communist as well.

The Japanese Colonize Korea

For most of its history, no outside power colonized Korea. In 1886, the Korean government had created a Royal Academy to educate young Koreans in western technology and thought. In the following years, the ruling Yi emperors created a new system of public schooling and welcomed Protestant missionaries who established private schools, many of which promoted western learning and democratic reforms.

Presbyterian and Methodist missions were especially prominent in Korea. Additionally, the YMCA and YWCA (Young Men's and Young Women's Christian Associations) exerted a powerful influence on Korea's young people and provided a setting for group meetings and study. In 1909, the "Million Souls for Christ" campaign successfully achieved mass conversions to Protestant Christianity. Many in the intellectual and business classes were also embracing Protestantism but most government officials clung to their traditional Confucian values.

Korean nationalism increased in reaction to the increasing foreign intervention in their country during the last decades of the nineteenth century. Japan, Russia, and the U.S. all competed for influence there, and Korea's independence seemed precarious. Ministers within the

Korean government, some of whom were pro-American, pro-Russian, or pro-Japanese, added to the confusion. Initially, the Korean king turned to the Russian legation for protection.

A group of Korean intellectuals, strongly influenced by Western ideas, formed the Independence Club in 1896. This club grew into a citizens' assembly that supported social and political reforms and it sponsored newspapers, debating clubs, and other nationalist projects. However, world events soon overwhelmed these early nationalist initiatives. After the Japanese defeated China in 1895, Russian influence in Manchuria expanded, threatening Korean independence. In 1904, Japan, fearing Russia's influence in the region, declared war on Russia.

The western powers were surprised that Japan won almost every battle during the Russo-Japanese war. President Theodore Roosevelt, the mediator of that conflict's peace treaty, believed that Japanese control of Korea was the best way to prevent further Russian expansion in the region. Once the international community accepted Japan's "guidance, control, and protection" of Korea, Japan became Korea's colonial master. In 1909, Japanese dissolved the Korean army, and on August 22, 1910, the Japanese forced Emperor Sunjong to renounce both his throne and his country. The Treaty of Annexation, which the Korean Prime Minister signed that same day, formally proclaimed that Korea had become a Japanese colony.

Koreans Lose Their Identity

The Japanese immediately sought to assimilate the Koreans to Japanese culture. Hardly any facet of Korean culture and society was left unaffected. Schools taught only the Japanese language and Japanese history; teaching Korean history was forbidden. Koreans had to choose new Japanese names and learn to speak Japanese. Soon young children did not realize they had ever been Koreans. Religious and government schools had been teaching about democracy, self-determination, and other western values. Now the Japanese rulers demanded that private schools use only Japanese-approved textbooks and curricula, and they imposed a new educational policy in all the Korean government schools.

Most Korean groups profoundly resented Japanese rule. Soldiers from the disbanded Korean army joined Korea's "Righteous Army." It was composed of freedom fighters dedicated to resisting against Japanese occupation. However, without training or adequate weapons, the Japanese easily controlled the Koreans.

Protestant missionaries, most of whom were Presbyterians, continued to have a strong influence on education and liberal political thought and most of them supported Korean nationalism. However, there was a split among the Confucianists: the more liberal wing was dedicated to reforming the traditional philosophy to fit better with the changing times and the crisis of meanings. Those Koreans who remained faithful to their neo-Confucian traditions tended to be more conservative. They were wary of modernization, even though they disliked the Japanese and being under foreign rule.

Under Terauchi Masatake, the first Japanese governor-general (1910–1916), assimilation to Japanese ways accelerated. Masatake justified his radical changes in the name of modernity and progress, but the results were just the opposite. The Korean language was banned and the thousands of schools that were built across Korea were supposed to promote Japanese culture and transform Koreans into loyal Japanese subjects. Although land reform was needed, Koreans were required to have written deeds to prove land-ownership. Since the majority of farmers tilled their lands by hereditary rights and had no deeds, most lost their land. Japanese developers soon bought it. The new realities impoverished the Korean tenant farmers, who were the vast majority of all Koreans and who paid about half of their meager earnings in taxes.

The Masatake "reforms" sparked a violent reaction among Koreans, but the Japanese military forces suppressed all opposition. At the same time, the Japanese colonial administration grew. In 1910, approximately 10,000 officials governed Korea; by 1937 the administration had 52,270 Japanese and 35,282 Korean officials. The Japanese also maintained a large police force in Korea that had grown to over 60,000 by 1940.[7]

Koreans refer to the years between 1910 and 1919 as the "Dark Period" because of the almost complete suppression of the Korean identity and any legitimate Korean political or cultural life. The Japanese-imposed educational system was transforming young Koreans into thoroughly Japanese young people. During that time, the only real Korean nationalist organizations were among Korean exiles in Manchuria, in the Russia Maritime provinces, and in China, Hawaii, and several large American cities. These diaspora Korean communities lobbied foreign governments to support Korean independence. They also collected funds for nationalist projects, and elected leaders who they hoped would one day govern their homeland.

Korean response to Wilson's Fourteen Points was immediate. The Korean National Association in Hawaii voted to send Syngman Rhee to the Versailles Peace Conference to plead for Korean independence. In Shanghai, expatriate Koreans from the Korean Young Men's Association in China sent Kim Kyu-sik to Paris to lobby for Korean independence. But Wilson and the other European delegates turned a deaf ear to the Korean delegation, as they had done to Ho Chih Minh. Within Korea, the Protestant churches increased their appeal for a peaceful settlement of disputes while many nationalist leaders called for stronger methods.

The state funeral for Emperor Kojong of Korea in January 1919 provided the nationalists with an opportunity for mass action against Japanese occupation: on March 1, student-led demonstrations were organized throughout Korea. Student "national representatives" signed their Declaration of Independence and a student representative carried the document to the Japanese governor-general. At the same time the Declaration was read in central Seoul. In hundreds of cities, marchers paraded through streets shouting "Tachan tongnip manse" (Long live an independent Korea). Following these massive demonstrations, a nationwide independence movement sprang up.

These demonstrations surprised the Japanese, because they did not think the Koreans were capable of this kind of planning or such courage. The Japanese hastily and brutally suppressed the incipient nationalist movement.

Although the March 1st Movement failed to influence any of the great powers, it did inspire other nationalist movements. It also helped unite many different factions of Korean society and the nationalist movement itself. The March 1st Movement remains a central symbol of Korea's collective will and courage in organizing a genuine revolt against Japanese colonial rule.

The March 1st Movement also spawned cultural nationalism (*munhwa undong*) during the 1920s to fight against Japanese efforts to eliminate Korean culture. Korean cultural, religious, academic, and other voluntary organization focused on "enlightenment projects" such as self-improvement, education, and social welfare. Additionally, dozens of new magazines and newspapers were permitted some small degree of journalistic freedom and Koreans created a large number of novels, dramas, paintings, and films.

But the growing nationalist movements inside and outside Korea were not united. Korean students who had studied outside Korea were the most radical. They were attracted to Marxism, and when they returned home, they organized many study groups dedicated to radical thought. Those nationalists who disdained communism and remained moderate were dedicated to gaining more freedom legally.

In September 1931, the Japanese Army, acting on a trumped-up excuse, attacked and took control of Manchuria from the Chinese and made it a puppet state called Manchukuo. The Japanese then required large numbers of Koreans to work as forced labor in Manchuko. At the same time, a new Japanese governor-general in Korea ended the Koreans' cultural nationalist movement. He also imposed strict new economic policies aimed at increasing rice production, which vastly increased the number of tenant farmers. At the same time, the brutal assimilation effort, which sought to eradicate all things Korean and to turn Koreans into good Japanese in heart and mind, continued.

SCENE
TWO

NATIONALISM IN WEST ASIA

Setting the Stage

European colonization in West Asia followed a different pattern from that in Asia, and nationalism in this region also followed another course. One cause of the differences was the gradual weakening of the vast Ottoman Empire and the formation of new nations in the process. Another important difference was the role of the European powers. In West Asia, the Europeans preferred to exert indirect control over both the old states and the new nations. In the process, the Europeans hoped to avoid open conflict by creating a series of both open and secret treaties that parceled out among themselves spheres of influence in the region.

The Decline of the Ottoman Empire and the Creation of Mandates

The European victory against the Ottoman forces in Vienna in 1683 had marked the end of the Ottoman Empire's westward expansion. From then on, European imperial expansion would gradually chip away large areas of Ottoman land. The Ottoman armies could not afford the latest military weapons that their neighboring European armies were using. After Europe started industrializing, the Ottoman artisans could no longer compete with European weapons or manufactured goods. Ineffective sultans and corrupt local officials who cheated the government out of tax revenue also weakened the central government.

In the beginning of the nineteenth century, the Ottoman government disbanded what had become a corrupt Janissary system and instituted the Tanzimat reforms intended to make the government more efficient. Besides creating a Commercial Code in 1850 and a new Penal Code in 1858, the Ottomans attempted to democratize their government by introducing a Chamber of Deputies with representatives from the different religious and ethnic groups. The government also instituted a military draft and reformed the banking system. To strengthen its power, the government at times sought alliances with France, the Netherlands, Britain, and Russia. When the Ottomans failed to benefit from these alliances, a group of "Young Turks" championed establishing greater contact with Germany. That move would ultimately prove disastrous.

Although the Ottoman Empire's millet system had made ethnic diversity a strength rather than a potential weakness, during the nineteenth and early twentieth centuries, various ethnic groups within the large and diverse empire began to express national feelings. Arabs openly resisted Turkish rule. Robust nationalist movements were also on the rise in Armenia and among the Greek and Bulgarian populations. A major uprising took place in Serbia at the start of the nineteenth century. As a result of the Greek War of Independence in the 1820s, Greece won its independence from the Ottomans in 1830. Serbia became free in 1867, and in 1870, the Ottomans lost almost all of the Balkans. The Russian Czar Nicholas I derisively called the Ottoman Empire the "sick man of Europe." In spite of these challenges and changes, the empire managed to survive, although greatly reduced in size.

The Young Turks, a hypernationalist party that was in power from 1908 to 1918, wanted to weaken the influence of non-Turkish groups within the empire. They instituted a constitutional monarchy that gave special privileges to the Turks while reducing the sultan's power. These policies, which upset the non-Turkish population, led to war in the Balkans from 1910 to 1912 and the terrible tragedy of the forced evacuation of the Armenians from Anatolia during World War I.

The Ottoman leaders knew that Russia coveted access to warm water ports and had long wanted to control the Bosporus, which flows through Istanbul. The Ottoman government accused the Armenians of secretly helping the Russians achieve that goal from inside the empire. The Turks then killed or caused the deaths of approximately a million Armenians and forced another million to leave the country. Most of them died of starvation, thirst, or the cold. The Turks claim their actions were justified because the Armenians were like a disloyal fifth column inside their country, but the Armenians and most

Europeans and Americans insist this cruel policy was a genocide.

Turkish nationalist feelings increased as Ottoman authority weakened. During World War I, when the Ottomans sided with Germany, the British supported Arab nationalism because they hoped it would further weaken the Ottomans. In response, the Ottoman leaders tried to use force to destroy any sign of Arab nationalism.

At the end of World War I, the majority of Arabs were living within the Ottoman Empire. The Arabs wanted greater autonomy, the right to use Arabic in the schools, and a chance to serve during peacetime in the imperial army. Although efforts to assimilate Arabs into Turkish culture had the opposite effect, Arab nationalism had not become a mass movement. Many Arabs identified with their religion, their tribe, or their own local government. Pan-Islamic sentiment also competed with Arab nationalism.

In 1917 the British issued the Balfour Declaration, which stated the British government would support "the establishment in Palestine of a national home for the Jewish people, and will use their best endeavors to facilitate the achievement of this object, it being clearly understood that nothing shall be done which may prejudice the civil and religious rights of existing non-Jewish communities in Palestine. . . ."[8] A year later, the British Cabinet Eastern Committee clarified the rights guaranteed to the Palestinians, who were the majority population. The statement explained, "Palestine was included in the areas as to which Great Britain pledged itself that they should be Arab and independent in the future."[9]

Besides its fear that Russia might control the Bosporus, the Ottomans believed that if they could defeat Russia, they would have a chance to liberate the many Turkish-speaking peoples living in Russian-controlled areas in Central Asia. At the same time, the Arabs living under Ottoman rule saw an Ottoman defeat in World War I as a chance to gain their independence. The Arab ruler of the Hejaz (the area that includes Mecca and Medina) switched Arab loyalty to the British when the British promised the Arabs independence.

Because of its hostility to Russia, during World War I the Ottoman government joined the Triple Alliance, which included Germany, Italy, and Austria-Hungary. At the end of World War I, the victorious nations, especially Britain and France, wanted to divide the German colonies and the Ottoman Empire among themselves. But President Woodrow Wilson was promoting the principle of "self-determination," a policy that would allow the various ethnic and "national" groups to decide their own future. Finally reaching a compromise, the victorious European leaders and Wilson agreed to create a series of "mandates" out of the defeated lands that the British, French, and Americans would administer until they were "ready" for independence.

The Ottoman Empire was so weak that France, Britain, and Italy thought they could easily influence what happened in Ottoman territory.[10] But unbeknown to the other Allied Powers, during the war Britain, France, and Russia had made a secret agreement to dismantle the Ottoman Empire. Russia wanted to include Istanbul in its empire. During the war the British had incited the sharif of Mecca to lead an Arab revolt against the Turks, promising him Arab independence. In spite of this promise and although the sharif's son Faisal had actually established the Kingdom of Syria, the French and British had already decided they would share control of the former areas of the Ottoman Empire and the mandate system would enable them to do so.

The largest or Class A mandates were to become "provisionally independent" but would be "subject to the rendering of administrative advice and assistance by the Mandatory until such time as they can stand

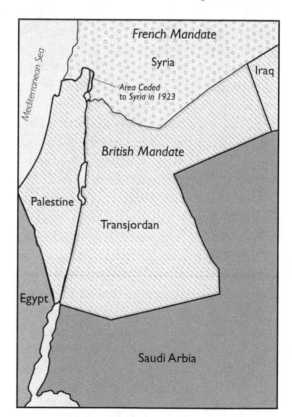

Mandates created after World War I

alone."[11] Most Arabs in the Class A mandates assumed this settlement was a promise of independence. The British mandates included Palestine (most of which is now Israel), Transjordan (Jordan), and Iraq, which became a new nation in 1921. The French were awarded Syria and Lebanon. Much of the land in the Arabian Peninsula that had been part of the Ottoman Empire became part of Saudi Arabia and Yemen.

The Class B mandates were former German territories in West and Central Africa. Class C mandates were territories that were very small or had very few people. They were to be treated as colonies under League of Nations supervision.

Hoping to claim even more Ottoman territory, French, British, Italian, and Greek forces invaded Istanbul in 1919. The Treaty of Sevres established an independent Armenia and a separate Kurdish region in eastern Anatolia.[12] A significant number of Greeks left Ottoman territory while Turks fled Greece. The treaty also gave autonomy and the option for eventual independence to the Kurds, the Sunni Muslims who were neither Arabs nor Turks and who lived in mountainous areas that are now part of Turkey, Iraq, and Iran.

Nationalist movements in these mandates developed slowly and were greatly encumbered by European occupation and indirect rule. Syrian nationalism was the most militant because Syrians wanted to create a "Greater Syria" that would include Lebanon, Palestine, and Jordan.

From the Ottoman Empire to the Republic of Turkey

The Ottoman decision to side with Germany in World War I proved disastrous. After the war, the once-proud empire was left with a mere shadow of its land, and the devastated Turks were at the mercy of the Allied victors. As the younger generation watched their helpless leaders meekly accept the conditions the Allied nations imposed, they grew more disillusioned and bitter. Their rich Arab lands had been taken away. The Armenians who had survived the massacre had fled east. Except for Kurdish settlements in northeastern Turkey, this transfer of populations all but eliminated the ethnic diversity that had been one of the strongest features of the Ottoman Empire.

A brilliant military leader named Mustafa Kemal took control of

what was left of the Ottoman Empire. He organized a rival government in the Turkish city of Ankara, in Anatolia. He hoped to restore
Turkish self-confidence and pride and to create a new, modern Turkish
nation that would glorify both the pre-Ottoman and pre-Islamic past.

In 1922, as his support increased, Kemal deposed the Ottoman sultan and proclaimed himself the president of the Republic of Turkey.
He had accepted the loss of Arab lands but was determined that
Turkey should include those areas where Turks were in the majority
as well as the Kurdish areas in the east. To accomplish these goals, he
led his army against both the Ottoman government and the Greeks
who were invading Anatolia. After successfully winning this Turkish
War of Independence, he helped found the Republic of Turkey. The
new nation was recognized in the 1923 Treaty of Lausanne. It also
included land west of the Bosporus and Istanbul.

Mustafa Kemal's goal was to modernize his nation. He proclaimed,
"We shall transplant western institutions to Asiatic soil. We wish to be
a modern nation with our mind open, and yet to remain ourselves."[13]
Almost single-handedly he instituted major changes at a breathtaking
pace. It was said that in a restaurant one evening, he figured out how
to write Turkish with the western alphabet instead of Arabic script. He
instituted civil marriage; outlawed polygamy; granted women equal
rights in divorce, child custody, and inheritance; abolished Islamic
schools and courts; and removed mention of Islam as the state religion
from the constitution.

Kemal's reforms were radical indeed, especially his attempt to
build a modern nation according to European models and to leave
behind its "Islamic past."[14] He required every family to choose a new
name, a dramatic way to symbolize the break with the past and the
creation of a new nation. Kemal chose the name Ataturk, which
means "Father of the Turks," for himself.

Egypt Seeks Independence

British forces had occupied Egypt in 1882 and ruled it as a puppet
state. British control led to increased foreign investment there, greater
public security, new public works to improve irrigation from the Nile
River, and lower taxation. These improvements resulted in greater
prosperity for the people. Nevertheless, many Egyptians felt that for-

eign domination was too high a price to pay for this prosperity. By 1892, Egyptian nationalists were demanding greater control over the ministries. Because the French and the Ottomans resented the substantial British role in Egyptian affairs, they aided the Egyptian nationalists.

When the Ottoman Empire entered World War I on Germany's side in 1914, Britain declared Egypt a protectorate, and legal ties between Egypt and the Ottoman Empire were formally severed. Britain promised Egypt an increased role in the government once the war was over. In the meantime, the British stationed more than 100,000 troops in Egypt, ostensibly to guard the Suez Canal from the Germans. Hoping to stifle any discontent, they imposed martial law.

The war years were difficult for the Egyptian peasants, who were conscripted to dig ditches while the army confiscated their livestock. Rampant inflation was especially difficult for people living in urban areas. As a result, resentment against the British increased.

After World War I ended in 1918, several Egyptian nationalist leaders asked the British High Commissioner for permission to go to London to negotiate an end to the protectorate. The British government not only refused to meet the nationalists, it exiled them. In March 1919, a nationwide revolt broke out, marked by random violence in the countryside, mass demonstrations in the cities, and expressions of national unity between Copts (Egyptian Christians) and Muslims.

The British freed some nationalists so they could go to the Paris Peace Conference. This delegation (*wafd* in Arabic) was called the Wafd Party. Although the victorious nations ignored the Wafd's demand for Egyptian independence, it grew to become the major voice for Egyptian nationalism and democracy.

Egypt's demand for independence continued between 1919 and 1922. However, the British wanted to keep their troops in Egypt so they could guard the Suez Canal, their airports, their radio transmitters, and their other means of communicating with India and the rest of their empire. In 1922, the High Commissioner offered Egypt qualified independence, subject to four reservations: the security of British imperial communications; the right of Britain to defend Egypt against outside interference; the right of Britain to protect foreign interests and minorities in Egypt; and continued Anglo-Egyptian control of the Sudan, which had been placed under the joint administration of Britain and Egypt in 1899.

In 1922, Britain declared Egypt an independent monarchy under Ahmad Fuad, who became King Fuad. However, the British reserved the right to intervene in Egyptian affairs if their interests were threatened. This stipulation robbed Egypt of real independence and allowed British control to continue unabated. In 1923, Egypt's politicians drafted a constitution that, if genuinely applied, would have made the country a constitutional monarchy.

The Wafd Party won the first parliamentary elections and the organization's leader, Zaghlul, became prime minister and formed a cabinet. However, the Wafd government did not last long. When the British commander of the Egyptian army was assassinated in 1924, the police uncovered a nationwide terrorist network with ties to the Wafd. Britain demanded Egypt to apologize and pay reparations. Zaghlul accepted some of Britain's demands, but he chose to resign rather than accept all of them.

King Fuad, who thought the Wafd threatened his power, replaced the 1923 constitution with a new law that enhanced the power of the monarchy. When Fuad died, the government immediately restored the 1923 constitution and held free elections. The Wafd was again victorious and it formed a new government.

It is important to note that in 1921, the British also had created the new nation of Iraq and installed King Faisal I. However, any genuine nationalist sentiment in Iraq was weak because of the state's pluralistic population: it included a majority of Shiite Muslims, a large number of Sunnis, and a third community of Kurds. Rather than promoting unity, the growth of nationalism actually served to divide the new nation and contributed to a long series of very authoritarian governments that used force to hold it together.

SUMMARY

Although most of the colonized peoples embraced the goal of national independence, each of them followed the path that best suited its own history and culture. The various movements were also shaped by the history and culture of their colonial masters. For example, the British frowned on intermarriage between Englishmen and colonial women, but the Portuguese, Spanish and French allowed it. Moreover, the fact that Britain was a functioning republic seemed to encourage the creation of more democratic nationalist movements.

Most of the nationalist movements were influenced by ideas borrowed from the European Enlightenment. The lofty goals of liberty, justice, and brotherhood were useful tools to use against colonial masters who practiced these values at home, but ignored them in their colonies.

Nationalist movements followed different paths depending on what their leaders took from other nations' experiences. The more democratic colonial powers such as Britain, France, and the United States were often looked to as examples of good government, but at the same time their reputations were severely undermined by their obvious hypocrisy in applying these principles among non-white peoples.

The Soviet Union's sudden rise in the 1920s and 30s from an agricultural society to a strong industrial power was a strong model for nationalist movements. As Eric Wolf has argued in his landmark book *Peasant Wars of the Twentieth Century*, communism had a strong appeal to peasant majority colonies because peasants saw this ideology as a way to rid themselves of the painful market capitalism implemented by the colonial nations. As we saw in this act, peasant societies in Russia, China, and Vietnam all embraced communism as a way to fulfill their traditional desire to own and farm their own land.

The Era of Disillusion, Depression, and War, 1920–1945

Following World War I, the Western World entered a long period of disillusionment with its long-standing values such as rationalism, democracy, and progress. New insights from scientists, psychologists, and artists such as Freud, Einstein, and Picasso in the early twentieth century further undermined these older values and also the confidence and certainty that had supported them.

Newly translated texts from Asia, Africa, and West Asia that gave information about people living in other cultural groups around the world helped erode the belief in the racial superiority of white people. As new knowledge of other cultures, many of them colonies, trickled into the Western consciousness, a growing number of artists, intellectuals, and average people began to adopt aspects of cultures outside the West and question the beliefs that Westerners were the most civilized people on earth. The catastrophic war brought about by hypernationalism also challenged the assumption of Western superiority. The general sense of unease and uncertainty is summed up in William Butler Yeats's elegant poem "The Second Coming," written in 1920.

> Things fall apart; the centre cannot hold;
> Mere anarchy is loosed upon the world,

The blood-dimmed tide is loosed, and everywhere
The ceremony of innocence is drowned;
The best lack all conviction, while the worst
Are full of passionate intensity.

Ironically, even as some were questioning the idea of Western cultural superiority, many were more convinced than ever that the "Rise of the West" was the best model for understanding recent history. As one example, in 1919 the administration of Columbia University introduced a new required course, "Western Civilization." This new course quickly spread to other elite universities and in the 1920s was also offered in thousands of high schools. The course stressed the unity of "Western Civilization," and explained the concept as consisting of a large number of diverse people in Europe, the United States, Canada, Australia, and New Zealand who shared a common heritage and set of values. The West, its proponents argued, was unique because it was the only truly modern civilization that was supported by a common belief in science, rationalism, and the persistent evolution of democracy. The long evolution of the West had emerged in Sumeria and Egypt, matured in Greece and Rome, had a few bad innings in "Medieval Europe," then went on to flower in Europe and reach its highest level in the United States.

Profound changes were also brought about by rapid industrialization, the ongoing development of new technologies, and together with the radical changes in collective worldviews, all contributed to questioning older assumptions and a growing sense of unease. These daunting developments and the human response to them ushered in new patterns of belief and social organization, not only in the industrialized nations, but by people in the many colonized areas as well. People all over the world were distressed and disillusioned because national leaders were not able to find successful alternatives to war and were not able to deliver more equality and social justice at home.

NEW CHALLENGES
TO EXISTING WORLDVIEWS

Setting the Stage

Among the most fundamental challenges were the new scientific discoveries that undermined the widespread belief in an orderly universe. These discoveries also threatened the belief in certainty, began to erode many institutions such as the family, education, and religion, and stimulated new art and literature.

For millennia, religion had served as the foundation of human "truth." Then, in the eighteenth century, European Enlightenment thinkers argued that truth could be found through reason and argued that good social institutions must be built on natural laws. Beginning with Darwin and later followed by other creative thinkers in science, art, music, and literature, a new generation emerged in the early twentieth century who challenged earlier Western worldviews.

As the new generation of scientists began carrying on experiments and making empirical observations that promised a more reliable truth based on scientific thinking and experimentation, their discoveries offered a new understanding that the universe was always in motion and every part of it, down to parts of the atom, was in constant motion. Their work also suggested that the orderly universe described centuries earlier by Newton was really far less orderly and more uncertain.

Looking Inside the Atom

By 1900, several European scientists were questioning the certainty of the world that Isaac Newton had bequeathed them. The growing skepticism led a group of European physicists to look for some of nature's mysteries inside the tiny atom. In 1900, the German scientist Max Planck (1858–1947) demonstrated a new theory that energy is not continuous like running water, but formed inside the atom in tiny separate packets he named "quanta" (plural of "quantum"). His quantum theory opened the door to a generation of new scientists.

Five years after Planck's discovery of quanta, the young German Albert Einstein (1879–1955) was working in a patent office in Bern, Switzerland, without university support, or a good laboratory to work in, or a decent library to consult. This truly amazing physicist worked out complicated mathematical explanations that revolutionized not only the world of physics, but modern culture as well. Einstein found that space and mass are far from fixed and stable, but rather all of them are related or "relative" to one another. He summed up this discovery in his famous formula $E=mc^2$: "E", which stands for energy, equals mass ("m") times the speed of light ("c") squared. This equation expresses that mass and energy are basically the same. Energy is matter freed, and matter is potential energy. The human observer is also relative to time, space, and mass. A scientist's observations will be determined by his or her position and speed.

Einstein demonstrated that time and space change with motion, but not the speed of light. He also demonstrated that while time slows down with motion, mass increases. Einstein's insight that time is not fixed, but that it changes with the speed of motion, has consistently been proven correct. In the twenty-first century it is still difficult to imagine that if during the night everything in the universe had become a thousand times larger, when you got up in the morning, you would not realize any change had taken place.

In 1911, Ernest Rutherford (1871–1937) proposed that the atom is made up mostly of empty space and that electrons revolve around the atom's proton nucleus just the way planets revolve around the sun. But other scientists wondered why the electrons didn't gradually lose their energy and become absorbed into the proton.

Niels Bohr (1885–1962) employed quantum theory to answer this question. He and his associates found that atoms have a dual wave-particle structure. Electrons move around the proton without loss of energy as long

Albert Einstein

as they remain in their orbits. However, if an electron jumps from an outer orbit to one nearer the proton, part of its energy is given off in the form of radiation.[1] It is impossible to assign electrons and protons to definite places within the atom. Bohr appropriated the Daoist symbol of yin and yang to explain his new discovery and found that light was simultaneously made up of both waves and particles. For his work, he was awarded the Nobel Prize in 1922.

The proof that protons and electrons posses wave properties was strengthened by Werner Heisenberg (1901–1976) and others who postulated the Principle of Uncertainty. Building on the discoveries of his fellow quantum physicists, Heisenberg demonstrated one cannot at the same time determine the position of a body and its speed (or momentum) with equal accuracy.[2]

The work of these brilliant European physicists combined to shatter the predictable and stable world that Newton had formulated. In its place, they offered a material world composed of flying particles of uncertainty. The theory of relativity also meant that things are not as they seem and they change with the position of the observer. This new buzzing beehive of a universe, moving at incredible speeds, challenged scholars in all fields of knowledge to deal with the new realities that this generation of scientists had discovered.

Psychology

While scientists and social scientists were challenging scientific conclusions, several path-breaking psychologists were exploring the human brain. Some of their insights changed the way people thought of themselves and others.

Sigmund Freud and Karl Jung helped reveal the role that the "unconscious" plays in people's lives. Their insights gave a new understanding of the seemingly non-rational aspects of human behavior. Freud argued that society serves as a person's "superego," which dictates what he or she should or should not do. But there is another part of each person called the id. The id is our instinctive self that wants to satisfy all our immediate desires, the most important of which is the sex drive.

Freud believed human beings were constantly struggling between the id and superego and the unstable result was the person's ego. He explained that the ego is a complex of neuroses mostly rooted in our formative experiences in the family. Unlike the Enlightenment thinkers who stressed human reason, Freud focused on human irrationality and the role of emotion.

The idea that humans have an irrational subconscious further encouraged people in such fields as advertising, politics, and literature to use symbols and other means to appeal to the emotions, unconscious reactions, and instinctive human passions. If the Enlightenment had taught us that humans were capable of making rational decisions, Freud and Jung forced us to acknowledge the power of our subconscious and how traumatic experiences, especially in early childhood, might influence how we act for the rest of our lives. Insights from psychology and psychoanalysis began to influence novelists, artists, and poets such as Marcel Proust, Thomas Mann, James Joyce, William Faulkner, and Pablo Picasso.

The discovery of the unconscious and the psychoanalysts' stress on human irrationality also influenced economics and politics. Businesses began to rely even more on advertising to sell their products. Instead of focusing on the quality of a product, advertisements tried to tap into psychological associations the ads would create in the potential buyer's mind. Politicians seeking votes began to realize that their stands on issues were often less important than how the candidate connected with people on an emotional level.

Social Science

Many anthropologists sought to study human society with the same precision and rigor that physical sciences were using to study the natural world. August Comte (1798–1857), one of the founders of sociology, argued that humans had evolved through three historic stages: a religious stage, a philosophical stage, and finally a scientific stage. Comte believed that social scientists should try to discover "scientific" insights about the best way to live. He called his new insight Positivism.

Many path-breaking social scientists began to study human values and culture and to challenge Comte's certainty about the laws of progress. European social scientists such as Emile Durkheim (1858–1917) and Max Weber (1864–1920) analyzed how human groups behave. Durkheim argued that every human learns how to speak, how to behave, and what values to follow in his or her society. Each of these societies has a religion that expresses its basic values and reinforces its values through rituals. He advised anthropologists to treat the norms for behavior and the beliefs in each society as "social facts," and not judge them against any uniform abstract criteria.

Max Weber studied how cultural values influence the way people act, particularly how religious values can shape economic behavior. Weber suggested that humans are motivated to act by several different values. We may act out of raw emotion, because of long-held traditions, or sometimes by rationally thinking through consequences of our action. Finally, we may act out of commitment to some abstract value such as equality, market values, or sacredness of life. Followers of Weber in political science and economics argue that humans are not motivated by one thing alone, but by many factors including pure emotion and the hold of tradition. Many contemporary economists are still trying to analyze how personal and group values affect the economic decisions people make.

By the twentieth century, many social scientists, influenced by Einstein's insights that truth is relative, rejected Comte's concept that social science is pure science. After studying Eskimos, Franz Boas (1858–1942), an American anthropologist, concluded that the way they lived was no better or worse than our own way of life. He explained that people live in "culture groups" that share a way of life and a common worldview. Each culture makes sense to the people inside it, and no culture should be judged from the outside.

Boas's students, particularly Margaret Mead (1901–1978) and Ruth Benedict (1887–1948), carrying on his work in anthropology, established the concept of "cultural relativism": there is no superior group of people and all human groups have roughly the same distribution of intelligence. If all humans are intelligent, these social scientists proposed, then the human brain encourages them to create a cultural system that is suited to the time and place in which they live. This phenomenon explains the thousands of distinct cultures, each with its own language and worldview. This concept of cultural relativism proved to be a powerful force in challenging the concept of Western uniqueness and superiority.

Literature

The new insights from psychologists, sociologists, and anthropologists influenced writers in the early twentieth century. Edith Wharton's *The Age of Innocence* portrayed the sea change between the opulence of the Gilded Age in America and the less genteel twentieth-century world. Sinclair Lewis' *Main Street* offered a biting satire of small-town America. Willa Cather's many novels, including *Death Comes to the Archbishop, O Pioneers*, and *The Professor's House,* vividly portray life in the American Great Plains and the rapidly changing world of the early twentieth century. Demonstrating the growing awareness of cultures outside of Europe was the fact that the Indian writer Rabindranath Tagore won the Nobel Prize for literature in 1913 for his long poem *Gitanjali.*

The disillusionment following World War I spurred a wave of writing that focused on the evils of war, the blundering of political leaders, and the lack of faith in progress. Erich Remarque's classic *All Quiet on the Western Front* offers a realistic picture of men in actual warfare. T. S. Eliot's long poem, *The Waste Land*, presents a spiritually empty age. Revealing insights about the subconscious was a large group of writers such as James Joyce. His novel *Ulysses* follows one man through a single day. Freud's influence can be seen in the work of the British writer Graham Greene, the American playwright Eugene O'Neill, and in the American poet Edgar Lee Masters's *Spoon River Anthology*. F. Scott Fitzgerald portrayed the so-called Roaring Twenties as a time of shallow materialism.

The Great Depression led to a wave of realistic writers such as John Steinbeck and William Faulkner. Steinbeck wrote of average people struggling to understand the world in which they live. His *Grapes of Wrath* offers profound insights into the human cost of economic business cycles. Faulkner had an ingenious ability to mix the past and present, and he offered a penetrating glimpse into the American South and the burden of its tragic racial history.

The Arts

Painting, sculpture, music, literature, and architecture all underwent dramatic changes in the twentieth century. Vasily Kandinsky (1866–1944), the Russian painter, printmaker, and art theorist, introduced abstract art that soon attracted many followers. Marcel Duchamp (1887–1968) was a second pioneer of "modern art." His "Nude Descending a Staircase" was scorned in Europe, and when he placed that painting in the famous Armory Show in New York City in 1913, the New York Times art critic savaged the work, calling it "an explosion in a shingle factory."[3] Yet this painting went on to set the standard for a new wave of modern art that soon won a world wide following.

Nandalal Bose (1882–1966) is considered the leading spirit behind the renaissance of Indian painting. His innovative use of lines in his painting of Gandhi's famous Salt March in 1931 won him world acclaim. Max Ernst (1891–1976), from Germany, was an important member of the Dada school and a leader in the surrealist school of painting. He introduced the frottage method of placing a sheet of paper over an object and then penciling over the surface to make images.

Karoda Seiki's painting "Lakeside," with its image of a woman in a light summer kimono robe holding a fan, is a fine example of modern art. He is known as the father of modern Japanese Western-style painting. The architect Frank Lloyd Wright was also greatly indebted to Japanese style buildings and his houses reflect their use of wood and the fine simplicity of Japanese art.

Pablo Picasso was one of the most prominent artists of the twentieth century. Among his many innovations was his departure from portraying realistic figures and landscapes and his use of geometrical shapes instead, a style that came to be called cubism. Picasso owed much to the African artists and he incorporated some of their masks in his work. His enormous artistic output and constant experimentation place him at the forefront of twentieth-century artists.

The poet William Butler Yeats was strongly influenced by Indian philosophy. He studied with a Hindu guru and befriended Rabindranath Tagore. His debt to India is evident in his poem "The Second Coming." The image of a beast with a lion's body and the head of a man that is "slouching towards Bethlehem to be born" refers to the man-lion, the fourth incarnation of Lord Vishnu.

Thomas Mann and Herman Hesse were also influenced by Indian thought. Mann's *The Transplanted Heads* is taken directly from an

Indian tale, and Hesse's *Siddhartha* is a novel about the Buddha's life in a Western setting. T. S. Eliot, one of the twentieth century's greatest poets, was also deeply influenced by Hindu and Buddhist writing. He ends his poem *The Waste Land* with "Shanti, Shanti, Shanti," a formal ending to a Upanishad.

Economics and Politics in the Interwar Years

By the end of the 1920s, most of the major differences among the nations seemed to have been peacefully settled and Germany had been welcomed back into the community of nations. The urge for peace, prompted by the "lost generations" of young men who had fought in the Great War, appeared to have overwhelmed the lingering desires for revenge or national gain. However, world leaders soon realize that some of the fundamental problems left by World War I had not been resolved, particularly Germany's economic collapse and the ensuing struggle between socialists and fascists that would soon render the treaties of the 1920s a "paper peace" and bring the world to the brink of another war.

The United States quickly became the world's leader in manufacturing and finance. During the war, the United States had lent vast sums to various European nations. Now the U.S. wholeheartedly embraced conservative free market capitalism, abandoning the government's attempts to regulate the free market from 1890 to 1920 in favor of a rampant laissez-faire economy. The lack of government regulations spurred a return to mergers and monopolies and the "value" of American stocks between 1925 and 1929 rose from 27 billion to 87 billion dollars.

American corporations were legally designated "individuals," and their owners fought in the courts to have them treated as such. Modern corporations had such vast wealth and influence that they often shaped national policies. Corporation owners vigorously opposed unions. Skilled workers, such as loom fixers, mechanics, electricians, and plumbers, were generally able to bargain successfully for better pay and working conditions, but unskilled workers had little power. Management's goal was "to take the control of the machine-shop out of the hands of the many workmen and place it completely in the hands of the management."[4]

The Great Depression

The free-wheeling prosperity of the decade came crashing down in October 1929 when the New York Stock Exchange plunged nearly 12 percent. The lack of bank regulation and the ensuing rush to borrow money to buy stocks had led to the crash. As the price of stocks dropped, the people who had borrowed money to purchase them had no way to pay back their loans. By 1932, when Franklin Roosevelt was elected president in the United States, more than 30 percent of American workers were unemployed and the United States entered the worst economic depression in its history. Similar events brought the European nations into what became a worldwide depression.

Depression-era food lines

Although people in the United States suffered during the depression, the impact in other nations, especially Germany and Japan, was even worse. When German credit from the United States and Britain evaporated, Germany had nowhere to turn for loans. Massive inflation and rising unemployment led to widespread unrest. By 1932, thirty percent of German workers were unemployed.

Japan's economy had depended on an open export market, and after the war, the United States had been Japan's major customer. As a result, the higher tariffs imposed during the isolationist 1920s, Japan's exports plummeted 50 percent between 1929 and 1931. Japan also suffered high unemployment and armed groups threatened to subvert its fragile democracy. The depression also took its toll in Italy and most of the other European nations, and had a major impact in China as well.

Even before the economic crash, there had been significant inequality between the haves and have-nots in all the European states. Critics openly questioned whether their nations could survive if the inequality continued unabated. Public figures discussed the possibility of workers revolting. However, Marx's hope that members of the working class around the world would unite and work together to force change was not fulfilled.

Several factors explain why workers lacked political power. Even in the most industrialized societies, workers were never in the majority. Moreover, workers were not a homogeneous group: their ethnicity, language, and religion often were more important to them than their economic class. Additionally, workers were divided according to their skill level and their crafts. Skilled workers often thought they had a higher social status than unskilled laborers; coal miners didn't necessarily see themselves as in the same category as lumbermen.

Another major reason why workers had not achieved significant political power was that labor unions, especially in Europe, had gradually been winning benefits such as shorter hours, better safety standards, and higher pay, reducing the necessity for open conflict. Most of the nineteenth-century socialist writers such as Marx had not foreseen the success that labor movements would win and how the gradual lifting of their living standards would undermine revolutionary socialist causes.

THE CHALLENGE
OF FASCISM

SCENE
TWO

Setting the Stage

In the first half of the twentieth century, the two biggest threats to republicanism and democracy were Communism and Fascism. Fascism took its name from the Italian movement toward a strong authoritarian state where the government controlled economic, political, and social decisions.

Fascism was one of the major threats to world stability following World War I. Even though Italy had been experimenting with Republicanism since 1871, it never established a viable representative government. Italy's post–World War I democratic government was being undermined by rising inflation and food shortages, accompanied by major strikes and workers' attempts to take over factories. As Italians struggled under five inept premiers in four years, Benito Mussolini (1883–1945), a strong, charismatic leader, began his rise to power.

Germans were also struggling to build a more democratic government and find solutions to the severe economic problems their exhausted nation faced, and they followed closely what was happening in Italy. Germany had also had long experience with republican government, but was devastated by losses of territory imposed by the allies, angry over the reparations imposed, and suffering under hyperinflation after the war. Similar social and economic pressures also led to a fascist movement in Spain, Japan, and many nations in Latin America.

Fascism Spreads in Italy

Mussolini, a blacksmith's son, had been raised among left-wing politicians and in 1912 he became editor of a socialist newspaper. An avid enemy of capitalism, Mussolini had urged Italy to enter World War I on the side of the Allies. Because of his pro-war stance, the newspaper fired him and the Socialist Party expelled him.

Undaunted, Mussolini launched his own newspaper, *The People of Italy*. He was determined to get Italy to demonstrate its courage by entering the war. To achieve this goal, he organized young men into fighting groups called *fasci di combattimento*. These groups gave the term "fascism" to the world. The word, based on an ancient Roman symbol of a bundle of sticks wrapped around an ax, was meant to express power.

When Italy entered the war on the Allied side in 1915, Mussolini volunteered but was soon wounded. Returning home, he continued to recruit young men and war veterans for his fighting groups. He hoped to take over the national government, but his initial efforts failed. When the socialists won the 1919 national elections, Mussolini's Fascist Party did not win a single seat.

Despite this embarrassing loss, Mussolini won the support of rich industrialists and large landholders who feared Marxist socialism. With their support, Mussolini's soldiers, known as "Black Shirts," began breaking up workers' strikes and demonstrations. They beat their political opponents and forced them to drink large doses of castor oil, hoping to get them to drop out of politics or change their views. However, in the 1921 elections, only thirty-five members of Mussolini's Fascist party were elected to the Chamber of Deputies. While serving as a new member of parliament, Mussolini formed the National Fascist Party.

Like governments in Germany, Russia, and Spain, Italy's legislative body was unable to address the real problems the country faced. By 1922, the Fascists had gained significant support from the discontented middle classes, disillusioned intellectuals, and destitute workers. During a very large general strike, Mussolini's Black Shirts used force to end the strike, and a band of Fascists in Naples marched on Rome and seized the capital. In response, the powerless king invited Mussolini to form a new government.

Once in power, Mussolini rushed through a series of laws that gave him power and ended all the other political parties. The Fascists controlled the newspapers and outlawed the free expression of ideas, and the Chamber of Deputies withered away. Calling himself "Il Duce," the leader. Mussolini promised his subjects that if they gave up their meaningless commitment to democracy, he would restore Italy's dignity and greatness.

In complete control of the country by 1925, Mussolini created what he called a corporate state. Groups were identified by their economic functions, and each was to be a voting unit in the National Assembly. In reality, Mussolini's Fascist Party controlled all aspects of Italian life, and it promised each group something. The industrialists were granted a free hand to make profits without worrying about labor or any possible strikes. The workers were promised jobs and food.

Fascist ideology sought to elevate love of and loyalty to one's nation over religion or any other value system. Religion and unquestioned love of nation were often combined into a single ideology. In effect, fascism was "a cult of the state" and everyone should be proud to be an Italian. Mussolini's fascism celebrated war as the best method for achieving national greatness and advised attacking a small state that would be easy to humiliate.

In 1923, Mussolini focused on Greece, Italy's weak neighbor. He found an excuse to occupy Corfu and forced the Greeks to pay Italy a fine. Having found aggression profitable, Mussolini seized several Turkish islands and in 1935 invaded Ethiopia, a weak African state. The other European nations and the United States protested but did nothing to stop him. In fact, there was a growing sympathy for Mussolini-type fascism among many who were disillusioned with the other great powers. It was not uncommon to hear people say, "Mussolini has made the trains run on time."

Germany Follows Italy's Example

In Germany, Bismarck had led his country with an iron hand for many years. After Germany's defeat in the Great War, Bismarck resigned and Friedrich Ebert (1871–1925) and the Social Democratic Party took over the government.

Germany faced myriad problems after the war. It was deeply in debt and was experiencing hyperinflation that nearly destroyed the economy. The new government also had to deal with naval mutinies, popular uprisings, and the growing support for the Revolutionary Socialist parties that advocated Marxist Socialism. Many Germans probably believed their struggling nation would soon follow the path of Russia.

Despite the threats to democratic government, Ebert and other liberals founded the Weimar Republic in 1919. This new republic gave far more power to the Reichstag (the lower house of government), whose members were elected by universal suffrage. Under the new republic, the president had far less power than Bismarck had exercised, but in times of emergency, the constitution granted him extraordinary powers.

Hitler and Mussolini

Many challenges threatened the Weimar Republic's authority. There was widespread resentment against the government for signing the Versailles Treaty. Almost every German hated its provisions, and in 1920 hostility to it inspired an attempted coup. Moreover, many political parties developed all across the country, and the Weimar government did not have effective ways of dealing with the many other crises the nation faced. France's occupation of the Ruhr Valley helped ruin working class stability. The seeming weakness of the government coalition led an increasing number of people to drift toward the Italian model of authoritarian leadership.

In 1923, the new National Socialist German Worker's Party, known as the Nazi Party (a shortening of National Socialist), promised stability and a renewal of Germany's strength and greatness. The driving force behind this party was a charismatic politician named Adolph Hitler (1889–1945).

Hitler had carefully explained his governing philosophy and strategies in his book *Mein Kampf* (*My Struggle*), for which he was sent to jail. Initially, few in Germany or around the world took Hitler seriously. Many considered his book a racist rant and the meanderings of a deeply disturbed mind. However, *Mein Kampf* clearly explains Hitler's worldview as well as how he planned to achieve his goals.

Hitler championed the racism that informed many communities in both Europe and the United States. He believed Germans were members of the "master race." Misinterpreting Darwin, he concluded that evolution had resulted in pure Aryans who obviously should rule the world. Hitler thought the "Alpine" race, which included French, Italians, and Slavs, was degenerate, fit only to do the bidding of the master race. The lowliest race included Africans, Gypsies, and all Jews, for whom Hitler carried a special hatred.

Hitler's Nazi Party was gaining support when General Paul von Hindenburg, a distinguished war hero, took over as president of the Weimar Republic in 1925. Despite his honesty and good intentions, Hindenburg was an ineffective leader.

Whatever possible hope had existed for the Weimar Republic was dashed in 1929 by the American stock market crash and the Great Depression. Germany could no longer get American loans for its development and old loans were being called in, causing Germany's economic depression to be even deeper than America's. With huge business failures and massive unemployment, the Weimar Republic lost its legitimacy.

As the middle class lost faith in democratic solutions, many turned to either fascism or communism in hopes one of them could solve Germany's woes. In 1930, the Nazi Party had about 200,000 members, but by 1932, as the depression deepened, it had 900,000.[5]

Because the 1932 election was so close, the government called for a new election. The Social Democrats continued to be the most popular party, but the Nazis won enough seats to encourage them to continue. They began beating up rivals in the Reichstag and making it impossible for the government to lead. Unfortunately, no individual or group seemed capable of restraining Hitler and his decidedly undemocratic tactics.

In an effort to end the growing power of what he called the "Bohemian corporal," President Hindenburg used his constitutional powers to appoint Franz von Papen chancellor. Von Papen tried to undercut Hitler's rising popularity by jailing communists and appealing to German nationalism. But then Hindenburg made a fateful decision to replace him with General von Schleicher (1882–1934).

Angered by this decision, von Papen proceeded to organize a new coalition of nationalists, army officers, war veterans, the landholding aristocrats, and some powerful industrialists. Although he had little support from the vast majority of people or parliamentary leaders, von Papen proceeded to eliminate all liberal opposition to his rule and installed himself as a dictatorial leader. In January 1933, von Papen made his own fateful decision: he demanded that Hitler be appointed the new chancellor.

As chancellor, Hitler assumed complete dictatorial power and moved quickly to end all vestiges of democratic government. Hitler was a far more effective dictator than Mussolini, and Germany was more united. It sensed the possibility of reclaiming its earlier status as a world power. The German lower classes wanted leaders who exalted their nation, and Hitler and Goebbels, his Minister of Information, were skilled at arousing loyalty.

Hitler made liberal use of night rallies, athletic spectaculars like the 1936 Olympics, and military displays to attract millions of Germans to the "Fatherland." His use of "Fatherland" instead of the more common term "Motherland" signaled that his nationalism rested on "masculine" qualities of strength and virility and the subordination of women, who were to be the incubators of a new "master Aryan race." As the German nation became the essence of one's personal identity in the 1930s, Communism faded as a popular option.

Hitler was also skilled at making the German people furious over the humiliations they had suffered after the Great War. In speech after speech he focused on Germany's "fourteen years of shame and disgrace, the shame of the Ruhr" and other blows to German pride. Hitler's eloquence and unquestioned confidence in rebuilding German pride were key to his increasing popularity.

In his quest for absolute power, Hitler also appealed to the racial superiority of the German people. He envisioned a world where Germans, the purest of the "Nordic" races, would be in control while other "Aryan" nations would be supporting bureaucrats. Hitler wanted to destroy the unworthy races or to make them slaves. He especially drew upon the anti-Semitism that was already rampant in Germany and much of Europe, calling Jewish liberals weak and effeminate and claiming the Jews were responsible for "selling out Germany." He roused non-Jewish Germans to hate Jews and to destroy their homes and businesses.

Hitler's racism led to experiments in selective breeding in order to create an even purer Aryan race and he advocated eliminating Gypsies, retarded people, homosexuals, and the mentally ill. Hitler also thought Christianity was a rival to his German nationalism. The worship of the state reached its ultimate heights under Adolph Hitler.

In both Germany and Italy the Fascist leaders sought to instill nationalist ideals in the young. Teenagers were organized into paramilitary groups. The school curriculum taught the racial superiority of Germans and Italians and that racial and ethnic prejudice was a form of patriotism.

Spain Joins the Fascists

Although Germany and Italy were arguably the most important fascist states in the 1930s, other nations supported some form of fascism. Fascists in Spain had had difficulty establishing a stable republic with democratic rights. Miguel Primo de Rivera was Spain's military dictator from 1923 to 1930. In 1930, a general election brought a coalition of socialists and radical republicans to power and drove the king into exile. The radicals drafted a new constitution that gave far more autonomy to the various regions. New laws also stripped members of the nobility of their special privileges and restricted the power of the Catholic Church.

After the second Spanish Republic ended in 1933, José Primo de Rivera, the son of the earlier military ruler and an admirer of Mussolini, seized power. Various right-wing parties then merged into the Falange Española, named for the ancient Greek phalanx. The Falangist Party made the usual Fascist appeals: glorious nationalism, the unity of the people under one flag, and glorification of the Spanish Empire. The Falangists also promoted an economic policy where all classes were expected to cooperate in creating greater prosperity for the nation.

The Falangist reforms did not last long. In July 1936, an armed group of Republicans tried to restore a democratic government. When the coalition of socialists and republicans executed the Falangist leader, General Francisco Franco became the new Falangist leader. Franco was less ideological than his predecessor. With Franco in power, the supporters of a republican system mobilized their forces and launched a civil war against the dictator.

Japan Adopts Authoritarian Rule

Japan had been seeking to be admitted into the exclusive club of great powers for a long time. Initially, it had tried to imitate the script the powerful nations had followed, namely to defeat known powers and establish colonies. It had accomplished the first goal by defeating both Russia and China, and it had accomplished the second goal by colonizing Korea in 1910. But none of these accomplishments brought the desired results.

The Japanese people had also suffered greatly during the Great Depression of the 1930s. Japanese exports, the basis for Japan's economy, had decreased dramatically and the economic collapse led to disillusionment and the development of anti-democratic groups. Unemployment soared while wages diminished and workers staged strikes. Young people were especially frustrated because they could see no hope in their futures.

By 1929, Japan had successfully embraced liberal republicanism and had achieved a degree of stability. Under the leadership of Prime Minister Hamaguchi (1870–1931), Japan agreed to the various disarmament proposals the Allies had sponsored. However the Japanese military strongly opposed Hamaguchi. He was assassinated in 1930, and a group of strong nationalists from the military rose to power. Turning away from Japan's earlier willingness to negotiate and sign various peace treaties, the ruling elite began to expand its influence in China.

Japan occupied Manchuria and other parts of China that could provide manufactured goods and quantities of raw materials for this resource-starved nation. Japan, like Europe in general, was experiencing a rapid increase in population and her Korean colony provided new areas for Japanese settlement.

Japan was also strongly attracted to the concept of racial superiority, but instead of claiming membership in the "white" race, Japanese leaders argued that the Japanese were the most "evolved" Asians. Because of their superiority, the Japanese felt they should work to "uplift" other Asians. When Japan joined Italy and Germany's military alliance, the ultra-racist Hitler declared the Japanese "honorary white people" and called them "Yellow Aryans."

Under Prime Minister Fumimaro Konoe (1891–1945), the government nationalized all its strategic industries, took over newspapers, radio stations, and labor unions, and prepared for total war against China. When General Hideki Tojo, a brilliant military strategist, replaced Konoe as Prime Minister, Japan was moving closer to the fascist model of authoritarian leadership. However, the cult of the individual so prevalent in European fascism did not work very well in Japan, a society that focused more on the group than the individual. Instead, Tojo made the Japanese emperor the symbolic head of the Japanese nation and emphasized his divine status.

Latin America Seeks Stability under Authoritarian Leaders

By the 1930s, many Latin American nations that historically had been unstable were also turning to military rulers. In Central America this move toward authoritarian government was enhanced by United States policy in the 1920s. By 1940, American investment in the region had grown to $3 billion from only $1.3 billion in 1914.[6] The United States ended its expensive policy of intervening in the smaller Central American states and instead trained Latin American National Guard units that were pro American. As a result, several dictators, such as Somoza in Nicaragua, Trujillo in the Dominican Republic, and Batista in Cuba, gained power.

In 1925, conservative officers overthrew the regime in Ecuador. In Brazil, a military junta took over in 1930 and modeled their organization on Mussolini's Black Shirts. The military also seized power in Argentina and Agustín Justo ruled as a dictator in the 1930s.

A military group seized power in Chile in 1924, but it was overthrown by another military coup in 1925. All during the next two decades, military rulers frequently changed governments, all of which were authoritarian and dependent on the army.

By 1940, fascism also had gained many followers with Latin American leaders. Argentina under Juan Perón (1895–1974) was very attracted to fascism. In 1943, Perón led a military coup and took his country into the fascist camp. After his death he was succeeded by his wife Eva Perón.

The rise of authoritarian governments throughout Latin America demonstrated once again that the hierarchical social structures of many nations in the area had not substantially changed over the centuries. The nations in the region still suffered from the dominance of large landholders and industrialists. The majority of people were still relatively poor and the expansion of the middle class was slow. The growth of democratic government was further impeded by the great number of large American corporations that controlled many of the rich raw materials and often interfered in Latin American politics.

TOWARD A SECOND
WORLD WAR

Setting the Stage

Although the First World War was fought as a "war to end all wars," the victorious allies did very little to manage the intense nationalist rivalries that not only continued after the war, but grew even stronger. The vicious contest for power among Western nations and Japan greatly undermined the world trading system that had flourished before the war. During the 1920s, nations raised tariff barriers in order to pay off war debts, and the United States, after joining the Allies in 1917, retreated into isolationism.

The Treaty of Versailles, various other treaties in the 1920s, and the efforts of the League of Nations all failed to keep the peace. The Great Depression of the 1930s helped bring fascism to Italy, Germany, Spain, and Japan. The economic wreckage it wrought around the world demonstrated that there was no effective institution or method for managing international conflicts. As a result, as the fascist powers mobilized and prepared for war, the rest of the world preferred to take no notice.

Steps toward War

Japan's appetite for colonies had already brought it success in both the Sino-Japanese and the Russo-Japanese wars. But even after these stunning victories, the Japanese imperialists believed that the European powers failed fully to appreciate Japanese interests and were lukewarm about welcoming Japan into the exclusive club of world powers.

When Prime Minister Hamaguchi was murdered in 1930 and the military clique took over, Japan's foreign policy grew even more aggressive. In September 1931, Japanese troops moved into Manchuria. A weakened China could only appeal to an equally weak League of Nations to try to stop this aggressive move. The League's condemnation of Japanese aggression meant nothing because, by this time, the League was powerless. When China boycotted Japanese goods in 1933, Japan responded by attacking Shanghai. China was forced to accept a treaty that legitimized Japanese occupation of large areas in northeastern China. Again, the League's members, as well as the United States, did nothing.

Meanwhile, Japan, newly allied with Germany, continued to expand its empire in Asia. After 1931, Japan occupied Chinese territory from its base in Manchuria. China was further weakened by the civil war raging between Chiang Kai-shek's nationalist armies and Mao Zedong's communist forces. Only after the nationalists and communists forged a united but unstable front in 1936 could a united China effectively fight the Japanese invaders. The Japanese were also increasingly hostile to the United States because of its outright support of Chiang Kai-shek's nationalist government in China.

In 1936, a group of Japanese military officers overthrew the Japanese government, removing the last vestiges of Japanese opposition to war. In 1937, using a minor clash between Japanese and Chinese troops near Beijing as an excuse, the Japanese launched a full-scale invasion of China. With lightning speed they took Shanghai and then Nanjing, forcing the Chinese government to move their capital to Chongqing in the west. The desperate Chinese forces intentionally flooded the Yellow River to try to stall Japanese advances. However, nothing deterred the better-equipped Japanese army from taking Wuhan in 1938.

Although President Roosevelt made several harsh speeches against Japanese aggression, the United States, still mired in the decade-long Great Depression, was unwilling to act. Despite American outrage at Japanese expansion in Asia, Roosevelt was unable to move his country to a more aggressive policy toward Japan, and the United States did not cut off trade with Japan until July 1940.

By that time Italy, one of the last nations to seek colonies, decided to make a sliver of oasis land called Walwal in Abyssinia (Ethiopia), a small East African state, into an Italian colony. In 1934, Mussolini launched a full-fledged invasion of Abyssinia, commenting with fascist bravado, "War is to man what maternity is to woman." When Abyssinia appealed to the League of Nations, it got only an ineffective boycott and pious words against aggression. Using aerial bombs, poison gas, and tanks, the Italians easily overwhelmed the hapless Abyssinian forces and the emperor, Haile Selassie, fled into exile.

These aggressive actions encouraged Hitler to challenge his former enemies. In 1936, German troops boldly marched into the Rhineland, the area that the Versailles Treaty had clearly stipulated was to have no military presence. In response, France mobilized 250,000 troops while Great Britain did nothing to support France. Once again, naked aggression was met by inaction. Germany seized the opportunity to join Italy and Japan, and the alliance of Axis Powers was born.

The first real bloodletting in Europe came that same year during the civil war in Spain. Since their election in 1931, Spain's Republican government had instituted a number of basic reforms, including breaking up the large estates and establishing a modern educational system. However, the fledgling democracy faced militant aristocrats and army officers and an equally militant socialist movement that were committed to destroying republican rule. In 1936, a well-organized group of conservatives and military officers took up arms to overthrow the republican government.

Italy and Germany, the two fascist powers, realized they could strengthen their alliance by supporting the authoritarian government in Spain so they provided arms, money, and advice to the pro-Franco forces. Hitler and Mussolini also saw a splendid opportunity to test the new aircraft and bombs that they were giving Franco's forces. Backed by this aid and the Spanish military, Franco expected a swift victory. However, the republicans and socialists joined forces and raised a volunteer Spanish army. It was soon joined by thousands of anti-fascist groups from Germany Italy, Poland, Austria, Russia, Great Britain, and the United States.

The outpouring of support for the Spanish Republic from ordinary people around the world demonstrated the overwhelming opposition to fascism. But once again, the democratic governments did nothing to stop this aggression. Britain and France pledged non-intervention, and therefore support for the Loyalist army rested entirely on volunteers from many countries, while Italy and Germany enthusiastically joined the Fascists. The Spanish Republic finally fell to Franco's forces in 1939.

Neville Chamberlain (1869–1940) was elected Prime Minister of Britain in 1937. Unfortunately, this mild-mannered and ultra-appeasing leader believed he could negotiate with dictators and that they would observe the treaties they signed. He was probably also responding to a certain feeling of guilt among English people who realized that Germany had been badly mistreated by the Treaty of Versailles. In addition, many English men and women admired Hitler's and Mussolini's efficiency and ability to create stability and prosperity in their nations. Some political realists also thought that a strong Germany and Italy would be an effective barrier against expansion by the fledgling communist regime in Russia.

Watching the weak and tepid response to fascist aggression, members of some of the smaller nations dropped out of the inept League of Nations and sought ways to make peace with the Axis powers. Belgium abandoned its alliance with France; Poland agreed to a non-aggression pact with Germany; and Romania and Yugoslavia quit their alliance with Czechoslovakia, leaving that small nation alone in its alliance with France.

Germany Makes Its Move

By 1938 the Germans had become the world's most efficient military machine. The German Luftwaffe (air force) was larger than England's and France's air forces combined. Germany had used its enormous military buildup to pull itself out of a depression. No wonder the vast majority of Germans supported Hitler and his ability to regain lost territory and respect in the world.

In 1938 Hitler launched the "Anschluss," an all-out invasion of Austria, and occupied that country virtually unopposed, while the immobilized democracies looked on in disbelief. Claiming he intended to liberate his fellow Germans, that same year Hitler's armies marched into the Sudetenland, an area in Czechoslovakia where Germans were in the majority. On the eve of that invasion, after meeting with Hitler, Chamberlain had returned to England with a piece of paper on which Hitler had promised he had no further ambitions in Europe.

Representatives from Germany, England, France, and Italy then met in Munich, Germany, and awarded the Sudetenland to Germany with the understanding that this completed Germany's expansionist plans. Then they all signed a pact renouncing war. Chamberlain's acquiescence to Hitler's empty promises now seems highly naïve. However, the British Prime Minister had grown up in an age when diplomats assumed that European leaders and foreign ministers kept their word.

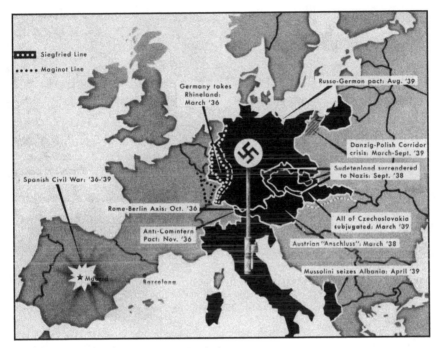

Prelude to war

But Hitler had had no intention of observing the non-aggression treaty that he had so willingly signed. Instead, in March 1939, he demanded that the Czech president allow the rest of his country to become a German protectorate. Soon after, Hitler was ready to reclaim the Polish Corridor and the city of Danzig.

The War Begins

This time the British and French warned Germany that they would defend Poland's independence. Biding his time, that summer Hitler

signed a non-aggression pact with Russia, a move that caught France
and Britain by surprise. Many nations as well as Pope Pius XI called
on Germany to avoid another great war, and the King of Belgium and
the Queen of the Netherlands volunteered to mediate.

On August 29, Hitler issued an ultimatum to Poland to cede Danzig
and the Polish Corridor back to Germany. When Poland refused,
Hitler launched a fierce attack. Finally, realizing Hitler's true ambitions, Great Britain and France declared war on Germany in September 1939.

Hitler's immediate goal, as World War II started, was to conquer
Eastern Europe and use it as an agricultural base to support German
industry. He called this plan *Lebensraum*, Germany's desire for "living space." At the same time Italy set its sights on acquiring more
African colonies, and Japan planned to create a "Greater East Asia
Co-Prosperity Sphere" that would bring China and Southeast Asia
under Japanese control.

Britain, France, and some of the smaller European nations were
united in their goal of stopping Hitler's moves. Poland was fighting
for its very existence as a sovereign nation, and England and France
were fighting to prevent Germany and Italy from taking over Europe
and spreading totalitarian rule there.

At the beginning of the war, the Allies planned to follow their
World War I defensive tactics, symbolized by the French-built Maginot line along its borders with Germany and Italy. However they
soon learned that Germany's huge armored vehicles, airplanes, and
rapid firing machine guns could run right around and through the
Maginot line.

World War II was the very opposite of World War I. This time the
technologically driven armies would fight an offensive war. The military could use dozens of different high-speed vehicles to transport
men, guns, and supplies over long distances. Tanks and airplanes
could deliver large bombs and small fighter planes could provide air
cover to advancing troops. Bombers and fighter planes could take off
and land on huge aircraft carriers. Massive bombings meant that civilians became prime targets and few groups were left unharmed.

In hopes that the nations with the greatest manufacturing capacity
would ultimately prevail, the warring nations focused on building

complex war machines. Initially the German armies were unequalled in their ability to move large armies and armaments very quickly. The Nazi *blitzkrieg* (lighting war) moved massive forces in record time. In Germany's first large-scale invasion using the blitzkrieg, its forces quickly overran Poland's traditional army. With Russians attacking Poland from the northeast, German troops conquered that nation in a matter of weeks. Meanwhile, Russia invaded tiny Finland.

In the spring of 1940, Hitler's armies quickly conquered Denmark and Norway. Sweden agreed to supply Germany with vital materials if Germany would respect Sweden's neutrality during the war. In May, German armies attacked Belgium and the Netherlands. Although the Dutch fought back, losing 100,000 men, they too soon succumbed to German firepower.

As the German army advanced, the British and French armies made their stand in Belgium and northern France. This time the disciplined German army out-maneuvered the Allied troops and took Calais and Boulogne, cutting off the French and British armies. On May 28, Belgium surrendered and the British army was pinned against the sea on the beaches of Dunkirk. In this darkest hour, the English mobilized every available boat that could cross the channel and rescue 338,226 of the stranded soldiers, leaving all their heavy equipment behind. For the British, the Dunkirk rescue was a miracle.

The Fall of France

France now faced the German armies in mainland Europe alone. Although the French army had an equal number of troops and good equipment, the Germans quickly broke their will and marched unimpeded on to Paris. Hitler forced the defeated French to sign an armistice in the very railway car in which the German generals had surrendered to the allies in 1918.

Many historians have pondered why the French army fought so poorly at the beginning of the war. After Hitler's invasion of Poland, the German border with France was almost completely undefended, yet the French armies did not attack Germany. The French had better planes, heavier tanks, and may even have had more soldiers, but they didn't attack. Perhaps, like the Belgians, they had suffered too much in the earlier war to muster the fighting spirit once more. The French may also have overestimated the strength of the German military because of the string of early German victories. The severe divisions in French society during the interwar years may be another explanation.

The victorious Germans installed the Vichy government in France and made 82-year-old Marshal Pétain its puppet president. For the rest of the war, the Vichy government fully cooperated with its German masters, imprisoning some 135,000 people, interning another 70,000, deporting some 76,000 Jews to Nazi death camps, and sending 723,000 French workers to Germany where they became virtual slaves.[7]

Germany's rapid victories encouraged Russia and Italy to go on the offensive. Mussolini wanted France's Mediterranean coastline and also France's colonies in North Africa. Meanwhile, Russia took control of part of Romania and all the Baltic states. The Axis powers reached their greatest expansion and power during the summer of 1940.

Britain Fights On Alone

Embattled Great Britain was now the last obstacle to German control of Europe. Promising the British people only "blood, sweat and tears," Winston Churchill, Britain's Prime Minister, called out to the British soul to "defend our island, whatever the cost may be. . . . We shall never surrender . . ."[8] Urging the British people to fight on, Churchill promised, "If we stand up to him, all Europe may be free and the life of the world may move forward into broad, sunlit uplands."[9]

Hitler wanted to destroy the English air force and "soften up England" before invading. In July 1940, he launched the "Battle of Britain," the intensive bombing of British land and civilians and the first step toward "Operation Sea Lion," the code name for Germany's invasion of the British Isles. The major part of the air war ended in October, but German raids lasted through December. The stubborn British resistance, greatly assisted by the newly invented radar that detected approaching German planes as well as Britain's effective fighter planes, saved the small island from defeat.

During the battle for Britain, Britain's Royal Air Force lost 1,023 fighter planes while the Germans lost 1,887 aircraft. British civilian deaths during the six months of bombings stood at 23,002 dead and 32,138 wounded. In a single raid on December 19, 1940, 3,000 British civilians lost their lives.[10]

Unable to bomb England into submission, Hitler became impatient and turned his attention to the Soviet Union. Even though Germany and Russia had signed a non-aggression treaty, invading Russia in order to secure needed grain, coal, and iron had long been part of Hitler's master plan. In June 1941, Hitler's armies, accompanied by soldiers from Romania, Hungary, Finland, and Italy—perhaps the largest armies ever assembled—invaded Russia. Some nine million men fought along an eighteen-hundred-mile front during the Russian campaign.

Initially, Hitler's forces moved deep into Russian territory, and by October they had almost reached Moscow. Then winter set in, dramatically slowing the German advance. To make matters worse, as the Russian armies retreated, they had moved heavy industries beyond the Ural Mountains and burnt and destroyed everything of value in their path. Unable to defeat the Russian forces, the German troops were caught far from their supply base and ill-equipped for winter warfare.

The Battle of Stalingrad, fought during that winter of 1942–43, was probably the turning point in the war in Europe. Although the German armies took much of the city by day, they lost those same areas at night. Finally about a million Russian soldiers surrounded the city and the German armies. The German commander probably could have broken out of the encirclement, but Hitler had ordered him to stay in the city and fight "until the last man." Stranded in the brutal winter of freezing weather and often without food, the German army of 91,000 surrendered in February, 1943, while remnants of the once-great force fled in full retreat. In this decisive battle, "the Red army suffered over a million casualties and the Axis an estimated 850,000. More than 40,000 Soviet civilians were killed in Stalingrad during the battle."[11]

Japan Brings the United States into the War

The United States managed to stay out of all the actual fighting until the winter of 1941. But as Britain was recovering from the relentless air attacks and Russia was beginning a counter attack, Franklin Roosevelt and his advisors were trying to move the United States toward war. Roosevelt, a master at shaping public opinion, had convinced the

U.S. Congress to pass the Lend-Lease Act in 1941. Accordingly, the
United States transferred U.S. naval ships to Britain and sent needed
munitions and other commodities to aid its war effort. The Americans
also aided Russia by sending supplies on merchant ships to the Baltic
ports, across the Pacific to Siberia, and through the Persian Gulf and
Iran.

Roosevelt and Churchill met and signed the Atlantic Charter on
August 14, 1941. It described their war goals and called for a peace
that would guarantee that all "men in all the lands may live out their
lives in freedom from fear and want." The charter also pledged that
"no territorial gains were to be sought by the United States or the
United Kingdom," and that "all peoples have a right to self-determination." This phrase rang loudly in the ears of colonial peoples around
the world, who took it as a promise of freedom after the war.

After Russia had agreed to a neutrality pact with Japan in April
1941, Japan, with Germany's full support, had begun to build its
"Greater Asia Prosperity Sphere," a slogan intended to spread a thin
veneer over Japan's intent to conquer most of Asia. When General
Hideki Tojo (1885–1948), a virulent Japanese imperialist, became

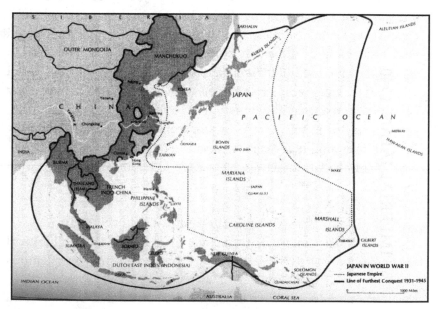

Japan in World War II

prime minister on November 1, 1941, Japan launched attacks on Southeast Asia and easily defeated the small British and French forces in their colonies. With their eyes fixed on the oil-rich Dutch colony of Indonesia that the Japanese so desperately needed to fuel its navy and air force, the Japanese high command began to plan an attack against the American base in Hawaii in order to seriously weaken if not destroy the U.S. Navy stationed there. Having called the American bluff so many times in the 1930s, the Japanese mistakenly believed that America was not willing to wage war and would leave Asia to feed the Japanese appetite for empire.

In December 1941, in one of the most daring naval operations in history, Admiral Yamamato ordered a fleet of Japanese aircraft carriers to sail undetected the 4,000 miles to Pearl Harbor. On December 7, Japanese planes from these aircraft carriers reached Pearl Harbor and all but destroyed the Pacific fleet and most of the American aircraft stationed there. Only the American aircraft carriers that were out at sea escaped unharmed. The following day, President Roosevelt, describing the Japanese attack as "a day that will live in infamy," declared war on Japan and Germany.

The American response to the Japanese attack on Pearl Harbor was to send most of the U.S. forces to fight against the Germans. The U.S. Navy and Marines were assigned to defeat the Japanese. The Pacific War against Japan focused on destroying the Japanese navy by hopping from one island to another across the Pacific until American planes were close enough to bomb Japanese cities. The Japanese had thought that the passionately isolationist Americans would make Pearl Harbor an excuse for neutrality and that it would take the United States years to rebuild its navy. Japanese intelligence was wrong on both counts. Once attacked, American public opinion fully supported an all-out war and demanded the Japanese surrender unconditionally.

The turning point in the Pacific was the naval battle of Midway Island in June 1942. Admiral Halsey, in one of the most brilliant campaigns in naval history, directed this major battle of aircraft carriers. The Japanese planned to capture Midway and use it as an advance naval base as they destroyed the U.S. Pacific Fleet. Instead, the U.S. Pacific Fleet surprised the Japanese forces and sank four of the

Japanese carriers that had attacked Pearl Harbor only six months before, while only losing one of their own carriers. Japan was left with only two aircraft carriers.

Following Midway, the Americans and their Allies took the offensive in the Pacific. Soon American and Australian forces defeated the Japanese at Guadalcanal in the Solomon Islands, checking Japan's advance to the south.

After Midway, the commander of the Japanese Navy informed Prime Minister Tojo and the Emperor that their navy could only hold off the superior American fleet for a year at best. Even so, the Japanese leadership, with the full support of Emperor Hirohito, decided to fight on; it desperately wanted to win at least one major victory against the Americans before making peace. Although Japan fought on for three more years, it never achieved that much-sought victory.

The War in Europe

While the U.S. Navy and Marines were fighting in the Pacific, the Army invaded North Africa in late 1942. By May of 1943, using their new American Sherman tanks, together with British forces, the allies succeeded in driving the Germans out of Africa. The American Army Chief of Staff, George Marshall, then wanted to launch a direct invasion in France that the Russians enthusiastically supported. However, Churchill, aware of a potential long-range threat from Russia, convinced Roosevelt to invade through Italy in order to keep the Russians out of southern and Eastern Europe, a strategy designed to weaken the Soviet Union as much as possible before the war's end.

The allied forces invaded Italy in September 1943, but it took nine months before they controlled the country. At the same time, American marines were continuing their efforts to take small islands in the Pacific. Once the Americans controlled Saipan in the summer of 1944, American bombers could reach Japan and they began frequent brutal bombing raids. Firebombings of Tokyo destroyed most of the city, took 97,000 civilian lives, and left 125,000 wounded.

In June of the same year, a massive allied fighting force landed in Normandy on the French coast. Four thousand ships, eleven thousand planes, eight hundred naval landing crafts, and 500,000 men arrived

The Normandy invasion

Churchill, Roosevelt, and Stalin at Yalta

just before dawn on June 6. Following a fierce bombardment by the large ships, British, U.S., and Canadian soldiers waded ashore. Despite withering German fire and staggeringly high losses, the surviving soldiers somehow managed to crawl up the steep embankments and secure a foothold.

Once this first line of Germany's defense had been breached, allied soldiers and equipment poured into France, and by August the allied armies had liberated Paris. In a last effort to save his Third Reich, Hitler launched the Battle of the Bulge in December 1944. The Allies slowly drove the Germans to the west while the Russian armies were advancing from the east. At a meeting at Yalta in 1945, Churchill, Roosevelt and Stalin had agreed that the British and American forces would allow the Russian soldiers to capture Berlin, which they did on May 2, 1945.

The War Finally Ends

During the last allied offensive in France and Germany, American forces were still fighting their way nearer Japan. In October 1944, the American navy destroyed what was left of the Japanese navy. The Japanese were using massive suicide bombing of American ships. Even without a navy or air force, the Japanese were still hoping to achieve at least one victory for their Emperor.

In June 1945, American forces invaded the island of Okinawa and fought the last and bloodiest battle of the war, where about a third of the population died.[12] At the Potsdam conference in July–August 1945, the Allies warned Japan that the attacks on them would increase with terrible vengeance.

That same month the Americans dropped two atomic bombs, one on Hiroshima on August 6 and another three days later on Nagasaki. Such a deadly weapon had never been used before. Three square miles of Hiroshima were scorched and 60% was obliterated. About 70,000 people were killed instantly and 100,000 were wounded; many of them died later of radiation poisoning. On September 2, 1945, Japan finally signed an agreement accepting unconditional surrender.

The consequences of the war were enormous and the numbers killed and wounded were greater than in any previous war. Twenty-two million military personnel and 28 million civilians were killed. For the first time in history, a war had killed more civilians than military.

The Soviet Union lost the most people: 13 million military and 35 million civilian dead.[13] Germany lost 4.5 million military and 2 million civilians, not counting the victims of the Nazi death camps. Japan suffered 2 million military deaths and 2 million civilian. Poland lost 4 million civilians and Yugoslavia lost 1.4 million. On the allied side, China suffered 2,500,000 military and 7,400,000 civilian deaths. Great Britain lost 300,000 military troops and 50,000 civilians. The United States lost 320,000 military personnel and very few civilians.[14]

During the last stages of the war, Allied troops liberated a number of concentration camps that Hitler had used to kill massive numbers of Jews and other victims. In the camps such as Buchenwald, Dachau, Bergen-Belsen, and Auschwitz, millions of innocent people had been gassed, tortured, and starved to death. This German holocaust was the most deadly case of genocide in human history. The Jewish population in Europe on the eve of the war had been 9,739,000, but in 1945 only 3,505,800 Jews remained. The Nazis had also murdered another 6 million Poles, Czechs, and Russians, and many others. Estimates of the total number of deaths due to Nazi policies between 1933 and 1945 amounted to some 20,956,000.[15]

SUMMARY

The generation born around 1900 had lived through the age of hyper-nationalism and radical changes in their collective worldviews. They had lived in nation-states that refused to find a peaceful method to settle their differences. They had fought in and sent their sons to fight the two bloodiest wars in history. They also raised their families amidst the worst economic depression in their history. The people of China and the Soviet Union experienced violent revolutions and wars that claimed some fifty million of their citizens.

The world after the war was a very different place than it had been at the beginning, and a large majority of the world's people were determined to build institutions that would avoid another such cataclysm and provide peace and prosperity for the world's people.

Not only were Japan and Germany defeated; their cities, economies, and social structures were in ruins. German civilians who had lived rather well during the war, thanks to large supplies of slave labor and the expropriation of food from conquered lands for their own use, now faced widespread starvation and homelessness as millions of refugees wandered around the countryside. Italy was without a legitimate government and was plunged into general poverty. Great Britain, the main victor in this horrible war, was not much better off. Its economy was in tatters and its people were tired and disillusioned.

The United States was the only country that emerged from the war in better shape than when the war began. Although it suffered 274,000 military deaths, the U.S. mainland had not been bombed and no military campaigns had taken place on its soil. Moreover, the huge demand for war goods had stoked American factories and provided full employment and a rising prosperity.

As horrible as it was, World War II ended the Great Depression in the United States. When the 13 million American servicemen flocked home, they were guaranteed jobs and subsidized education. With a weakened Britain and France and a totally defeated Germany, the United States emerged from the war as the most powerful nation in the world. For the first time in its history, the United States was the strongest power on the world stage.

ACT FOUR

The Cold War Era: Rebuilding and Reordering the World, 1945–1960

At the end of World War II, the most terrible war in history, much of the world lay in ruins and many cities resembled huge piles of rubble. Some 85 million people had died in the war. Thirteen million members of the Russian military perished and a staggering 35 million Russian civilians were killed, mostly because of deliberate German murders, deportations, and slave labor.[1] Allied bombings killed 600,000 German civilians and 900,000 Japanese. The war left 25 million refugees around the world and another 23 million who had been deported or resettled.[2] The United States was the only major power that came through the war without any fighting on its soil.

Millions of people who were disgusted by the constant wars and revolutions of the first half of the century looked to new ways to settle disputes peacefully and to transform their nations' seeming fascination with the military toward more compassionate efforts to provide social welfare and greater prosperity for average people.

The end of World War II also marked the beginning of the "Nuclear Age," when large and small powers raced to create nuclear weapons like those the Americans had dropped on Japan. Although atomic research at first was focused on developing atomic bombs, scientists also began to experiment with peaceful uses of atomic energy, including generating electrical power.

In this act we introduce "decolonization" as a new pattern. The fact that so many colonies, beginning with India in 1947 and ending with Zimbabwe in 1980, gained independence and became nation-states during this period is a significant development in world history. In analyzing the components of decolonization, we will examine the paths that many of the colonies took toward independence and their economic and political development after they became nations.

Some new nations chose some form of democracy as their governing philosophy and practice. Others chose some form of Communism or Socialism that featured leadership by a small group of party members and a command economy where the state owned and operated the means of production. Some of the nations that chose democracy also opted for elements of socialism: the central government owned some of the means of production while leaving other sectors of the economy in private hands. Some nations, especially those with close relationships with the United States, chose to pursue the capitalist path to development. Some of these nations built vibrant democracies while others lived under strong military-supported dictators.

Many nations in the process of decolonization were not completely free of great-power interference in their political and economic affairs. This form of "neocolonialism," where outside powers permitted political independence but still dominated the new nations' economies, was especially evident in the newly independent African nations, in Latin America, and other small states around the world.

Decolonization has also ushered in vigorous debates about the construction of knowledge. Different historians writing about the colonial experience often give very different interpretations about how the colonial powers and the colonial subjects acted and the reasons for their actions. In other words, the way we "construct" information about the colonial experience differs.

Some scholars from some of the former colonies, especially from India and West Asia, have rejected history altogether. They do not think stories about the past can ever be told objectively. In fact, they see the recent discipline of history as an attempt to justify Western colonialism and therefore they believe it cannot be unbiased. Many

Western scholars reject this interpretation. As you read on in this text, keep in mind this debate about the struggle for objectivity and accuracy in stories about the past.

Writers, artists, musicians, and intellectuals from former colonized nations have contributed a rich collection of films, novels, poems, and other expressions that reveal the exploitation of their fellow humans under colonialism. The many novels on the colonial experience are among the best ways for those of us living in the West to get a feeling for what it meant to be colonized. Chinua Achebe's *Things Fall Apart* and Kiran Desai's *Inheritance of Loss* are but two examples of this literature.

The contest to win the support of these newly independent nations, most of which emerged from the collapsing European colonial empires, played out in different ways in the many nations that both the United States and the Soviet Union sought to win over to their side. We will examine how Cold War rivalry gave these "Third World" nations the opportunity to play one of the great powers off against the other.

SCENE ONE

NATIONS REBUILD THE POST–WORLD WAR II WORLD

Setting the Stage

In the immediate aftermath of World War II, government leaders seemed willing to make a serious effort to end the international violence that had plagued the world for centuries. The victorious European nations, weary and exhausted after the devastating war years, realized that imposing a vengeful peace on Germany after World War I had been a mistake. They seemed eager to reject war as the solution to their conflicts and to concentrate instead on finding new ways to survive together and provide better lives for their citizens. As a result, France and Germany, historic enemies, took the lead in creating a common future.

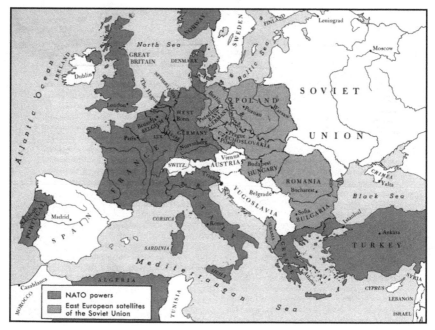

Europe after World War II

The victorious nations were nearly as devastated as the vanquished ones. Although technically the war was over, millions of people were without homes and still suffering from the war's effects. A severe drought in Europe during the summer of 1945 added to the destruction of farmland and resulted in major food shortages throughout Europe. As many as 100 million people were living on less than 1,500 calories a day. During the winter of 1945–46, millions were without heat.

But Europe was not only physically devastated and economically weakened by the war. It was no longer the world's power center. Instead, the United States, already the acknowledged economic power in the first half of the twentieth century, became the major political power, replacing Britain, France, and Germany. China, the most populous nation in the world, was caught in the midst of a bloody civil war.

The Reconstruction of Japan

Japan and China were even worse off than Europe. Many Japanese cities lay in ruins; two had been all but destroyed by atomic bombs. Only the ancient capital of Kyoto had escaped massive bombing.

The Japanese, having been forced to accept unconditional surrender, feared the worst. For Japanese leaders and military officers, the loss of face proved overwhelming. As many as 500 officers committed suicide while others were tried and executed for war crimes. Japan had to relinquish all the territory it had conquered since 1894. Japan was also required to disarm completely. Shintoism, which the Japanese had used during the war to deify the nation, was banned as the official state religion. Although Emperor Hirohito was stripped of all his political power, the Americans let him remain on the throne and serve as a unifying symbol, but he was only allowed to conduct ceremonial events.

The surrendering Japanese expected the victorious Americans to take revenge on the Japanese population by looting and raping. To prevent the possible exploitation of Japanese women, the Japanese authorities recruited a corps of young Japanese women to provide sex for the American soldiers who were occupying the country. However, unlike the Korean "comfort women" who had been forced to serve the Japanese soldiers during the war, these women volunteered, but many of them did not know what they would have to do. (When President Roosevelt's wife Eleanor learned about this project, she immediately demanded that it be ended.)

The Japanese were surprised that their worst fears were unfounded and that American troops did not take advantage or try to exploit them. General Douglas MacArthur, the Supreme Commander in charge of the Japanese occupation, promoted reconstruction and Japan began to rebuild its industry, reinstitute democracy, and carry out a number of reforms.

From the American perspective, the Japanese occupation went smoothly. It proved relatively easy to eliminate Japan's standing army, introduce educational reforms, and give small farmers plots of land. The new Japanese constitution, adopted in 1947, provided for universal suffrage that meant women could vote, and it guaranteed basic human rights. Under American guidance, the Japanese Liberal Democratic Party won the first parliamentary election and continued to dominate Japanese politics until 2009.

The American occupation ended in 1951. The peace treaty that the Japanese signed in 1952 allowed Japan to have Self-Defense Forces but no regular army. It also stipulated there were to be several American military bases in Japanese territory and a large military presence in Okinawa.

The Japanese quickly realized that the United States was serious about aiding Japan's reforms and reconstruction. Even so, it is somewhat astonishing how quickly the Japanese accepted the new reforms, elected a parliament, carried out land reform, established a free public education system, and set about rebuilding their battered nation.

One probable reason for Japan's relatively quick recovery was the indomitable energy and tenacity of the Japanese people. They have many words for extended effort; one is *gambaru*. Gambaru means something like "keep trying" or "stick to the task no matter what happens." Instead of wallowing in self-pity, the generation that came to adulthood in the late 1940s and early 50s decided to work even harder to regain their own and the world's respect; that is, they decided "to gambaru."

The Japanese also continued to nurture their long-standing traditions. The family remained the basic unit of society. Shinto practices, along with Buddhism and a strong Confucian element, continued to inform their values and actions. In most aspects of public and private life, the Japanese continued to submerge individual desires to the greater good and sought to establish harmony in their society. A common Japanese saying is: "The highest nail gets knocked down."

Japanese culture flourished after the war. Central to the Japanese tradition is aesthetics. Japanese poetry, art, films, and gardens all express a deep sensibility to nature. Writers like Yukio Mishima, Yasunari Kawabata, and Junichiro Tanizaki have been recognized around the world as major writers. Japanese films directed by Akira Kurosawa and Kon Ichikawa have also won worldwide praise. Popular support for baseball gradually resulted in excellent Japanese baseball teams.

Japan's sense of harmony had played a critical role in Japan building one of the world's most powerful economics. From 1950 to about 1990, the promise of lifetime employment led to worker satisfaction and greatly reduced the labor-management tensions that were so common in other industrialized nations.

Allied Powers Oversee the Creation of the Federal Republic of Germany and the German Democratic Republic

At the end of the war, Germany, like Japan, lay in ruins. Forty percent of the country had been severely bombed. The brutal ground war destroyed most of Germany's infrastructure and left the defeated survivors devastated. During the Soviet army's advance into Berlin, it was estimated that at least two million German women were raped.[3] Heroic German women, using mostly hand carts and paid very little, cleared the rubble from the Berlin's streets so vehicles could travel freely.

German recovery was made more difficult by its division into East Germany, occupied by the Soviets, and West Germany, under the shared occupation of France, Britain, and the United States. The Allies quickly turned the areas they occupied into the Federal Republic of Germany, while the Soviet-occupied zone became the German Democratic Republic (GDR).

After placing a number of German war criminals on trial, the Allied command in West Germany encouraged the German people to resume their prewar lives and to develop a working democracy. In the process of democratizing German politics, a large number of former Nazis, especially those with scientific and other expertise, were quietly welcomed back into society. Germans who wished to keep their jobs, such as teachers and other public servants, had to convince the Allies that they had not been Nazis, even though this process of "denazification" was very degrading for them.

Millions of Germans fled or were expelled from Eastern Europe. Hundreds of thousands of Jews who had survived the Holocaust sought secure homes beyond their native lands. (See the extended discussion of the Holocaust in Act 7, Scene 2.) Many refugees in Eastern Europe rushed to escape from the newly installed Communist regimes. The resulting population movements were the largest in European history. By 1950, approximately 11.5 million Germans had been expelled from Eastern Europe or had left voluntarily.

Many Allied leaders wanted to de-industrialize Germany completely so it could never threaten Europe again. More realistic American diplomats realized that Soviet expansion might become a major concern, and they wanted to be able to enlist German support against it. Accordingly, in September 1946, the American government supported reindustrializing West Germany and creating a democratic government there.

France and Great Britain Rebuild

In 1946, the French people created a new constitution that established the Fourth Republic with a parliamentary government. However, France had had difficulty maintaining a consistently democratic government for over two hundred years. It had also suffered major destruction and loss of life during World War II. Moreover, humiliated by German occupation, France had to face a future as a second-class political and economic power.

For the next 16 years, a sequence of coalition governments presided over the liquidation of the French colonial empire, particularly Vietnam and Algeria. The battles to maintain control of these two countries were a huge economic drain and resulted in the loss of thousands of soldiers.

Charles de Gaulle came to office in 1958 as a strong president with considerable new power. As part of his effort to renew French greatness, he authorized developing a French nuclear bomb that he boasted could kill eighty million Russians. While talking tough, de Gaulle ended the Algerian War in 1962, a controversial decision that effectively ended France's colonial empire. During the de Gaulle era, France grew increasingly nationalistic and often opposed the United States in international matters.

Great Britain emerged from the war both battered and facing a severe loss of its share of world trade. Long dependent on global economic activity, British leaders desperately tried to restore their country's global commerce. However, without its colonial empire, Britain no longer had sources of raw materials, and it had to import cotton, oil, timber, iron ore, and 75 percent of its food.[4] For the first time in centuries, Great Britain became a debtor nation.

Despite Winston Churchill's plea in 1945 that the war coalition of Britain's major parties continue, he was turned out of office and was succeeded by the Labour Party's Clement Attlee. The Socialist governments imposed austere programs that asked the citizens to postpone their own needs in order to build up their export market. As part of their programs, the government nationalized basic industries such as banks, power, railroads, and iron and steel. In 1949, the government took over 92 companies involved in steel production.[5]

The Socialist governments also introduced several welfare measures, including a government-sponsored universal health system that provided free medical care for all British citizens. They passed a social security retirement program, lowered school fees, and opened up university admissions to many more students, particularly those from the working classes. However, Britain's welfare state did not deliver robust economic growth or restore Britain's economic superiority. By 1960, its sluggish economy was lagging far behind both Germany and Japan.

The Soviet Union Attempts Reforms

Although the Soviet Union was technically one of the victorious nations, the Russians and their allies suffered more from the war than any other people except the Chinese. At least 60 million had been killed, major cities were destroyed, and rich farmland had been torn apart by the prolonged fighting.

Stalin, who was still in power at the war's end, had overseen the industrialization of the Soviet Union in the 1930s. Ever the realist, Stalin knew that Britain and the United States wanted to limit Soviet influence in Eastern Europe and the Balkans, but he was also committed to maintaining firm control of the Soviet people. When he died in 1953, the Soviet leadership considered basic reforms in their system.

However, the promised loosening of Stalin's iron grip was short-lived. Thinking Khrushchev's reforms were genuine, mass protests in Poland, Czechoslovakia, and Hungary in the 1950s and 60s threatened to launch a general uprising in the Soviet-controlled states in Eastern Europe. However, Khrushchev did not hesitate to send tanks and armed forces to all of those areas, and the uprisings were quickly put down.

The United States Faces Growing Tension with the Soviet Union

The United States emerged from the war a stronger economic and military power. After four long years of shortages while the economy was retooled for war, American consumers were hungry for both new durable goods, like cars and refrigerators, and new clothing styles, vacations, and entertainments.

Traditionally isolationist and separated from Asia and Europe by two vast oceans, the United States had joined World Wars I and II only reluctantly. However, American leaders were now forced to face the realities of the new world order that thrust their country to the forefront of Western leadership.

Franklin Roosevelt, the only American president to be elected four times, was a committed internationalist, in spite of his country's isolationist sentiment. His leadership in World War II, as well as Republican internationalism, helped create a new foreign policy. Harry Truman, who became president when FDR died in 1945, had given the order to drop atomic bombs on Japan. Truman championed strong involvement in world politics.

President Truman faced public demands for a rapid demobilization of the armed forces and an end to the wartime price controls. The transfer to a peacetime economy led to rampant inflation and labor unrest. Despite these challenges, Truman pursued liberal domestic and foreign policies. He promoted civil rights for African-Americans, supported the Full Employment Act, liberalized the Social Security program, and supported federal aid to education, low-cost housing, and raising the minimum wage.

In 1952, as Truman's public support waned, the American voters turned to General Dwight Eisenhower, a popular wartime leader. Eisenhower was a moderate Republican and a convinced internationalist who carried on Truman's foreign policy. Eisenhower managed to forge a bipartisan consensus between Republicans and Democrats on several major issues, including a shared internationalist foreign policy and the preservation of the social and economic reforms of the New and Fair Deals.

During the Eisenhower years, competition with the Soviet Union fostered fear of communism and raised suspicions about potentially disloyal Americans. Senator Joseph McCarthy exploited this fear by leading public investigations to discover communist sympathizers among professors, teachers, and even government workers. Most of these accusations were false or greatly exaggerated and destroyed the reputations of many innocent people. In 1957, the Russians launched Sputnik, the first earth satellite. The shock of this astounding Soviet achievement intensified American determination to keep up with the Soviets. When John Kennedy was elected president in 1960, he promised to send an American astronaut to the moon in a decade.

AN UNEASY PEACE
DURING THE COLD WAR

Setting the Stage

The first five years after the end of World War II was a period of growing competition between the Soviet Union and the United States. In fact, the tensions between these two major powers gave birth to the term "Cold War." Despite several armed conflicts, both sides generally respected the existing balance of power and these years passed without open warfare between the two superpowers and their allies. New institutions and efforts to avoid war were also developed.

The Cold War period produced a large number of alliances and international relationships as each side tried to maximize its influence and power around the world. Beyond the alliances, both sides used various means to win over public support for their competing ideologies and political systems. Each side also used generous amounts of foreign aid to win and maintain the support of friendly factions and nations.

The Creation of the United Nations

In the immediate aftermath of World War II, government leaders seemed willing to make a serious effort to end the international violence that had plagued the world for centuries. The victorious allies realized that the harsh punishment they had imposed on the defeated nations after World War I had increased conflicts and that the refusal of the United States to join the League of Nation had crippled that organization from its inception.

During World War II, President Roosevelt had urged the Allied Powers to consider creating a new organization of nations to replace the defunct League. After serious planning, the United Nations was formed and its charter was ratified on October 24, 1945. Its preamble states:

We the peoples of the United Nations determined:

- to save succeeding generations from the scourge of war, which twice in our lifetime has brought untold sorrow to mankind, and
- to reaffirm faith in fundamental human rights, in the dignity and worth of the human person, in the equal rights of men and women and of nations large and small, and
- to establish conditions under which justice and respect for the obligations arising from treaties and other sources of international law can be maintained, and
- to promote social progress and better standards of life in larger freedom,

and for these ends:

- to practice tolerance and live together in peace with one another as good neighbours, and
- to unite our strength to maintain international peace and security, and
- to ensure, by the acceptance of principles and the institution of methods, that armed force shall not be used, save in the common interest, and
- to employ international machinery for the promotion of the economic and social advancement of all peoples,

have resolved to combine our efforts to accomplish these aims.[6]

The United Nations is composed of a General Assembly, a Security Council, a staff of bureaucrats who handle the organization's routine business, and several special agencies that deal with specific areas of world interest and concern. The General Assembly has representatives from all the member nations. With the great wave of decolonization beginning with India in 1947 and continuing through the remainder of the century, membership in the General Assembly has more than doubled.

The Security Council has five permanent members—China, France, Great Britain, the United States, and the Soviet Union—plus representatives from seven other member nations, selected on a rotating basis. Each of the permanent members may veto any Security

Council decision. The General Assembly discusses and ratifies all decisions over which the U.N. has jurisdiction. However, the Security Council has the last word on matters relating to relations among nations and issues of war and peace. Special agencies include the United Nations Children's Emergency Fund (UNICEF), the Food and Agriculture Organization (FAO), the United Nations Educational, Scientific, and Cultural Organization (UNESCO), and the International Labor Organization (ILO).

The member nations renounced war and territorial conquest and charged the Security Council with keeping the peace. Its job is especially important because from its inception, it was clear that the world was dividing into competing factions. One initial contentious debate was over how China should be represented on the Security Council. Should the People's Republic of China or Taiwan, be seated?

Following the Communist defeat of the Kuomintang in 1949, many of Chiang Kai-Shek's followers had fled to Taiwan, a small island off the coast of China. With United States support and protection, they declared themselves the Republic of China, totally independent from mainland China but hoping one day to return and rule the mainland. The Allied Powers had backed the Kuomintang during the Chinese Revolution, and they successfully argued that Taiwan should be the Security Council member. As a result, initially the much larger Peoples' Republic of China was denied membership on the Security Council, and Taiwan was seated. It was not until 1972 that the PRC finally replaced Taiwan as a permanent member.

Relations between the Soviet Union, Great Britain, and the United States, which had often been strained during the war, soon broke out into outright hostility. Stalin, the leader of the Soviet Union, argued that it should have influence over most of Eastern Europe. He was suspicions of the true motives of President Roosevelt and Britain's Prime Minster Churchill, and soon after the war, he moved swiftly to secure Soviet interests throughout the Balkans and Eastern Europe.

Stalin also supported Communist movements in Greece and seemed ready to move into Turkish territory in order to fulfill Russia's long-held desire for a warm water port. Because large areas of Soviet land on which the war against the German forces had been waged were no longer fit for farming, Stalin felt fully justified in taking land from the Eastern European nations that his forces had freed from German occupation.

In addition, Churchill had never told Roosevelt that during the war, he and Stalin had agreed on a division of influence over several European states. After the war, the Soviets quickly established socialist republics in the eastern European nations of Czechoslovakia, Romania, Bulgaria, Albania, Poland, and Hungary, and they transferred machinery, food, and manpower from these states to the Soviet Union in order to rebuild Soviet cities and industries. By 1948, Poland, Hungary, Romania, Bulgaria, and Czechoslovakia were all under direct Soviet control and Greece was in the midst of a civil war between King Geiorgios II's forces and the Communists. The one exception was Yugoslavia: after the Communist dictator Marshal Joseph Broz Tito had declared independence there, he proclaimed his independence from Soviet control.

The Iron Curtain and the Cold War

Less than a year after the end of the World War II, Winston Churchill described his view of Europe:

> From Stettin in the Baltic to Trieste in the Adriatic an iron curtain has descended across the Continent. Behind that line lie all the capitals of the ancient states of Central and Eastern Europe. Warsaw, Berlin, Prague, Vienna, Budapest, Belgrade, Bucharest and Sofia; all these famous cities and the populations around them lie in what I must call the Soviet sphere, and all are subject, in one form or another, not only to Soviet influence but to a very high and in some cases increasing measure of control from Moscow.[7]

Churchill's identification of an "iron curtain" was the first major public admission of the gulf between the democratic nations and the Soviet Union. Britain feared that the Soviets planned further expansion into Eastern Europe and knew that the Turkish government was too weak to repel Soviet efforts to gain control over the Dardanelles. However, the war had left Britain too devastated and its economy too weak to aid either Greece or Turkey.

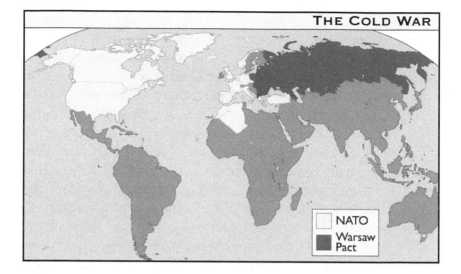

When Britain announced that it would withdraw aid to these two countries, President Truman realized the United States would have to act to prevent further Soviet expansion. In March 1947, Truman asked Congress for $400 million in military and economic assistance for Turkey and Greece. In announcing what became known as the "Truman Doctrine," the line between the United States and the Soviet Union was firmly drawn and the "Cold War" between the U.S. and the Soviet Union had begun.

Later that same year, the United States announced the Marshall Plan, an ambitious program to promote European industrial production, to bolster European currencies, to facilitate international trade, and, indirectly, to check the growing Soviet influence in Eastern Europe. Germany and Italy received Marshall Plan aid, a radical departure from the punishment administered to Germany at the end of World War I. By 1952, the Marshall Plan had contributed about $17 billion to Europe's economic recovery.

It wasn't long before Germany became the center of tensions between the NATO and Soviet nations. According to the Potsdam Agreement reached at the end of the war, the United States, Great Britain, France, and the Soviet Union were to share the occupation of Germany. As we have seen, these powers had divided Germany into four areas. However, given the Cold War tensions, Germany was soon divided into East Germany, the German Democratic Republic controlled by the Soviets, and West Germany, the Federal Republic of Germany, a fledgling democracy under French, British, and American protection. The city of Berlin, the German capital, which lay deep inside the Soviet Union zone, was also to be divided into two zones: West Berlin under Allied control and East Berlin controlled by the Soviets.

A West German looking over the Berlin Wall into East Berlin, 1961

Upset that the three Allied powers that controlled their portion of Berlin had created one political authority, in 1948 the Soviets closed off all roads, rails, and river access to Berlin. Without basic food supplies, rations in Berlin were cut to 900 calories a day. In a daring effort to aid West Berlin, the United States and its allies launched a round-the-clock airlift to supply West Berlin with food and other necessities. The Berlin airlift flew over two million tons of supplies during its 270,000 flights, many made during the particularly harsh winter. Daily flights of supplies for the beleaguered West Berliners went on until the Soviets finally lifted the Berlin blockade in May 1949.

In April 1949, the United States and representatives from Europe created the North Atlantic Treaty Organization. NATO promised to provide armed assistance to any member state that was threatened. By 1953, NATO had stationed fifty military divisions in Europe. In response, in 1955 the Soviet Union created the Warsaw Pact, which included all eight of the Soviet-controlled Eastern European nations from Poland to the Balkans, as well as East Germany. In 1955, West Germany was invited to join NATO, demonstrating that the member nations believed it was a dependable member of the Cold War alliance. From this time onward, both the United States and the Soviet Union would continue to sign on new allies in their continuing Cold War struggle.

By 1948, the removal of German industrial assets and payment of reparations had ended. With generous investments of capital from the Marshall Plan and the currency reform of 1948, the West German people began rebuilding their shattered nation. With the acute shortage of workers due to the number of men who had died in the war, the new German government welcomed many "guest workers," particular Turks, to work in factories. As a result, Germany's industrial output increased dramatically after 1948. By 1960, the West German economy had become the world's third largest.

The West Germans also created a genuinely democratic government. Because Berlin, the former capital, was well within the Soviet zone, Bonn was established as the provisional capital of the Federal Republic of Germany. The Christian Democratic Party won the first election and Konrad Adenauer (1876–1967) was chosen as Chancellor. By 1960, West Germany was a stable democracy and one of the world's major industrial powers. The Christian Democrats dominated the government from 1949 to 1966.

To contain the Soviet Union, the United States was creating an elaborate systems of alliances based on so-called "front line" states that would encircle the Soviet Union. These states included the members of the North Atlantic Treaty Organization (NATO) and a necklace of other U.S. allies from Turkey all the way to Taiwan and South Korea. The U.S. relied on Israel, Saudi Arabia, Turkey, and Iran as loyal allies against Soviet expansion in West Asia. By agreeing to supply generous military and development aid, the United States gained strategic military bases in Pakistan, Thailand, and Taiwan, and later the Philippines, including many large air bases. After World War II, the United States was already the major occupying power in Japan, South Korea, and West Germany. With this dramatically enlarged system of alliances, the United States could count on a very large number of nations to support its Cold War aims and strategies.

During the Cold War, the U.S. also kept B-52 planes armed with nuclear bombs in the air at all times, ready to attack the Soviet Union if it made a first strike. Later, American submarines armed with Polaris missiles and intercontinental missiles capable of carrying nuclear warheads to Soviet territory supplemented the B-52s. The presence of American military bases, missile sites, and troops understandably caused the Soviet Union to position its own forces along the perimeters of the countries that had established alliances and military pacts with the U.S.

Some Hot Spots during the Cold War: Korea and Egypt

Despite the informal arrangement of America's containment policy, several flash points during the forty years of the Cold War burst into open warfare and very nearly sparked a nuclear exchange. The first of these crises occurred in Korea only five years after the conclusion of World War II.

Shortly before the end of the war, Soviet troops had invaded and occupied the northern part of Korea. An informal demilitarized zone at the 38th parallel divided the country into North and South Korea. When the Japanese surrendered, American troops were occupying the southern part of the peninsula.

The Soviets immediately established the Socialist Republic of North Korea. Its communist-led political organization, called the United Democratic Front, seized the large estates and divided them among the peasants. It also took over the major industries that the Japanese had controlled, and raised an army. Once North Korea's socialist government was firmly established, the Russian forces withdrew.

During the same time, the South Koreans established a democratic government in the Republic of Korea and held free and open elections for all South Koreans. In the 1948 elections, Syngman Rhee (1875–1965), with strong United States support, was chosen president. The following year the American troops left the south, even though the South Korean security force it left behind was not nearly as powerful as North Korea's military.

In May 1950, President Rhee invited North Koreans to participate in an all-Korea election and promised the Socialist leaders that they would receive the "appropriate positions." In response, the North Koreans attacked Kaesong, an industrial city near the 38th parallel. In spite of abortive negotiations and the promise of American aid, North Korean armies invaded the south in June 1950 and nearly drove the South Korean army off the peninsula. While the Soviet Union's delegation was absent, the United States convinced the United Nations Security Council to condemn the North Korean attack.

Meanwhile President Truman initiated air and sea support for the South Korean forces and ordered General Douglas MacArthur to wage a full-fledged war to defend the Republic of Korea. By October, 1950, MacArthur's troops had driven the North Koreans back across the 38th parallel. Unfortunately, MacArthur did not agree with just containing communism. He hoped to bring China into the Korean War so he would have an excuse to invade China; he was even willing to use nuclear bombs against the Chinese. Toward that end, MacArthur pushed his troops all the way to the Yalu River, Korea's boundary with China.

MacArthur's actions not only brought China into the war, they changed the entire conflict. What was intended as a limited attempt to contain the Communists became the Korean War. After Truman finally fired MacArthur, South Korean and American troops regained the offensive. The truce that was signed on July 27, 1953, reestablished the 38th parallel as the border between North and South Korea, but no peace treaty was signed. As of 2010, the Korean War, which cost hundreds of thousands of lives, including those of about 49,000 Americans, has never officially ended.

Other crises also threatened the Cold War's uneasy peace. In 1956, perhaps encouraged by American's anti-communist statements, Hungarians revolted against Soviet rule and declared their independence from the Soviets. However, Russian tanks and armies quickly crushed this popular uprising and reestablished Soviet control. Adhering to Cold War agreements, the United States did not interfere.

In 1956, the United States got another shock, this time from Egypt, one of its major allies. Earlier, the U.S. had tried to convince the British to remove their forces from the Suez Canal and allow Egypt to control this vital waterway. However, shortly after the British left in 1956, the Egyptian government nationalized the canal. At the same time, Israel wanted some way to prevent Egyptian raids against its territory. On October 29, following prearranged plans, Israel invaded Egypt. British and French forces then attacked Egypt, claiming they needed to protect the Suez Canal.

The United Nations quickly passed a resolution calling for an immediate cease-fire and the evacuation of all foreign armies from Egypt. America's closest allies had planned and executed an invasion of a nation that was a key target of both American and Soviet planners. This event clearly revealed that the United States was the major power in the new Cold War world.

Nuclear Threats and the Cold War

The post World War II international system and the Soviet-American nuclear arms race were further complicated by the fact that the Soviet Union, Britain, France, and later Israel and China all had nuclear weapons. To attempt to limit the spread of nuclear weapons, in 1968 the member nations on the UN Security Council that already had the bomb proposed the Nuclear Non-Proliferation Treaty (NNPT). It was intended to limit the spread of nuclear weapons. Since 1968, 189 nations have adopted the NNPT treaty. Five of those countries already had nuclear weapons in 1968. India, Israel, Pakistan and North Korea did not sign the treaty, and all of them had developed nuclear weapons by 2000. South Africa, Libya, and Iran have also worked to develop nuclear capacity.

The threat of an atomic attack spread fear throughout the world. Frightened citizens in both the United States and the Soviet Union anxiously tried to protect themselves and their families. Public basements were designated as air raid shelters. People built bomb shelters in their back yards, filled with dried food, flashlights, and other necessities, in case of attack. Children in schools in the U.S. were told to "duck and cover," as if hiding under their desks would protect them from atomic radiation.

In 1956, Nikita Khrushchev, who succeeded Stalin, had begun began to liberalize the Soviet Union. He believed that imperialism and capitalism could coexist peacefully because the Communist system was growing stronger. Under Khrushchev, the Soviets ushered in a period of liberalization and stability. They launched a successful space program and financed better education and working conditions for their citizens.

Perhaps the closest the world came to a nuclear war was in 1962. In 1959, Fidel Castro, an avowed Communist leader, had deposed the Cuban president and established himself as Cuba's sole leader. The United States almost immediately put trade restrictions on Cuba and tried to isolate the small island in any way it could. But in October 1962, Soviet ships sailed toward Cuba with nuclear equipment.

President Kennedy felt that he could not allow Cuba to house nuclear warheads that could easily reach major American cities. Several days of intense debate ensued. About half of the major U.S. policymakers wanted the United States to use military force to destroy the missile sites in Cuba. After all, they argued, they were only ninety miles from the coast of the United States. When President Kennedy stated that unless the ships turned back, the U.S. would fire on them, many feared a nuclear war was about to begin. Many students who left their classes that Friday afternoon feared they would never see one another again.

After listening to all sides, Kennedy decided Khrushchev's messages indicated a willingness to negotiate. After numerous exchanges, the Soviets agreed to remove their missiles from the island if the Americans would withdraw its missiles from Turkey. Since the U.S. had already determined that the missiles in Turkey were obsolete, the U.S. agreed.

Perhaps the most important legacy of the Cuban Missile Crisis was the fact that both the Soviets and the Americas tried to lessen the possibility of nuclear attacks. In 1963, the United States and the Soviet Union signed several minor agreements, and in 1967, President Lyndon Johnson met with Soviet Prime Minister Aleksei Kosygin in Glassboro, New Jersey. Although none of these meetings produced serious treaties, the leaders did agree that the boundaries of the Cold War would continue to be respected. The two superpowers entered a period of détente that lasted into the 1980s.

Toward Greater Cooperation in Europe

The European nations made a remarkable recovery in the years after World War II. Weary from 500 years of warfare, Europeans seemed willing to reject war as the solution to their problems and to concentrate instead on finding new ways to survive together and provide better lives for their citizens in a common European society. They realized that the vengeful peace imposed on Germany after World War I had been a mistake. Instead, France and Germany, historic enemies, took the lead in creating a common future. Western Europe welcomed Germany into the European Union. A general Christian Democratic movement that swept across Europe also contributed to harmony.

Certainly the generosity of the Marshall Plan was a huge boost to Europe's economic recovery. In addition, the nuclear shield the U.S. built to contain Soviet aggression and the transfer of world power from Europe to the United States provided relative security for the Europeans so they could concentrate on rebuilding their cities and industries rather than on defense.

In 1949, ten European nations formed the Council of Europe. The loose federation emphasized a common set of values and a shared cultural tradition. The next year, the French foreign minister, Robert Schuman, offered a plan to merge the French and West German coal and steel industries into a single governing authority.

Later, four other countries—Belgium, Luxembourg, the Netherlands, and Italy—joined France and West Germany to form the Common Market. The new arrangement facilitated the free flow of economic exchanges among the members and established several other methods of mutual cooperation.

These nations continued to work toward combining their national economies into a single European economy that encouraged free trade and economic cooperation. The Common Market Council set common tariffs between the Common Market and the outside world. It also established a bureaucracy in Brussels that was to administer the various cooperative efforts.

The Brussels Treaty (1965) created the merger of the Council of Europe and the Common Market into what came to be known as the European Union. The EU further strengthened a united Europe by establishing a system of commercial courts to rule on disputes and also created a special fund to be used to encourage economic growth, especially in the underdeveloped areas of the various member nations.

The Union expanded again in 1973 when Britain, Ireland, and Denmark joined. Later, Greece in 1981 and Spain and Portugal in 1986 were added. Finally, after the German unification of 1990, the former East Germany was accepted as a member.

The Single European Act (1987) strengthened the organization's ability to create one internal market. The Treaty of European Union, signed in 1992 and ratified in 1993, provided for a central banking system and the Euro, a common currency, that replaced the national currencies. In 1995, Austria, Finland, and Sweden, all joined the EU, but Norway did not.

In 2004, ten non-EU European nations—Estonia, Latvia, Lithuania, Poland, the Czech Republic, Slovakia, Hungary, Slovenia, Cyprus, and Malta—also joined the EU, increasing its population by 20% and its land area by 23%. Most of the newer member nations were significantly poorer than the older members.[8]

In recent years the greatly expanded EU has attempted to create a common military force. The member nations have also opened their universities to one another's students and encouraged travel within the Union. Despite several disagreements and a few crises, the European Union has succeeded in forming one of the largest economies in the world and is also a formidable force in international relations.

SCENE THREE

A PROLIFERATION OF NATIONS JOINS THE WORLD SYSTEM

Setting the Stage

If anyone doubted that the European model of the nation-state was appealing, he or she would probably have been convinced of the popularity of this political organization by world events after World War II. Beginning with Indian independence in 1947, up until 1980 when Zimbabwe gained its freedom, more than ninety new nations had been formed. As of 2009, there were 195 independent nations in the world.

As we saw in Act Nine, colonized people reacted to colonization in a variety of ways. While some groups willingly cooperated with their colonial masters, increasing numbers fought against their foreign rulers. Anti-colonial activity slowed during the Second World War, but after the war, all the remaining the colonized states strove for independence and the right to form their own governments and develop economically.

In 1945, colonial powers controlled about three-fourths of the world's land, hundreds of millions of people, and most of the world's resources. Great Britain still had colonies in the Indian subcontinent and in Africa. France had colonies in Southeast Asia, and it also controlled Algeria in North Africa. Belgium ruled extensive territory in Central Africa. The Netherlands controlled land in both Asia and the Americas. Germany, a latecomer to the scramble for colonies, controlled territory in Africa. Even the United States had become a colonial power when it occupied the Philippines and Caribbean islands.

Once they became free, the newly independent nations faced many challenges. For one thing, poverty, diseases, and harsh living conditions that had resulted from colonization had stimulated high birth rates in an effort to compensate for the low life expectancy. After the 1940s, with better medicine, better technology, higher literacy, and improved living conditions, the population of some of the nations

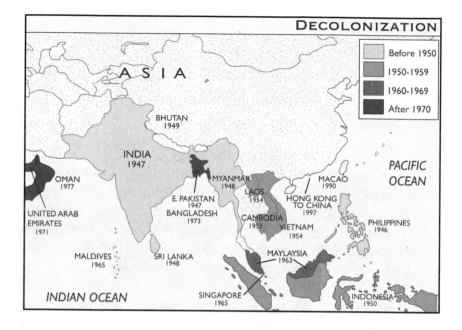

was growing four or five times as fast as in the industrial nations.[9] The increasing number of people tended to negate a lot of the economic growth these societies were striving to achieve. The first group of new nations emerged in Asia in areas that had first been colonized in the eighteenth century.

New Nations Are Formed in the Indian Subcontinent

During the nineteenth and twentieth centuries, Great Britain's power and wealth was fueled in large part by its colonies, particularly India, the "Jewel in the Crown" of its empire. But for nearly a hundred years, Indian nationalists of all faiths and regions had been agitating unsuccessfully for independence. Not even pitting Hindus and Muslims against each other distracted the nationalists from their goal of independence.

The end of British rule really came during World War II when the nationalists staged the Quit India Movement and the Indian Nationalist Congress refused to cooperate with the Allied effort unless Britain promised to abide by the Atlantic Charter and promise the country its freedom. Although Gandhi, Nehru, and many other nationalist leaders were imprisoned during the war, British rule was nearing its end in India.

By the end of the World War II, an exhausted and economically strapped Great Britain decided that it would be fruitless to try to continue to hold the subcontinent by force. Instead, the British were willing to divide the subcontinent into two nations. At independence, at the insistence of Muslim leaders and despite Gandhi's resistance, the British created India and Pakistan, two independent nations. On August 15, 1947, India's first Indian Prime Minister, Jawaharlal Nehru (1889–1964), stated: "Long years ago we made a tryst with destiny, and now the time comes when we shall redeem our pledge. . . At the stroke of the midnight hour, when the world sleeps, India will awake to life and freedom."[10]

Refugees trying to escape Partition riots

Unfortunately, it its rush to negotiate independence, the British had failed to develop adequate plans for the violent reactions that were about to erupt as a huge transfer of people began. Hindus living in what was to be Pakistan and Muslims living in India fled to be with their co-religionists. According to the Indian census in 1951, 7,226,000 Muslims left India for Pakistan and 7,249,000 Hindus and Sikhs left Pakistan for India. In this bloody transfer, between five hundred thousand and a million people lost their lives, and ever since, these two new nations have been hostile neighbors.

The Indian constitution established a federalist system: the 25 states and the central government share power. Federalism seemed logical given India's size and extraordinary pluralism. As of 2009, there were 23 official languages, the same number as in all of Europe. States such as Uttar Pradesh are larger than many nations, so balancing state and central power has proved challenging.

The Indian constitution established a secular state. Its Directive Principles require the government to promote the welfare of the people by affirming social, economic, and political justice, and economic equality. B. M. Ambedkar, an ex-untouchable who had a major role in writing the Indian constitution, helped make sure that in addition to affirming human rights, the constitution requires that government jobs and places in the universities be reserved for ex-untouchables.

Pakistan and Bangladesh

The partitioning of the subcontinent at independence created the new state of Pakistan. Despite the pledge of democratic rule promised in the Pakistani constitution, attempts to establish democracy in this new country proved difficult. Muhammad Ali Jinnah, the architect of the Pakistani nation, died only one year after independence, and a series of military dictators, supported by the army, took control. The struggle for democracy was further complicated by the fact that Pakistan was divided into two parts, with a thousand miles of Indian territory in between.

After partition of the subcontinent in 1947, the 563 princely states were given the option of joining either India or Pakistan or remaining independent. At the time, Kashmir was ruled by a Hindu prince even though more than 70 percent of the population was Muslim. When

Pakistani-backed militants invaded the Kashmir Valley right after partition, the Hindu ruler signed an agreement with India making the state legally part of the Indian Union. Pakistan argued that since a majority of Kashmir was Muslim, the state logically should be part of Pakistan. Hostilities ended in a truce, with India occupying two-thirds of the state and Pakistan holding the rest. After three wars and continual unrest, as of 2010, Pakistan still insists on renewed negotiations over this disputed territory.

Relations were further strained in 1971 when India gave financial and military backing to the groups in East Pakistan who were fighting for independence from West Pakistan. As a result of this war, Bangladesh was formed and Pakistan was reduced to its western territories.

Pakistan made a fateful decision in 1954 when it chose to join the United States in a military alliance supposedly against the Soviet Union. In 1954 Pakistan accepted U.S. military and economic aid and agreed to allow American spy planes to use Pakistani bases. Pakistani leaders saw their new friendship with the United States as a way to counter the power of India and help them in their quest for Kashmir, most of which India controlled.

As a result, U.S. aid poured into Pakistan, including modern military weapons and aircraft. Pakistani leaders looked on American military aid as a bulwark against India, while the United States believed its generous aid would make Pakistan a force against Soviet expansion. Ayub Khan acknowledged the far different purposes of the military pact when he stated, "There is no such thing as a gun that shoots in only one direction."

Since their partition into two nations, India and Pakistan have fought three wars, and they continue to look on each other with mutual suspicion and hostility. The dispute over Kashmir has kept their tense relations boiling. Strengthened by generous U.S. aid, the army began to control Pakistani politics. For its first ten years as an independent nation, Pakistan held no elections, and it held only six up to 2010. Moreover, the army has overturned the results of many of these.[11]

During its war against the Soviets in Afghanistan in the 1970s, the Pakistanis used billions of dollars of American aid to help create the Mujahideen, a militant Islamic group that began to destabilize Afghanistan. As the Taliban, a radical Islamic militia, moved to take over Afghanistan, Pakistan gave them full support. However, by 2000, the Taliban began attacking Pakistani troops and sending suicide bombers into highly populated areas in Pakistan, threatening its very existence. Further, Taliban-controlled areas in western Pakistan were used as bases for military campaigns in Afghanistan. In the fall of 2009, with strong backing by the United States, the Pakistani army finally launched an all-out assault on the Taliban stronghold in South Waziristan. However, by 2010 Pakistan appeared to be secretly supporting the Taliban while accepting billions of dollars in U.S. aid to help put down the Taliban occupations in western Pakistan.

Palestinians and Jews Claim the Same Land

Palestine, a province that was part of the Ottoman Empire, was made up of about a thousand villages and several larger towns and cities including Jericho, Nazareth, Jerusalem, and Haifa. Most of the Palestinians who lived in the area were Arab farmers, merchants, and craftsmen. In 1914, the population of Palestine included about 525,000 Arabs and about 94,000 Jews.

The modern Zionist movement, which was formed in the 1890s in Europe, called for a Jewish homeland in Palestine, and interest in a Jewish homeland began to grow among European Jews. In 1915, during World War I, the British promised independence to their Arab allies living in Palestine. However, the British issued the Balfour Declaration two years later that promised Jews a "national home" in Palestine as long as "nothing should be done which might prejudice the rights of existing communities there." The British government's stance was certainly murky: it had promised the Arabs they could live in the area and promised the Jews a homeland on the same land. There was no mention of a "state" for either group.

In the 1930s, Jewish immigration to Palestine increased. In 1931, there were 174,616 Jews and 750,000 Arabs. Watching the increasingly violent clashes between Jews and Palestinians, as the Jews continued to settle on Palestinian land, in 1937 the British Parliament concluded that Arabs and Jews could not live peacefully together. Instead, they suggested partitioning Palestine into two states. As of 1948, the population of Palestine included about 1.35 million Arabs and 650,000 Jews.[12]

Unfortunately, the British were too preoccupied during World War II to act on the "Palestine Question," although they did try to cap the number of Jewish immigrants to Palestine and they sent 80,000 troops there in an attempt to control the increasing violence. Jews were vigorously insisting they deserved a state on the land that historically had been their "promised homeland," but the Palestinians resisted the creation of any kind of Jewish state on what they also considered their homeland.

Jews and millions of non-Jews around the world were devastated by news of Hitler's death camps and how people in many European nations had willingly rounded up Jews for extermination. The Holocaust intensified the Jews' desire for a safe haven away from the persistent anti-Semitism in Europe and increased the support of non-Jews for the creation of a Jewish state.

In November 1947, the United Nations passed a resolution calling for independent Jewish and Arab states, with Jerusalem under international jurisdiction. Great Britain, which had promised land to both groups, abstained. The new nation of Israel was born as fighting between Jews and Palestinians increased. Israeli forces, including several future prime ministers (among them Yitzhak Rabin and Menachem Begin), drove about 800,000 Palestinians out of Israel.

Terrified Palestinians fled from their homes, often with their clothes still hanging in their closets and their cars in the driveways, and 84% of the Palestinians became refugees. The United Nations set up major refugee camps in Gaza and the West Bank, and these camps remain today.

Israeli settlers, especially those from Europe, were committed to democratic socialism and they established a vibrant parliamentary democracy in their new nation. In the early years, the Labor Party dominated Israeli politics, but with the immigration of many more Jews from West Asia and the Soviet Union, the Likud Party, a more conservative and militant group, gained power.

The Arabs in the Middle East were totally opposed to the creation of the state of Israel and announced their intent to drive the Israelis into the sea. As hostilities continued to intensify, Israel in 1967, fearing an Arab attack, launched a preemptive war against Egypt, Syria, and Jordan. The Israeli air force destroyed most of the Egyptian air force on the ground. In less than a week, Israel took Jerusalem and the West Bank, Gaza and the Sinai Peninsula.

New Nations in Southeast Asia

As a result of the Japanese victories in Southeast Asia from 1940 to 1942, the Dutch, American, British, and French colonial powers lost their control over those areas. Japan quickly occupied Hong Kong, Malaya, Singapore, Dutch East Indies, Indochina, and Burma. The Japanese occupation helped convince nationalists in these colonies that European military power was not invincible. As a result, in many of these areas, local leaders were willing to work with the Japanese to set up new governments.

The Southeast Asian colonies were among the first to gain independence after 1945. Although the British had willingly freed their possessions, the French, Dutch, and Portuguese were far more reluctant to do so. Their reluctance was probably strengthened by the rise of the Cold War and the growing importance of Europe in American foreign policy. Since these European states were all willing participants in the North American Treaty Organization, the United States was less willing to push them to free their colonial possessions.

When the European powers tried to reestablish their control over their colonies, local nationalist leaders drew on the intense anti-colonial feelings for support. The British, realizing they were quickly losing their imperial authority in Burma and Ceylon, negotiated independence for these two countries but hoped to keep them both tied to the British economic system. Unlike their British colonial neighbors, the Vietnamese and the Indonesians fought protracted wars against the French and Dutch. The Portuguese were the very last colonial power to free their colonies.

In the British colony of Malaya, a powerful Chinese Communist–led guerilla army tried to make that small country a Chinese satellite. However, because of its rich tin and rubber resources, the British were determined to hold on to the Malaya peninsula. By posing as defenders of the Malay people, most of whom did not want to be under Chinese control, the British military defeated the Chinese guerillas and maintained their economic interest in Malaya. They even kept a military base in Singapore after granting the people independence as a sovereign nation. Meanwhile, the Americans, who had never been very dedicated colonialists, granted the Philippines complete independence in 1946.

Vietnam Joins the Communist Bloc

France's determination to regain control of Vietnam led to the bloodiest of the nationalist struggles in Asia. By the time of the Japanese surrender, the Vietminh under Ho Chi Minh, who had had full American support during World War II, controlled the area in North Vietnam around Hanoi, while the French occupied the south. During the war, President Roosevelt had pledged to support Vietnamese independence and had promised Ho Chi Minh, the Vietnamese nationalist leader, that the U.S. would honor this pledge.

After Japan surrendered to the Allies, Ho's troops entered Hanoi. On September 2, 1945, before an enormous crowd gathered in Ba Dinh Square, Ho Chi Minh declared Vietnam independent and read his Declaration of Independence, a document that owed much to the American Declaration of 1776.

Despite Ho's enormous popularity with his people and Roosevelt's tacit promise of independence, the British army welcomed the French back to rule Vietnam. After all their efforts, it appeared that the Vietnamese had merely traded one imperial ruler for another and that the Allied war in the "defense of freedom" did not include freedom for the colonized people.

The French offered Ho Chi Minh a federated Indochina under French control that would include Laos and Cambodia as well. Free Vietnam would include only the north, which the Vietminh nationalists already controlled. To force Ho Chi Minh to accept this plan, the French bombed Hanoi and occupied the city in February, 1947. This ill-advised move led to an all-out guerrilla war that soon resulted in the Vietminh controlling most of the northern part of the country. In 1954, in one last desperate attempt to hold on to their prize colony, the French made a stand at Dien Bien Phu. Defeated, the French army surrendered in May 1954.

But the major world powers did not let the Vietminh have a total victory. Led by the United States, they organized a peace conference in Geneva that divided Vietnam at the 17th parallel and required it to hold free elections in 1956. The Americans became the "protector" of South Vietnam and attempted to install a series of puppet governments there, none of which had the support of the people in the region. The promised elections were never held, and as the Vietminh trickled into the south, they created popular support for their Communist cause.

South Vietnam had difficulty establishing a stable government. Ngo Dinh Diem (1901–1963), an authoritarian Catholic who believed he was following Confucian principles of centralized control, did not wholeheartedly support democratic principles. Despite this fact, the United States supported him with nearly a billion dollars in aid, most of which was used to build up his military force.

Foreseeing a victory at the promised general election in 1956, Ho sent thousands of northerners to live in the south and organize for the Communists. After the North Vietnamese invaded Laos in 1959, the United States increased its aid to the South. In the 1960s, President Kennedy increased the number of American advisors from 685 to about 16,000, even though American support was going to the unpopular South Vietnamese government. Despite many urgings, Diem refused to carry out the kind of land reform that Ho had already insti-

A Vietnamese soldier in a tunnel

Vietnam War Memorial, Washington, D.C.

tuted in the north. Meanwhile, Kennedy was arranging a behind-the-scenes overthrow of Diem.

American military forces were increasingly drawn into the struggle; in 1964, Lyndon Johnson, using the pretext that South Vietnamese forces had fired on American ships, asked Congress to authorize an increased number of troops for the expanding conflict. Before long the United States was committed to a major war against North Vietnam and was sending hundreds of thousands of troops to fight its largely peasant society. The war lasted from 1964 to 1973. Following North Vietnam's victory, what had been South Vietnam was incorporated into the Socialist Republic of Vietnam. The Vietnamese who were loyal to the Americans were "reeducated" and assimilated back into society.

Over the next several years, the Vietnamese nationalized all private industries and resettled farmers on state cooperatives. However, Vietnam's collectivization, like China's in the 1950s, was an economic disaster that resulted in severe food shortages. Thousands of Vietnamese became refugees who attempted to find new homes in any nation that would take them. Meanwhile, Vietnam grew closer to the Soviet Union, and benefited from approximately $3 billion a year in Soviet aid throughout the 1980s.

Indonesia Joins the Western Bloc

The Dutch were also adamant about trying to maintain their colonies in Indonesia. After the Japanese surrender in September 1945, the Dutch tried to regain control over Indonesia. However, Sukarno had already declared his nation's independence. The Dutch encountered armed opposition to their efforts to regain control of Indonesia. Javanese nationalists and the Dutch fought fiercely for another four years and terrible atrocities were committed by both sides. Finally, after intense pressure from the United States, the Dutch decided to give up the battle. In August 1949, a weak Dutch-Indonesian Union allowed the Dutch to save face in the wake of their impending military defeat.

Creating a functioning nation-state out of the very diverse people living on the many islands that had been under colonial rule for over a hundred years was a formidable challenge. For Sukarno (1902–1970), the country's first president, establishing democratic principles was secondary to creating and retaining national unity.

Sukarno was a charismatic leader who could inspire his audiences, but his economic policies were both poorly thought out and ineffective. He found it difficult to create a functioning parliament that represented the many large groups with varying ideologies and faiths. The three major political groups each had a different objective. The Communists enjoyed wide public support and sought to establish a Soviet-style state. The Muslim leaders wanted to create a Muslim state, while the military focused on maintaining order and stability.

Indonesia had historically been a rice-surplus area, but by 1965, it was importing rice. The once-lucrative tin and rubber export industries were in shambles, and only exporting oil brought the new country any income. The corrupt government ran huge deficits and inflation was making it almost impossible for average people to survive. The Indonesian government spent seventy-five percent of its budget on the military, and Sukarno's followers were living the lush life. All these factors threatened to tear the young nation apart.

The Communist Party (PKI) was present in all levels of government. Fearing a Communist coup, in 1965, General Suharto mobilized forces under his command, overthrew Sukarno, and declared himself the new ruler. American leaders, always fearful that a "third world" nation might become Communist, aided the army officers and later openly supported General Suharto. The backlash against what was perceived as an attempted Communist coup resulted in an orgy of violence against the Communists and those suspected of being Communists. Mobs of young people filled the streets of the capital with signs reading "Crush the Communists."

Once in power, the new Suharto Government dismissed all the Communists and other ministers involved in the attempted coup. The new dictatorship then killed more than 400,000 workers and peasants suspected of being members of the Communist Party. Hundreds of thousands more who were suspected of being Communist sympathizers lost their jobs and lived under constant surveillance. Suharto's troops also killed thousands of Chinese merchants whom they considered rich, elite, and non-Indonesian. It is estimated that between 500,000 and one million suspected Communists and ethnic Chinese were killed.

Indonesia became part of the Western bloc. Supported by the United States, General Suharto installed a military-backed, authoritarian regime in Indonesia and called it the "New Order." During his rule, Indonesia enjoyed significant economic growth and industrialization and made improvements in health, education, and living standards. However, basic human rights, including free expression, were drastically curtailed, and the government's efforts to improve the economy also caused it to destroy significant portions of the country's rain forest.

Thailand, the Philippines, Malaysia, and the Association of Southeast Asian Nations

Thailand has never been colonized or been under foreign control. It is a predominantly Buddhist nation with profound reverence for its king. While respecting authority and seeking harmony in society, the Thais have tried to create a genuine democratic system. However, because their nation includes a large Muslim population, the close identity between the nation and Buddhism has sometimes caused friction. This internal struggle helps explain why Thailand has frequently had a military ruler and why Thai students have periodically agitated for more human rights. In many of these demonstrations, students have been arrested and even killed.

Following the example of the European imperial powers, the United States had become a colonial power when it took control of the Philippines after the Spanish-American War (1898–1900). During World War II, the Japanese easily overran the Philippine islands, defeated the American forces there, and took thousands of prisoners.

After the war, the United States had little desire to maintain a colonial empire and it made plans to free the Philippines on July 4, 1946. However, several factors undermined the American plan for the new nation to function as a viable democracy. Under American rule, a new upper class of industrialists, bankers, and large landowners had prospered at the expense of everyone else. The United States used this group to retain power and rewarded them with wealth and prestige.

In the first attempts at democracy, these elites threatened, bribed, and rigged elections in order to stay in power. The far-from-free elections disillusioned the majority of Filipinos and made them fear the United States was continuing its imperial control by other means.

Critics pointed to the many U.S. airbases that formed a ring around their small nation. Further, the Filipino media was saturated with American films, TV shows, and American popular culture, making it difficult for the Filipinos to forge a unique national identity. The quest for identity has been further complicated by the fact that the north is predominantly Catholic, while Muslims are concentrated on the southern islands. Over the years the Christian north has fought Muslim guerilla forces in the south.

The political result was support for a strong dictator. In seizing power, Ferdinand Marcos (1917–1989), pointing to the chaos and instability that democracy was causing, promised to bring law and order. The dictatorship of Marcos and his wife Imelda, who was known for her lavish spending, lasted until 1986. When the couple abandoned the palace, Mrs. Marcos left behind 2,700 pairs of shoes.[13]

Their successors have fared little better at installing democratic institutions. Civil strife between the Muslim south and the Christian north has deepened in the years since independence. With the election of Maria Aquino in 1992, the prospects for democracy were significantly enhanced. Under her leadership the Fifth Republic was formed and a new constitution was adopted. The Philippines have enjoyed relatively free elections since then. In 2001, Gloria Macapagal-Arroyo and her coalition won an overwhelming victory, and this popular president remained in power until 2010.

Malaysia gained its independence from Britain in 1957. Like the Philippines and Vietnam, Malaysia had a significant Communist movement. However, British forces, applying effective anti-guerilla strategies, were able to defeat the rebels until 1957. Since then, the Malay political party has managed to build a vibrant democracy. This predominantly Muslim nation has successfully conducted free elections and is prospering in the global economy.

The tension between the large overseas Chinese merchant community and local traders was resolved in 1965 by making Singapore a separate city-state. It now has one of the highest standards of living and one of the best educational systems and is a center of world finance.

With the surge of nationalism and rising standard of living in Southeast Asia, Malaysia, Indonesia, Thailand, Singapore, and the Philippines formed the Association of Southeast Asian Nations (ASEAN) in 1967. After the Vietnam War, Cambodia, Laos, Vietnam, Burma, and Brunei all joined ASEAN. The organization is more like a political and economic cooperative agency than a military pact and it has given the entire region of Southeast Asia an important united voice in world affairs.

The Cold War and the Wider World

While the Soviet Union and the United States faced each other along a jagged line that ran from the Baltic Sea all the way to the Pacific Ocean, both powers invested much energy and wealth in trying to attract the newly independent, former colonial nations to their respective sides.

The Soviets made the most of several powerful arguments in their favor. Communist leaders tried to befriend the various independence movements around the world and stressed that the Soviets had not conquered foreign lands and turned them into colonies. Despite the fact that the Soviet Union had openly occupied the Baltic States, many Eastern European nations, and a large part of Germany, this argument had appeal in the new states of Africa and Asia.

As we have seen, the Soviet Union could also point to its rapid and successful industrialization and modernization at the very time of a deep economic depression in the capitalist countries. The Soviet model of development had significant appeal to many new nations who adopted various forms of a planned economy.

The Soviets also held out the promise of foreign aid and modern military weapons, and Soviet officers were dispatched to help create new armies in newly independent nations. Moreover, the Soviets invited young students to study at their universities and sent experts to help potential allies build dams, airports, and other important infrastructure.

The United States offered many of the same gifts to the wavering nations. The U.S. advertised itself as the beacon of democracy in a world that had seen republican forms of government threatened and overwhelmed by fascism and what they called totalitarian communism. As self-appointed defender of the "free world," the United States mounted a worldwide campaign to promote its image. The American government established the United States Information Agency, which built libraries and cultural centers and sponsored educational exchanges around the world. The U.S. also sponsored the Voice of America broadcasting service, which provided news to those behind the iron curtain, and it supported journals, newspapers, and student conferences in many nations, all calculated to promote American values.

The government even subsidized art shows and encouraged new wave of abstract expressionist artists like Jackson Pollack. Further, the Fulbright programs brought thousands of young students from around the world to attend American universities and colleges while American scholars were sent to teach and lecture wherever they were invited.

Like the Soviet Union, the United States offered large amounts of military and development aid to potential allies in the Cold War and used the Central Intelligence Agency to help install friendly governments in the newly independent nations. Sometimes, as in the cases of Guatemala, the Congo, and Iran, the CIA participated in planning the removal of governments that the United States thought anti-American.

The Cold War struggle for the "hearts and minds" of the world ran the entire spectrum from offering student scholarships to sending covert forces to overthrow and establish governments. This intense competition between the two superpowers lasted until 1989. The constant covert Soviet and American involvement in the affairs of the Third World left a trail of bloodshed and factional struggles in many of the weaker states, especially in Africa.

The contest to win the support of the newly independent nations, most of which emerged from the collapsing European colonial empires, played out in different ways in the many nations that the United States and the Soviet Union each sought to win over to its own side.

Because most of these nations were economically very poor, mostly because of centuries of European exploitation, the Western powers called them "undeveloped" nations. More recently, they have been called "developing" nations or "Third World" nations. The Cold War rivalry gave these "third world" nations a measure of power because both the U.S. and the Soviet Union promised them foreign and military aid and strong support in the United Nations, where each possessed veto power.

In 1954 the new nation of Pakistan accepted U.S. military and economic aid and agreed to allow American spy planes to use Pakistani bases. Pakistani leaders saw their new friendship with the United States as a way to counter the power of India and help them in their quest for Kashmir, most of which India controlled.

By 1960 the United States had already convinced some of the newly independent states to join it in a series of alliances. In 1953, American and British operatives engineered a coup in Iran to remove a popularly elected Prime Minister, Mohammad Mosadegh, and replace him with Shah Pahlavi, who was quite willing to join the U.S. side in the Cold War in turn for receiving military and development aid that would keep him in power until 1979.

As the Cold War competition heated up in the 1950s, several new nations reasoned that their own hard-won independence would be short-circuited if they took sides in the Cold War. Fearing this trend, the Indian Prime Minister Jawaharlal Nehru (1889–1964) and several other Third World leaders worked to discover an alternative to backing either the Soviet Union or the United States. In an effort to institutionalize their common concern, in April 1955, Nehru, President Nasser of Egypt, and Marshal Tito of Yugoslavia created an organization of nations that were not aligned with any of the American-led anti-Soviet alliances or the Soviet-sponsored alliances. At the first conference, China also participated, and Nehru and the other leaders tried in every possible way to convince the largest nation in the world to continue in the organization. However, China soon decided to follow its own policy even as its tensions with the Soviet Union mounted.

The non-aligned nations have numbered over a hundred members at various times. Most of them have been most concerned about their own economic development and their precious, newly won independence. From time to time, some have moved closer to the Soviet Union or the United States, depending on how much that change would benefit their own development. These nations also gained significant influence in the United Nations by forming the "Group of 77," a powerful voting bloc in the organization.

Although the non-aligned nations sought to avoid taking political sides in the Cold War, many of the these states wanted to combine features of the Soviet planned economy with aspects of the free market system. India, which combined a Soviet-style planned economy and a commitment to democracy and democratic rule, has been a democracy for all but a year and a half since independence. Nehru believed India could have both socialism and democracy and he was also determined to help his nation become a first-rate industrial power.

SUMMARY

The disillusionment and pessimism that flourished around the world in the wreckage of World War II soon gave way to a burst of hope and optimism among the world's people. The tenacity of the human spirit was proved once again as millions of average people in the war-devastated nations moved rubble by hand and plunged into the daunting task of rebuilding their nations. The energies that the Japanese and Germans had invested in waging war were suddenly focused on the job of rebuilding, and in each nation a hatred of war developed that has lasted until our own time.

The victorious nations had also learned a lesson from their vindictive treaties after World War I. This time they heeded Lord Keynes' advice to invest in the defeated nations and help them rebuild instead of punishing them. As a result, Japan, Italy, and Germany soon joined the family of nations as responsible and productive societies.

In the United States, the thirteen million returning war veterans were quickly absorbed into the peacetime economy and many took advantage of the free higher education provided by grateful American taxpayers. This massive infusion of first-generation college students created a social revolution in the United States and moved millions of members of the working class into the middle class. During the period from 1945 to the late 1970s, despite an outbreak of strikes in the years immediately following World War II and the civil discontents of the 1960s, the United States enjoyed a long stretch of prosperity.

In Europe, where much damage had been sown by the war, a vast majority of people faced the future with a keen hatred of war as a way of life. There was a consensus in much of Europe that the huge debts and enormous loss of life brought on by wars they had lived through for centuries resulted from the pursuit of folly. Instead of continuing on the same path, postwar Europe opted for investments in peaceful development and an increase in social benefits such as stable incomes, vacation time, and access to healthcare and free education.

Even though the Cold War lines drawn between the United States and the Soviet Union symbolized a static division of the world, there were rapid changes going on everywhere. Sputnik surprised many people, but soon the United States was also sending satellites and manned missions into orbit, and, in 1969, the U.S. landed a man on the moon. Moreover, hundreds of new nations were joining the world community, and their citizens were demanding their share of the world's wealth. New technologies were radically altering human life, and new ideologies and worldviews were competing for supporters. These issues we now take up in the acts that follow.

ACT FIVE

Patterns of Development, 1950–1990

 As newly independent nations joined the world system after World War II, people around the world were already debating the best way to create modern industrialized societies. The former colonized nations could draw upon the experiences of Europe, the United States, and Japan, which had already undergone industrialization. The European nations seemed determined to hold on to their colonies and redirect the huge investments they had made in war machines to supporting more social benefits for their citizens. The United States seemed convinced that free markets were the best path to prosperity and power.

Following World War II, both the industrialized and developing nations pursued their own interests and debated the best ways to rebuild their economies and establish stable political systems. Further, new nations, mostly in Africa, continued to join the nation-states system. Both old and new nations had many possible options from among the political and economic systems around the world. They could look to the socialist command economies where the central state owned the major means of production and set production goals, wages, and consumer prices. They could copy the capitalist economies where market forces were allowed to determine the founding and operation of industries and services and to establish prices and wages. Finally, they could opt for mixed economies, where govern-ments owned some of the industries and financial institutions but pri-vate enterprise controlled the rest.

Besides various approaches to economic development, there were also several ways to organize the governments and the roles that citi-zens would have in shaping their nations' political decisions. Usually nations that had command economies chose more authoritarian gov-ernments and their citizens had little power.

In states rich in natural resources such as oil and rare metals, eco-nomic development was usually inhibited because foreign corpora-tions controlled drilling rights and the mining industries. Because the industrialized economies depended on these resources, especially oil, they often became deeply involved in the resource-rich nations' poli-tics as well.

SOCIALIST STATES
CHOOSE COMMUNIST
STRATEGIES

Setting the Stage

In the choice of economic theories leading to modern development, two of the world's largest nations opted for the Communist models outlined by Karl Marx and Friedrich Engels. Interestingly, the founders of the Communist movement believed that their model would be applied first in the advanced capitalist nations of Europe. However, Russia under Lenin and Stalin was the first to apply their writings to a large agricultural society.

Other primarily agricultural societies such as China and Vietnam soon followed the Soviet example and by the 1950s, nearly two billion people lived under some form of Marxist-Leninist socialism.

China Struggles to Reconcile Ideology and Economic Growth

Probably no nation in the world made such revolutionary changes as China experienced in the years after 1949. During World War II, the Chinese had fought both a defensive war against Japan and an internal civil war. The National Kuomintang under Chiang Kai-shek had enjoyed the full support of the Western allies during the war. In the civil war between the Communists and the Nationalists that followed, few people outside China expected the Communists to win. The United States had invested nearly a billion dollars to support Chiang Kai-shek, and Mao Zedong's defeat of the American-backed Kuomintang came as a shock to the United States and soon dramatically changed the international political order. Once victorious, Mao and his forces created the People's Republic of China (the PRC).

Marxist-Leninist Communism was an attractive model for leaders of colonial nationalist movements in many areas of the world. Many in the colonial countries agreed with Lenin that colonialism was the last stage of capitalism. They believed that their independence depended on the overthrow of both capitalism and foreign rule. By World War II, most colonial nations had active Communist parties, but few expected that Marxist strategy could apply to peasant-based societies such as China that were not industrialized. How, then, can we explain the adoption of communist theories in China?

Eric Wolf, one of the major scholars of peasant revolutions, argued that peasant wars in countries like Russia, China, and Vietnam were very different from communist movements in industrial countries. Most peasants are farmers and their goal is to acquire their own land. Wolf argued that it is capitalism, not communism, which causes revolutionary changes in peasant societies. Capitalism results in peasants losing their small plots of land when investors and managers claim the land in order to grow commercial crops on large, industrialized farms.

By contrast, communist movements in peasant societies are committed to giving land to the peasants, especially landless peasants. The Chinese communists promised to confiscate the large estates and capitalist enterprises and redistribute their land and the wealth to the peasants, either as direct owners or on collectivized farms where everyone shares in both the production and the produce. It seems very probable that the overwhelming support for Mao Zedong was rooted largely in the peasants' hope of acquiring their own land.

Of course, Mao's programs and reforms were not all about economics. Mao had been able to don the mantle of nationalist and unifier once the Japanese invaded China. This helps explain why his picture is still hanging in Tiananmen Square.

Once Mao had declared the independence of the Peoples' Republic of China, he and his followers immediately began to institute radical domestic reforms. In the first few years he made sure that most of the large landlords were killed, jailed, or sent for "reeducation." Villages established Village Tribunals that acted as informal courts where peasants could insult, spit upon, and even sentence to death the landlords who had exploited them for so long. In the process, somewhere between 800,000 and 3,000,000 landlords and their supporters were killed. Mao's commitment to the peasants was the foundation of the land reforms that followed. The majority of peasants were given plots of land to till. In 1950, Mao also introduced Soviet-style cooperative farms, and he offered average people education and health care. For three years the peasants owned their plots of land.

Within the first decade of Communist rule, cordial relations between China and the Soviet Union began to fray. Disputes over boundaries, China's refusal to subordinate its interests to the Soviet leaders, and meager Soviet foreign aid led to a breach and sometimes open battles. Mao and his colleagues, like Nehru in India, also believed that China must rapidly industrialize if it was to become a true world power.

Following the Soviet model, Mao launched a series of five-year plans intended to invest resources from the countryside in urban factories. But expecting the peasants to set aside their own needs and contribute to the industrial projects instead of devoting their attention to their own farms was highly unpopular. At the same time, the Communist leaders had to give privileges to technical experts, managers, and workers who could implement the industrial program.

Upset that he was creating a privileged urban class at the expense of the peasants who had been responsible for the communist victory, Mao changed course in the mid-1950s. He was opposed to a ruling party that did not have to answer to anyone. He firmly believed in the peasants' intelligence and values and honored their judgment over intellectuals who had never worked with their hands. In 1955, Mao concentrated on peasant welfare, and he hoped to establish huge agriculture cooperatives to improve farm production.

In 1956, Mao announced a new openness with the poetic name, "Let a hundred flowers bloom." His invitation to speak out against the government let loose a perhaps unexpected flood of criticism from intellectuals, writers, and artists. Upset, Mao immediately clamped down on the dissenters, jailing many, banishing others, and demoting still others. The flowers did not have the chance to set roots, never mind bloom, before the program was over.

Mao's biggest gamble was the "Great Leap Forward" in 1958. This ill-advised experiment was supposed to enlist every loyal Chinese person in a massive effort to industrialize the nation. Mao identified grain and steel production as the keys to rapid economic development. He forecast that within 15 years, China's steel production would exceed Great Britain's.

The idea was to involve every able-bodied citizen, including women and children, in a common effort to industrialize by transferring manufacturing from the cities to the countryside. Farming communes were to produce tractors and steel. Villagers, using backyard furnaces, were assigned steel-making quotas. The goal was to make most communes self-sufficient and to avoid the formation of bureaucratic elites that had, in Mao's mind, ruined the first attempts at industrialization.

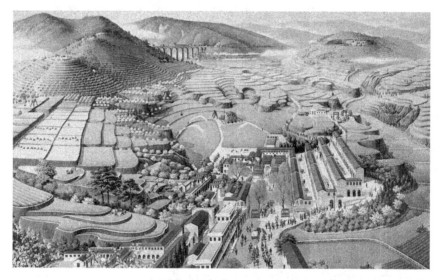

Mao's ideal commune

Unfortunately the equipment available for these efforts was out of date and very labor-intensive. In a few months it was apparent to any objective observer that the plans to collectivize agriculture and at the same time embark on rural industrialization projects were turning into a disaster. Birth rates were soaring and the rural communes could not even produce enough food to feed their own members. The resulting major human-made famine forced the government to import food. The industrial projects fared no better. Steel production fell drastically and the steel produced in the makeshift rural factories was almost useless.

The Great Leap Forward was an economic and human disaster. Not only had rural and manufacturing production plummeted, millions of people needlessly died in the process. Estimates of the costs of Mao's grand experiment range from 27 million famine deaths to 40 million. Mao's colossal failure resulted mainly from his unrealistic goals, poorly planned collectivization of farming, and a disastrously low harvest in 1959.[1]

Assuming that he would take the most blame for this disaster, Mao stepped down as State Chairman in 1959, but he kept his position as Chairman of the Chinese Communist Party (CCP). Liu Shaoqi and Deng Xiaoping assumed responsibility for developing new plans for economic recovery. While the top leaders worked to find a way back to economic growth, Mao and his radical supporters stayed in the background.

In the wake of the Great Leap disaster, ideological struggles broke out within the ruling Communist Party. Zhou Enlai, Mao's longtime and loyal companion, and Liu Shaoqi and Deng Xiaoping all pre-ferred a more pragmatic approach to development. Deng's 1961 dec-laration, "It makes no difference if the cat is black or white as long as it can catch mice," symbolized their willingness to include market incentives and their readiness to seek new ways to encourage eco-nomic growth and more local control of the economy.

But Mao and his wife Jiang Zing could not accept this new prag-matism and they continued to promote grassroots support for their cherished continuing revolution. Mao refused to accept Deng Xiaop-ing's plan to reduce the large communes and allow peasants to farm private plots. He also opposed pursing economic growth without the proper ideological underpinnings.

By the mid-1960s, Mao believed he had enough support to initiate another chapter in his "permanent" revolution. His goal this time was a Cultural Revolution that would reeducate the growing bureaucracy and technocrats who had come to power since the revolution. Believ-ing that the young, especially students, were purer than adults, Mao urged them to turn against their parents, teachers, and anyone in authority whom they thought might be a "capitalist roader." The vol-unteer army in this revolution consisted of student volunteers known as Red Guards, backed by the Peoples' Liberation Army. The gospel for the revolution was Mao's *Little Red Book*, a simple compilation of Mao's thoughts about almost every issue.

The Red Guards acted as police, courts, and sentencing agencies. Liu Shaoqi was murdered and Deng Xiaoping escaped to the south, where he survived with the protection of friendly military leaders. Even Zhou Enlai was removed from power and marginalized. In the large cities, particularly Shanghai, workers took over factories and the local government.

"Long Live Chairman Mao and His Little Red Book"

The students' main targets were university professors, industrial managers, bureaucrats who they thought were not true Maoists, and members of China's middle class. Although many were killed or imprisoned, the preferred punishment was to send the guilty ones to work in the countryside and "learn from the peasants." The slogan "Better red than expert" underscored their preference for ideological purity rather than advanced skills and knowledge.

After two years of chaos, many army officers concluded that the revolution had gone too far, and they persuaded Mao to call of his permanent revolution. The Red Guards were disbanded and the officers regained control over the army. Students were told to return to schools and universities. Gradually, technocrats, professors, and middle-class exiles began to reclaim their positions. The Cultural Revolution proved to have been another expensive experiment that not only set back development but also led to the deaths of between 400,000 and 850,000 people.[2]

The energy let loose by the Cultural Revolution took some time to recede, but by 1973, the old pragmatist Deng Xiaoping rose again, phoenix-like, to lead the nation, and many of his allies had also crept back into power. Mao's death in 1976 finally ended the long era of the Cultural Revolution; once again the new leadership sought to industrialize China by restoring scientists and intellectuals to positions of responsibility. Although Deng launched what amounted to a second Chinese Revolution, he did not reverse the real gains of Mao's revolution, including a genuine redistribution of power and wealth, free health care and enough food, and education through the university level for all qualified students.

Reforms for women also continued. Chinese women had already gained equal political and economic rights and were regularly employed outside the home. Women also became cadres, even though men still held most of the higher positions. As birth rates soared, the government introduced strict new birth control programs. In 1965, each urban couple was limited to two children, and rural families to one child each. By the 1980s the limit was lowered to only one child per couple and was strictly enforced.

In 1978, Deng introduced Four Modernizations, first in agriculture, then in industry, technology, and national defense, and opened the Chinese economy to the global system. The move from state planning to a more free-market economy was called a "Socialist Economy with Chinese Characteristics." With the resurgence of the remarkable Deng, China moved ever closer to a free-market economy, but a strong central government still guided it.

Under Deng, small farmers could sell their products at market prices. He encouraged the revival of handicrafts and the opening of private retail shops. The government also began to create "special economic zones" where entrepreneurs were permitted to use market principles and to get rich. China's promise of political stability and a decent standard of living for every citizen gained overwhelming public support.

The Soviet Union Chooses Reform

After the Cuban missile crisis in 1962, both the United States and the Soviet Union realized that they would have to take steps to avoid a nuclear catastrophe. During the 1970s, Soviet–U.S. relations grew more cordial, and the two nations held summit meetings and negotiated a series of strategic arms limitation agreements. In 1973, Leonid Brezhnev, who ruled the Soviet Union from 1966 to 1982, proclaimed that peaceful coexistence was the normal, permanent, and irreversible state of relations between imperialist and communist countries, although he warned that conflict might continue in the Third World.

Although the policy of peaceful coexistence offered more stability, the Soviet economy stagnated under Brezhnev. The consumer economy was suffering because of the huge military investments. Some consumer products disappeared from the markets, and long, slowly moving lines outside food shops were common. The vast farm collective system was not producing enough food to feed the people, and workers in the state-owned factories were not very productive.

In addition, the Soviets brutally put down rebellions in Hungary, Poland, and Czechoslovakia and suppressed any open dissent or serious discussion at home. To make matters more unstable, the majority of its citizens were against Russia's war in Afghanistan in the 1980s, which was draining the country of wealth, resources, and lives. Moreover, unrest in the Soviet satellite nations was growing. Popular democratic movements were developing again in Poland, Czechoslovakia, and Hungary, and the nations under Soviet control were openly agitating for reform.

By 1985, the Soviet leadership finally decided to reform aspects of the Soviet system. Mikhail Gorbachev (b. 1931), who became the General Secretary of the Communist Party in 1985, announced two programs he called *glasnost* (openness to the west) and *perestroika* (restructuring the economy). Under glasnost, people were given more access to information, and libraries offered previously banned books. This reform also granted more freedom of speech and even allowed newspapers and television to criticize the government. Perestroika was intended to improve peoples' living standard. To achieve this, Gorbachev tried to reduce corruption and introduce incentives, risk, and some private ownership into the command system. In addition, students, religious organizations, and other discontented groups the Soviets had previously restricted could now travel abroad and make international investments and loans.

Looking back on his reforms with pride, Gorbachev explained that glasnost had succeeded to the point that by "March 1989 . . . for the first time in Russia's history democratic, competitive elections took place."[3] However, despite his noble intentions, Gorbachev proved to be a weak leader, unable to carry out his reforms without presiding over the sudden total collapse of the Soviet Union that led to cruel deprivation for millions of Soviet citizens.

Under Communist rule in the Soviet Union and China, the majority of people enjoyed more social services than they had ever known, such as guaranteed jobs, free health care, and a right to an education. However, providing social services and building a powerful military depended on ever increasing production and the Socialist systems did not result in the necessary economic growth to support these benefits. As a major scholar has written: "The Communist states of the mid-twentieth century sought to match the economic and military successes of capitalist societies, while avoiding the inequalities inseparable from capitalism. But they did not succeed in keeping up with their rivals or in creating societies that offered attractive alternatives."[4]

THE ATTRACTION OF
FREE-MARKET CAPITALISM

Setting the Stage

In the decades after World War II, the United States was at the pinnacle of economic and political power in the world. Only the Soviet Union, with its nuclear arsenal and large standing armies, could rival American power. At home, President Truman, confronted by public demands for a rapid demobilization of the armed forces and an end to the wartime price controls, successfully led the national transformation to a booming peacetime economy.

The American automobile industry dominated the world market. American electronics, information technology, financial services, and universities were unequaled. By the 1960s, American workers were rapidly acquiring middle-class living standards. Unionized workers earned paid vacations and holidays, worked eight-hour days, got extra pay for overtime, and had safer working conditions and generous retirement packages. Unionized auto workers, who were being paid more than university professors, were often able to send their children to college.

Further, New York and other U.S. cities had moved ahead of Paris as centers of the arts. All these successes tempted some Americans to think of themselves as an exceptional nation whose citizens had the good fortune to be living in what one of the major magazine publishers had named "the American Century."[5]

The United States Debates Economic Theories

Truman had difficulty when he tried to continue the New Deal programs. The transfer to a peacetime economy led to rampant inflation and labor unrest in the USA. Despite these challenges and the fact that his approval rating plummeted, Truman courageously clung to his domestic policies, which included civil rights for African-Americans, the Full Employment Act, a liberalized Social Security Program, federal aid to education, low-cost housing, and a higher minimum wage.

Presidents Eisenhower and Kennedy continued many of the New Deal programs without greatly expanding them. However, this moderate expansion of social welfare programs changed dramatically when Lyndon Johnson became president. In 1964, Johnson launched his Great Society programs, which included universal health care for those over 65, medical coverage for young children, voting and other rights for African-Americans, expanded aid to education, and a pledge to end poverty.

It was a testament to the vitality of the American economy that it could finance all these expensive social programs and at the same time pay for an ongoing war in Vietnam that would end up costing about $584 billion. At the same time, the United States was investing what would amount to over $13.1 trillion between 1945 and 1995 to build the world's largest military machine.[6]

However, fissures began to spread in the United States economy after President Nixon ended the Bretton Woods Agreement of 1944 that ensured that gold guaranteed the value of the U.S. dollar. In the 1970s, due to the massive cost of the Vietnam War, the United States withdrew that guarantee. As a result, a large number of the world's currencies began to "float," meaning they had no common standard of value. Instead, their value would now rise and fall in the free market's supply-and-demand system.

The industrialized world soon plunged into a long economic slump. The high inflation coupled with slow growth and recessions that characterized this period was called "stagflation." Stagflation spawned high unemployment, stagnant growth, and static wages and prompted many to question the U.S. government's economic policies during the postwar period.

In the 1920s, John Maynard Keynes had advised that during economic recessions, governments should pump money into the financial system and into creating jobs. Even if these emergency moves caused large government deficits, Keynes believed these deficits were better than a long recession or a possible depression. Conversely, in times of economic prosperity, governments should raise taxes and pay off the deficits that the efforts to stimulate the economy had created.

But just as stagflation was causing a dramatic downturn in the U.S.

economy in the late 1970s, many Western economists were calling for a reduction in the size of government and suggesting that most economic decisions should be left to the "free market." They assumed that private enterprise would create robust growth, solve inflation, and create general prosperity. Most conservatives believed that except for financing defense and other necessities, any government intervention in the economy would impede economic growth and undermine prosperity. Instead, they wanted "free market solutions" for all aspects of public life, from public schooling to raising armies.

This faith in the free market was named "neoclassical" economics because it meant returning to the philosophy of Adam Smith. Both the Conservative Party in Britain and the Republican Party in the United States strongly advocated this philosophy. Many political leaders and public intellectuals rallied to the free-market cause. To others it seemed that belief in free-market economics in the United States, Britain, and other societies increasingly "took the form of a religion."[7]

Resistance to what many Americans perceived as a growing American welfare state brought Ronald Reagan and the Republicans to power. They were committed to a classical, conservative laissez-faire economic system with minimum government intervention. As followers of the American economist Milton Friedman, these new conservatives believed that the free market would solve the economic problems of boom and bust. This conservative movement, carried on by the two Republican presidents Bush and the Democratic president Bill Clinton, continued to support free-market economics by removing most of the regulations on banks passed by the New Deal, while reducing government welfare programs, protection for unions, and other reforms associated with the New Deal. Reagan's political success also heavily depended on attracting millions of evangelical Christians who championed social values such as outlawing abortions, strengthening families, and personal responsibility.

The East Asian Tigers

After 1980, neoclassical economics, often called market capitalism, not only prevailed in the industrialized societies, but was also increasingly appealing to the newly industrializing nations where growth rates had been very low. Three East Asian states and one city-state—

Japan, South Korea, Taiwan, and Singapore—earned the label the "East Asian Tigers." All four chose to follow the capitalist development model. Japan flourished under a parliamentary system established by the U.S. occupation team. Authoritarian rulers governed Taiwan and South Korea until the 1980s. For several years Singapore was part of Malaysia, but now it is an independent state.

The three nations were closely tied to the United States in several ways. The United States occupied Japan for several years after World War II and insisted that it adopt both democracy and capitalism. The U.S. also occupied what became South Korea and oversaw its political and economic development. The United States had backed the Kuomintang government in China, and after its defeat by the Communists in 1949, the U.S. helped Chiang Kai-shek and his followers evacuate to the island of Taiwan, where they founded the Republic of China. The U.S. government continued to offer strong support for the Taiwanese government. Singapore had long been a British colony and an important commercial center for centuries. Once it gained its freedom from Britain, it easily adopted a capitalist system,although under a strong totalitarian government.

Cold War realities certainly benefited the Asian Tigers. The U.S. was dedicated to turning Japan into a model of capitalism and democracy that would be a dramatic contrast to the People's Republic of China. To achieve that goal, the Americans opened their consumer markets to anything that Japan, and later South Korea and Taiwan, wanted to sell them. During the Korean War, the U.S. purchased lots of supplies from Japan. When President Eisenhower wondered if this policy might take jobs away from American workers, his Secretary of State informed him that Japan might have shirts, pajamas, and "perhaps cocktail napkins" to sell, but not much else.[8] But Japan was soon producing much more than bargain-store trinkets. What the Japanese had failed to gain through war, they began to win economically.

Japan's Economic Miracle

In the 1950s, after the United States promised to buy Japan's exports, the Japanese economy began to grow at an astonishing rate. In 1951, Japan had a GNP of only $14.2 billion, half that of West Germany, one-third that of Great Britain, and only 4.2% of the size of the U.S.

economy. By the 1980s, this small country, with almost no natural resources and devastated by war, had become a major economic power. As of 2010, it had the third largest economy in the world.

It is hard to pinpoint any one reason for the Japanese postwar economic development miracle. Japan certainly benefited from American military protection and the fact that it did not have to invest in the military. The government's role in securing loans, mediating potential disputes, and making investments were also major factors. The close relationship between bankers and industrialists has also been a positive force. The supreme dedication of the workers and managers to building the economy was perhaps the most important factor in Japanese economic development.

Japan was able to achieve economic growth along with a genuine democratic system. Its 1947 constitution guarantees freedom of speech and the press, and all citizens may vote. With United States backing, Japan's Liberal Democratic Party won early elections and remained in power for most of the rest of the century. Japan's highly educated and competent bureaucracy plays an important role in its democratic system. Civil servants are recruited from the top universities and elected officials welcome their knowledge.

Japan has a free-market economy with a lot of active government participation and supervision. The government carefully manages the competition and negotiates decisions among many interlocking interests of the leaders in the universities, government, banking, and industry.

The intellectual center of Japan's economy is the Ministry of International Trade and Industry (MITI), established in 1949. This agency attracts some of the brightest graduates. It sets planning goals, encourages economic sectors, enforces regulations, and oversees financing. One of the leading scholars of the Japanese economy has written, "The particular speed, form, and consequences of Japanese economic growth are not intelligible without reference to the contributions of MITI."[9]

The Japanese people have had one of the highest rates of savings in the world, allowing Japanese businessmen to borrow heavily from the banks holding these savings. The government also followed a consistent policy of inflation that made payments of these loans easier. This system worked well until the "bubble" burst in 1990, which left the banks with many bad loans and bankruptcies that required government bailouts.

The devotion of the "salarymen" also helps explain Japan's dramatic recovery. They worked hard all day and into the evening, often not returning home until 11 o'clock at night, too late to see their children. They worked part of Saturday and had only Sunday free for perhaps a game of golf or rest. Japanese wives and mothers carried the main responsibility for raising the children and supervising the home. It was really this generation's sacrifices that rebuilt Japan and laid the groundwork for its impressive economic recovery.

Japan's excellent educational system has been another reason for its dramatic economic development. Every school is under the supervision of the central government; all the schools across the nations follow the same curriculum and pay the teachers the same excellent salaries. Frequently, when young students are ill, their mothers will attend the children's classes and take notes. Students can also watch the content being taught on television.

Many called the Japanese emphasis on doing well on the tests so you can get into the right college "examination hell." But Japanese students continued to score at or near the top in international math and science examinations almost every year. Universities are free, so Japan can draw on its best talent and select the best graduates for the government bureaucracies. This system makes it possible for the finest minds to be in positions where they will make important decisions that the elected officials generally follow.

The Republic of Korea

The dramatic growth and success of the South Korean economy was no less a miracle than Japan's successful development. While they controlled Korea, the Japanese rulers tried to eradicate any memory of Korean history and culture. But in 1945, after having been a colony of Japan since 1910, the independent Southern Koreans have struggled to revive their own culture and to develop a democratic system.

For three decades after independence, the military backed a series of harsh dictators who controlled most of the political power in the country. Syngman Rhee, whom the Americans installed as president, governed with an iron hand from 1948 to 1960. When popular protests over his rigged election threatened to disrupt the country, he fled to Hawaii, where he later died. Following Rhee, a series of authoritarian leaders backed by the army continued to suppress the demands for a more democratic government. However, during this period, public protests, particularly by university students, that continued to gain momentum ultimately led to genuine reforms.

In 1987, soon after the president was found to have tortured a university student to death, the Koreans elected Roh Tae-woo, a committed democrat, president. His election marked the beginning of Korean democracy. A year later, when South Korea was hosting the Summer Olympics, its democracy seemed well established.

Both South Korea's authoritarian rulers and democratic presidents emphasized economic growth. The government encouraged the formation of very large industrial firms like Daewoo and Hyundai and gave them generous support. By the 1970s, Korea's growth rates were catching up with Japan's. Korean industries were able to win over a large share of Japan's textile trade and also a large share of the world's steel production. By the 1990s, Korean automobiles had a good share of the world automobile market as well.

South Korea's economic success can be attributed to close government–industry cooperation, a highly qualified core of engineers, skilled workers, and a strong work ethic. Korea's commitment to excellent public education is another major reason for its economic growth. As of 2010, South Korea was investing more per pupil in public education than any other nation.

Although most South Koreans are pleased with their new democratic reforms and vibrant economy, they still yearn for the reunification of their divided country. Because the Korean War was never officially ended, many of the families that were separated from one another when the country was divided have never been allowed to contact or visit one another. Moreover, when North Korea under Kim Jong-il began developing nuclear weapons and flew rockets capable of carrying nuclear warheads over South Korea, strained relations between the two Koreas intensified.

The Republic of China (Taiwan)

The Republic of China, often identified as Taiwan, became a nation in 1949 when the Kuomintang fled to that island. Since its inception, the nation has experienced significant economic growth. Soon after its founding, the government carried out a sweeping land reform program that gave plots of land to individual farmers and encouraged them to grow commercial crops. The Taiwanese government also established close relations with large industries and business firms and passed legislation that would help them grow. The Taiwanese also invested heavily in education at all levels, which helped them create a literate workforce and a pool of skilled engineers and technicians.

Despite the 1971 decision that transferred Taiwan's United Nations seat to the People's Republic of China, Taiwan's leaders have established close relations with its neighbors and even with the PRC. When Chiang Kai-shek died in 1978, he was succeeded by his son Chiang Ching-kuo, who allowed greater democratic participation. However, the Kuomintang continued its authoritarian rule until the 1990s.

In the 1980s, the American government had led the move toward a freer global economic system and had tried to persuade other nations to open their economies to global competition. In general, nations seeking membership in the global economy had to reduce government subsidies, diminish the power of labor unions, control their national debt, and, above all, reduce government regulations on business and let the market work. This movement, sometimes called the "Washington Consensus," was advanced by the World Bank and the International Monetary Fund, international agencies that regulate the financial activities of each nation that joins the global system.

Following the lead of Japan, Korea, Taiwan, and Singapore, several other Southeast and East Asian nations have joined the global system. With the wider acceptance of the so-called "Washington Consensus" in the 1980s, these nations sought exchanges of capital among nations without tariff barriers. Both authoritarian states, like Indonesia, Thailand, and the Philippines, and the more democratic societies, like Malaysia and Singapore, have benefited greatly from the new global economy. Vietnam, healing from its generations of war, also opted to join the global system; so did neighboring Cambodia.

The new economic boom in these countries was often led by the large Chinese diaspora communities who traditionally were the merchants and bankers there. The new economy also led to massive migrations from countryside to cities as millions of farmers sought jobs making Nike sneakers, clothing, and other export products that were sold in Europe and the United States. In many of the new money economies, the rising prosperity has also been accompanied by an underworld of corruption and prostitution and traditional values have been severely challenged.

STRATEGIES FOR MIXED ECONOMIC AND SOCIAL DEVELOPMENT

Setting the Stage

Rather than choosing between Soviet-style communism and American capitalism, many nations saw fallacies in both capitalism and the socialist economies and attempted to adopt the best practices of each. Many of the newly independent nations also tried to avoid direct involvement in the Cold War as they tried to combine the benefits of capitalist economic growth and socialist commitment to human equality. In this search for a "middle way," India was an acknowledged leader.

India Chooses Democracy and a Planned Economy

After achieving independence, Prime Minister Nehru chose to create a "mixed economy that combined major features of both the Soviet and Western economic systems. Following the Soviet model, India embarked on a series of five-year plans that identified specific goals for each sector of the economy. Despite major achievements in heavy industry, irrigation projects, and electrical production, Nehru's planned economy only grew about 3 percent a year. Furthermore, it neglected fundamental investments in agriculture that would have improved the lives of Indian farmers who make up the majority of India's citizens.

Prime Minister Nehru then championed a policy of import substitution. This meant India would try to produce most of the manufactured goods it needed while using tariffs to keep out foreign products such as Coca-Cola. By the 1970s, largely due to Nehru's foresight, India had become one of the ten largest industrial nations in the world. Although it became relatively self-sufficient, poverty continued to increase and economic growth was meager. Further, the huge government bureaucracy often stood in the way of entrepreneurs starting new businesses. The stifling bureaucratic rules and countless permits that businesses had to get became known derisively as the "License Raj." As a result, many innovative ideas and entrepreneurial ventures were not implemented.

When Nehru's daughter Indira Gandhi (1917–1984) was elected prime minister in 1966, she tried to move India to a more centralized political system. Mrs. Gandhi, like her father, was also a dedicated socialist. She nationalized the banks and increased the role of government in the economic system. Both the Socialist and Communist Parties supported her, but she encountered serious opposed from a strong faction in her own Congress Party that wanted to move India toward a free market system.

In 1969, Ms Gandhi nationalized banks, mines, and oil companies and abolished the titles and privileges of the former maharajas. After another victory in 1971, she issued her famous slogan, *Garibi Hatao* ("End Poverty"). However, her socialist policies resulted in sluggish economic growth that did little to end poverty.

Ms. Gandhi's popularity was at an all-time high when she supported the secession of West Pakistan from the Pakistani nation and the creation of Bangladesh. However, in 1975, facing criticism over her increasingly strong leadership, corruption, and the lack of eco-

Indira Gandhi

nomic progress, she declaration an "emergency" that allowed her to act without any checks on her power. The emergency lasted until 1977, when Mrs. Gandhi, confident of her popularity, called for a new national election. Much to her surprise, she lost. However, the majority of Indians, apparently forgiving her for her transgressions, voted her back into power in 1980, and she served until her assassination in 1984.

Ms. Gandhi tried to follow her father's commitment to the non-aligned movement, but her hostility to American policies drove her closer to the Soviet Union, and India's relations with the United States were frequently strained. Soviet leaders provided India with modern military equipment and some development aid. The Soviet veto in the United Nations Security Council also meant India could keep the U.N. from passing resolutions on Kashmir.

Indian leaders found it difficult to implement an effective family planning program. Although the government birth control campaign promoted "Two or three children, enough" and encouraged sterilization, India's population grew from 369 million in 1950 to about 1.2 billion in 2010. Unfortunately, aborting female fetuses has become a serious problem. As of 2008, there were only 933 live female births for every 1,000 male births. Projected increases will make India the most populous country in the world by 2050.[10]

Despite her often-quoted promise, to end poverty, India's economic growth remained low and the deadening effects of its centrally controlled economic system were becoming more obvious. During her son Rajiv Gandhi's years as Prime Minister, 1984–1989, most Indian leaders were questioning the socialist planned economy that India had followed since independence. He lifted some government restrictions on private enterprise and he vigorous supported the new information technology sectors. Following his defeat in 1989, Rajiv ran for Prime Minister again, but while campaigning in 1991 he was assassinated by a suicide bomber, who was protesting his attempts to mediate in the Sri Lankan civil war.

Europeans Create Welfare States

Although Western European nations achieved remarkable growth in the decades after World War II, their earlier world political power was diminishing. As the United States began to assume a greater world power status and provided a nuclear shield against potential Soviet threats, Europeans were free to invest more in non-military sectors.

Since World War II, the Western European states have mounted a major effort to promote maximum economic growth and also to provide maximum human equality. The European states also sought to find a middle way between the rigidly controlled socialism of the Soviet Union and the more laissez-faire capitalism of the United States. The major exponents of this synthesis were the Social Democrats, who insisted on democracy but at the same time wanted to use various taxes to give the state the resources needed to provide more social benefits to its citizens. These nations had a long history of integrating socialist values into their capitalist systems. Most of them supported active labor parties that pressed for better working conditions, higher wages, a shorter work day, paid vacations, and guaranteed benefits such as free education and universal health care. The political systems the Europeans developed to achieve these goals are often called social democracies or welfare states.

The European nations differed markedly from the United States in their attitude toward socialism. For many Americans, socialism evoked images of Karl Marx and the Russian Revolution. Americans assumed this ideology was a bitter enemy of free-market capitalism and antithetical to democracy. In 1919, the Americans had purged all potential socialists and communists from their government and rounded up hundreds of suspected communists for being unpatriotic. In the 1950s Senator Joseph McCarthy embarked on another anti-communist fear campaign. He accused state department officials, university professors, and officers in the army of being communist sympathizers. Even Robert Oppenheimer, the father of the atomic bomb, was denied security clearance. As the overheated atmosphere of McCarthyism abated, it became increasingly clear that the vast majority of those tainted by McCarthy's allegations were, in fact, innocent of any unpatriotic behavior.

By contrast, most Europeans supported democratic governments that used socialist ideas to promote the welfare of their citizens. Following World War II, socialist parties regularly competed in European elections; several socialist governments were elected in Europe and also in Australia, Canada, and New Zealand.

Socialist values are embedded is what is known as the "welfare state," the belief that government has a responsibility to ensure that all its citizens have health care, insurance, a living wage, safe working conditions, and access to education. In addition to ensuring that all citizens have enough to meet their basic needs, welfare states seek to lessen the gap between the very rich and the poor. Welfare states usually have a low poverty rate. They commonly offer parental leave for both fathers and mothers and free childcare for working parents.

Some of the first government welfare programs in Europe were intended to support women after childbirth while they were caring for infants. Efforts were made to ensure that men with young wives were paid enough to support their families. However, because welfare payments were given to the husbands, this policy actually increased women's dependency and helped keep women's wages lower than men's.[11]

In the European movement toward Social Democracy, the Scandinavian nations led the way. Iceland, Finland, Sweden, Norway, and Denmark all worked to expand social democracy and create welfare programs that came to be known as the "Nordic Model." These reforms aimed to enhance individual autonomy, ensure universal human rights, and stabilize the economy, while expanding economic benefits to all citizens. The Nordic Model also sought to expand the number of people involved in economic decision-making, especially for women and workers.

Generally a variety of taxes, often amounting to fifty percent of one's income, were imposed to pay for the government's services. Despite high taxes, most Europeans were able to take long vacations and have more leisure time than most American workers had. The thirty-five-hour week was common and so was a five-week paid vacation. European social democracies also provided free university education for all qualified students and universal health care.

From 1960 on, France, Germany, and Britain were the major political players in Europe. In these states, conservatives and social democrats often took turns leading governments. The governments that had names like Christian Democrat, or Conservative, tended to favor business and allocate less money for welfare programs. The center-left parties, called Labour, Socialist, or Social Democrats, alternated in power. During these decades the British welfare state continued to expand and Conservative governments did not succeed in reducing it.

However, after a prosperous period in the 1950s and 60s, the growth rate of the British economy in the 70s was slower than that of any other European economy. Margaret Thatcher, a conservative who served as Britain's prime minister from 1979 to 1990, believed private incentives would promote economic growth. She wanted to reduce government regulations on the market and give entrepreneurs a free hand. Thatcher supported the privatization of most British industries, and during the 1980s, Britain experienced the longest period of economic growth it had had for more than 150 years.

In France, Charles de Gaulle served as president from 1958 to 1969. Under his leadership, France managed to find stability and accept the loss of its colonial empire, particularly Algeria. After de Gaulle, France generally followed the same alternating pattern as Britain, and from 1957 to 1981, no socialist party won an election.

Francois Mitterrand, a socialist, served as president from 1981 until 1995. During that time France expanded its welfare system by nationalizing industrial companies and thirty-six banks, increasing the minimum wage by ten percent, reducing the work week to thirty-nine hours, and guaranteeing a yearly five-week vacation. These generous benefits increased further when unemployment rose and the devaluation of the franc failed to stem rising inflation.

Remarkably, Germany, which had suffered more than any other western European nation during the war, achieved significant economic growth. German voters, following the general European pattern, chose between center-right Christian Democrats and the left-of-center Social Democrats. By 1960, West Germany was well on its way to being an economic power and its prosperity continued throughout the twentieth century. Germany's economic prosperity and its competitive advantage in Europe has greatly strengthened the people's commitment to democratic rule.

Most of the European workers have middle-class lifestyles. From 1980 to 2010 the United Nations' quality of life index consistently

A bombed church and modern skyscraper in Berlin

identified the Scandinavian nations as well as the Netherlands and Costa Rica as having the highest quality of life in the world. The European welfare states also enjoyed the most freedom of the press, freedom of assembly, and privacy. All these welfare states provide free health care, and France's health system is generally regarded as the best and most efficient in the world.

Although the world economic downturn after 1980 caused many European nations, particularly Great Britain, to reevaluate their social welfare systems, none has taken away major benefits such as health care, free education, or assistance for the poor, and none of them is characterized by the large class divisions and income inequalities that are common in the United States.

A New World Order, 1989–2010

The sound of hundreds of sledgehammer blows could be heard around the world as the German people pounded against the Berlin Wall on November 9, 1989. The fall of the wall signaled the end of the Cold War. The destruction of this divisive symbol of the two German nations, which had existed since 1961, was soon followed by the entire Soviet empire coming apart, with almost no violence. The consequences of this process have reverberated around the world ever since.

Since 1990, twenty-eight new nations have joined the expanding nation-state system. Most of these new states were carved out of the former Soviet Union. With some one hundred and ninety-three nation-states now in existence, the challenge of regulating and mediating international conflicts has increased exponentially.

This act focuses on the dramatic changes to the world since 1989. The Eastern European former Soviet satellite nations are free to choose their own destiny. The United States has emerged as the preeminent superpower. India and the PRC have experienced rapid economic growth and begun to reclaim the economic power they had enjoyed before European colonialism. At the same time, globalization is fundamentally changing individual lives all around the world.

RECONFIGURING THE MAP OF EUROPE

Setting the Stage

Although Gorbachev's glasnost and perestroika were meant only to reform a troubled Soviet Union, an unintended consequence was the unleashing of the pent-up frustrations of millions of people living in Soviet-controlled Eastern Europe. The March 1989 elections in the Soviet Union resulted in the old guard Communist leaders losing power. These cracks in the Soviet Union, the second most dominant power in the world, quickly turned into chasms. When Gorbachev announced the results to the party leadership, they replied, "What kind of communists are they?"[1]

In a matter of months, the members of the minority communities, who together outnumbered all the ethnic Russians, began to rebel. As Gorbachev relaxed travel restrictions, thousands of people in the Soviet-controlled states began to flee, and the citizens of East and West Germany tore down the Berlin Wall. After seventy-two years of firm Communist Party control, the Soviet empire completely collapsed in only a few months.

The Aftermath of the Disintegration of the Soviet Union

After the fall of the Soviet Union in 1991, the map of Europe was redrawn. Fifteen independent countries were free to decide what kind of governments they would establish. The two large Slavic republics, Ukraine and Belarus, both became new nations. Mass protest movements in the Ukraine indicated growing popular support for democratic rule there. However, few of the former Soviet republics managed to install anything like democracies. International organizations have criticized Armenia, which is operating under a democratic constitution, for its lack of democratic procedures. Similarly, Moldova, also a constitutionally based parliamentary system, has been charged with having a poor human rights record. The government controls the Moldovan press, its system of justice is weak, and as of 2010, police brutality was quite common.

Belarus has remained a totalitarian state with close relations with Russia. In the "stans" that had been part of the Soviet Union—Kazakhstan, Kyrgyzstan, Tajikistan, Turkmenistan, and Uzbekistan—harsh authoritarian governments prevail. The military also backs Georgia's and Azerbaijan's leaders. By contrast, the Baltic states of Lithuania, Estonia, and Latvia all embraced democratic rule, and up until the economic crisis of 2008, they were participating in the global system and their standard of living was rising.

In 1991, in a modern replay of the Balkan crisis of the early twentieth century, Yugoslavia was breaking up and Slobodan Milošević, the Serb leader who had long encouraged Serbian nationalism, now emerged as the protector of Serb identity. Milošević opposed the dismemberment of Yugoslavia, but he could not stop it. Slovenia and then Croatia were the first to break away, and that led to violent conflict with Serbia. The war in Croatia resulted in hundreds of thousands of refugees.

In 1992, a more violent war broke out when Bosnia declared independence. The Serbs who lived there, urged on by Milosevic, were determined to remain within Yugoslavia and help build a greater Serbia, but the European Union and the United States immediately recognized Bosnia. This new nation had about 1.3 million Serbs who were Eastern Orthodox Christians, more than a million Muslims, and 700,000 Roman Catholic Croats.

The Bosnian Serbs fought hard to gain control. As they conquered territory, they removed or killed thousands of innocent civilians, most of whom were Muslims. The Serbs marched thousands of women and children into concentration camps; they trucked 7,500 men and boys into the countryside and killed them. Another 3,000 who attempted to escape were shot and decapitated. The Serbs called this "ethnic cleansing"; many call it genocide.[2] For more than a decade, the United Nations and the European community have been responsible for the country's security, but ethnic tensions still dominate any attempts at a peaceful settlement in Bosnia.

In the mid-1990s, the Serbs also tried to take over Kosovo, a small state with an Albanian majority. This time the United States and

NATO intervened and Kosovo remained independent. Since then, NATO peacekeeping forces have helped keep the fragile peace in the historically troubled Balkans.

Areas beyond the Soviet Union also claimed their independence. The Versailles Treaty had created Czechoslovakia and Yugoslavia, two multi-ethnic states that were comprised of six separate ethnic groups. These states, together with Poland, Hungary, Bulgaria, Romania, and Albania, had also gained their independence by 1992. Most of these reconstituted states were able to create democratic systems with various types of multiparty parliamentary governments. In 1993, Czechoslovakia peacefully split into the Czech Republic and Slovakia. Both these new democratic nations enjoy cordial relations with one another and with the rest of Europe.

The Russian Federation

After the collapse of the Soviet Union in 1991 and the creation of the Russian Federation, Boris Yeltsin was elected the Russian Federation's first president and people attempted to build a viable democratic system. Their new constitution guarantees free elections, basic human rights, and rule by law. Initially, President Yeltsin worked for closer relations with the United States and also hoped Russia would move closer to Western Europe. However, when the United States expanded NATO by including nations on Russia's borders, relations between the two countries cooled considerably.

After centuries under the Czarists and more than seventy years of communist totalitarian rule, most Russians lacked many of the civic values that underpin democratic rule. Perhaps their long totalitarian experience, coupled with a low standard of living, also helps explain why the Russian people have had difficulty creating a genuine democracy. With the sudden privatization of industry and finance after 1990, many of the former communist leaders and military officers simply took over factories and banks and ran them as their own businesses. By 1995, the Russian economy was in a worse depression than the Great Depression of the 1930s.[3] However, the Russian economy recovered, thanks mainly to a steep rise in oil prices. Since then, Russia has depended on its rich natural resources to repay its debts and raise its growth rate.

Russia has also faced several ethnic challenges. Chechnya, a largely Muslim province, has been the most problematic. Chechnyan guerrillas bombed a Moscow opera house in 2002 and have carried out many terrorist attacks around the country. The Russian army got bogged down fighting in the Chechnyan civil war, and by 2004, the Russian people were turning against the war.

When Vladimir Putin, a former secret police official, was elected president in 1999, Russia drifted back toward a more authoritarian government. Many former KGB members became political leaders and several former Communist Party members took over industries and banks. In his second term, Putin gave up the earlier goal of joining the Western nations. Instead, returning to the idea of Russia becoming a great world power, he appealed to Russian nationalism and rekindled memories of Russia's imperial past. He has consistently contested the growing influence the United States achieved in Europe by expanding NATO.

While running for president in 2004, Putin publicly called the demise of the Soviet empire a national tragedy from which "only the elites and nationalists of the republics gained."[4] Putin's chosen successor, Dmitri A. Medvedev, promised to continue Putin's major policies, and Putin became the prime minister. Russia's decision to emphasize economic growth without developing industrial power or empowering its fragile democracy remains problematic.

Europeans Struggle to Maintain Their Welfare States while Remaining Globally Competitive

After 1989, the European nation-states, freed from the fears of the long Cold War, worked to strengthen the European Union. In 1992, France joined the EU, and in 1999 the EU adopted the Euro as its common currency. Although France continues to celebrate its rich history and most of its citizens consider their culture superior to any other, its leaders see France as an important member of the European Union and it is involved in many joint European projects.

With the expansion of the European Union in 2004, when ten new nations joined, the older members, with more stable economies and generally more wealthy, were forced to come to the aid of some of the weakest nations. By 2010, Germany and some of the other more developed economies were investing hundreds of billion dollars to save the Greek economy, while Portugal and a few other new members were also on the verge of serious economic crises, largely because of their growing national debts.

After 1980, because they were having trouble balancing strong welfare programs and also staying competitive globally, many of the European states elected more conservative governments. Jacques Chirac, elected president of France in 1995 and again in 2002, symbolized this growing conservatism. Chirac promised to reduce France's high unemployment and streamline the economy. He promised to lower tax rates, end price controls, extend privatization of industries, and stiffen penalties for crime. He also supported closer relations with Britain and the United States. But Chirac was no great admirer of the free-market approach; he wanted the government to

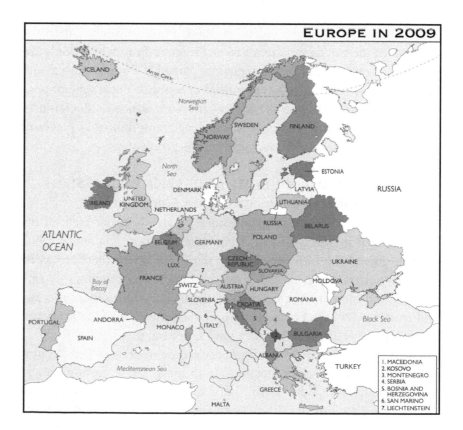

maintain a strong presence in French life. Gordon Brown, then Britain's Prime Minster, played an active role in the European Union's efforts to combat the long recession that followed the near-collapse of the world financial system in 2008.

Most of the more industrialized members of the EU have faced a delicate balancing act trying to maintain their many social welfare programs and still keep a competitive advantage in the global system. Despite high levels of unemployment and rising national debts, most of the member nations have maintained universal health care and offer parental leave, maintain excellent working conditions, enjoy good educational systems, and have a skilled workforce. With nearly 25 percent of its jobs in manufacturing, compared to only 12.5 percent in the United States, Europe has remained competitive, although it is losing manufacturing jobs to the developing nations.

In the 2007, Nicolas Sarkozy turned France toward a free market economy and a more disciplined workforce. He pledged to rekindle the French work ethic and support new business initiatives. Worried about France's very large national debt and the seeming lack of productivity of French workers, he called for extending the work week beyond 35 hours and stimulating economic growth.

After 1989, the two German nations were united and the newly unified German nation had to merge West Germany's capitalist economy with East Germany's socialist economy. Many West Germans resented having to assist the East Germans, while many East Germans thought their West German brothers and sisters were too materialistic and individualistic. However, by supporting the East German economy and mollifying the West Germans' anger at the welfare payments being given to the East Germans, Germany has succeeded in rebuilding a strong, stable democracy.

Since unification, Germany has taken an active part in both the European Union and NATO. German troops served on peacekeeping missions in the Balkans in the 1990s and in Afghanistan in the early 2000s. By the end of the first decade in the twenty-first century, Germany was a prosperous, stable, and powerful nation with the strongest economy in Europe and had regained its historic position as a world power.

In Britain, when Tony Blair became prime minister in 1997, he kept many of his predecessor's free-market reforms and continued to rely on free-market principles, even though he did not increase working-class benefits. When Gordon Brown followed Blair in 2007, Brown took an active role in designing the European Union's stimulus and financial reform projects to combat the 2008 recession, but by 2010 he had lost much of his support at home. In 2010 Brown was defeated by a conservative-liberal coalition.

The European Union's population in 2010 was about 492 million and its 2009 GDP was nearly $15 trillion.[5] Its stronger integration has made Europe a major participant in the global economy.

SCENE
TWO

ASIAN STATES JOIN
THE GLOBAL ECONOMY

Setting the Stage

One of the greatest surprises during the late twentieth century was the resurgence of India and the People's Republic of China as major world economies. Although both of these civilizations were prominent world economic centers from ancient times to 1750 and led the world in manufacturing until at least 1800, many contemporary leaders and opinion makers argued that both nations were "backward" societies that would have to significantly change their "traditional" values if they hoped to compete with the West.

With their rapid rate of economic growth after 1980, the balance of power in the world has undergone a major shift. India and the PRC have returned to the economic forefront, and many small Asian states such as Japan, Malaysia, Vietnam, South Korea, Singapore, and Taiwan have joined in Asia's economic growth boom.

India Excels in Information Technology

By 1991, the planned economy Nehru had championed was nearly paralyzed. When a balance of payments crisis occurred that year, India had to airlift most of its gold reserves to Britain, and the International Monetary Fund required basic reforms in return for loans.

As a result of the economic crisis, Dr. Manmohan Singh, the finance minister, realized he would have to institute some radical economic reforms. He ended the "license raj" and instituted a market economy based on free enterprise, opened India to international trade and foreign investment, and privatizing banks and basic industries. He made the value of the rupee, India's currency, "float," meaning its value was allowed to change in relationship to the other world currencies.

India also significantly lowered tariffs, freed up borrowing, and encouraged foreign investments. The Indian GDP steadily increased, and by 2010, India had become the world's fourth-largest economy and a major world power as well. India, unlike China, achieved significant economic growth while maintaining a vibrant democracy that guaranteed a free press, the people's right to vote, and diverse political parties.

India's dramatic economic growth has pulled hundreds of millions of Indians out of poverty and spawned a new class of rich businessmen. Entrepreneurs have launched new companies, especially in the new field of information technology (IT). One impressive example is Narayana Murthy, who started out by borrowing $250 from his wife to launch Infosys, an information technology company in 1981. By 2009, Infosys was worth almost $30 billion. More than 300 million people are now in India's middle class, almost equivalent to the total population of the United States.

Narayana Murthy with Nandan Nilekani

When President Bush visited India in 2006, the two nations began to develop closer relations. The United States accepted India as a nuclear power and agreed to furnish nuclear fuel for its peaceful projects. The two nations also began to coordinate military activities in the region and the U.S. recognized India's preeminence in South Asia.

Taiwan and the People's Republic of China Thrive

By 1987, Taiwan had ended its long period of authoritarian rule, and in the early 1990s, along with freedom of the press, speech, and assembly, the Taiwanese got the right to organize political parties. In March 1996, Taiwan held its first presidential election. Although the PRC still insists that Taiwan is a vital part of the People's Republic, informal exchanges, tourism, and financial investments between these two nations have been established.

In the People's Republic of China, the transition to a market economy that started in 1978 resulted initially in an enormous displacement of people and in much corruption. Communist Party officials, who were the first to become entrepreneurs, had a huge advantage because they could buy materials at state-controlled prices and sell them at market prices. Soon members of the People's Liberation Army were also buying land, building factories, and investing in the new global economy.

Despite the problems caused by the rapid economic growth, during the 1990s, the PRC enjoyed growth rates of over ten percent. In the process, the PRC created a large middle class and ushered in a consumer revolution. By the turn of the twenty-first century, China had become the world's third-largest economy and it was exporting more than any other country. The United States, its main consumer, bought about $1.5 trillion worth of Chinese products in 2008. China has used part of its enormous dollar surplus to buy large parts of the burgeoning American debt. It is now the largest holder of U.S. dollars and owns the largest share of the United States' national debt.

Without foreign aid, the Chinese Communist party has managed to transform the country into a world power and an industrial giant. By 2005, Shanghai, China's largest city, had 4,000 skyscrapers, "almost double the number in New York" at that time, and it was planning "to build 1,000 more by the end of" 2010. According to one scholar, "There's no doubt what is happening in parts of China is on a scale we've never seen before."[6] Another writer predicted that "in the coming decades" China will create "coastal megacities" will probably have "an urban population of one billion" by 2030, and will "possibly" be "the world's biggest economy."[7]

Although Deng Xiaoping and his supporters were enthusiastic

Shanghai skyline in 2008

about the new global market economics, they were not receptive to political reforms. Instead, Deng promised the Chinese people that they were free to get rich, but they were not to make any serious attempt to democratize the Chinese system. This policy formulation is often called "Deng's bargain": You can try to get rich, but keep quiet about expanding human rights.

What Deng's bargain really meant become clear in 1989. That year, Hu Yaobang, a long time champion of economic reform and political liberation, died. Hu had also spoken up for student rights, including the right to criticize the government. At his funeral, thousands of student sympathizers publicly expressed their desire for an end to political corruption and in favor of a more open society. Once the funeral was over, students filled Tiananmen Square in Beijing, and some even carried a Chinese-style Statue of Liberty. However, the students had no clear leaders or reform program. After seven weeks of daily demonstrations and speeches, the government sent in armed troops who violently ended the demonstrations. A *New York Times* report estimated that between 400 and 800 students were killed.[8]

Even though the PRC has not instituted democratic reforms, its free-market economy has resulted in a gigantic increase in China's middle class, and thousands of Chinese entrepreneurs have started export businesses. As of 2009, China had the second-largest number of billionaires (measured in U.S. dollars) in the world: 130 known bil-

Chinese soldiers during Tiananmen Square demonstrations

lionaires, compared with 101 in 2008.[9] In 2010 China moved ahead of Japan to become the second largest economy in the world.

The PRC is moving quickly to regain the kind of economic power and international status that it enjoyed before 1840. The spectacular Chinese performances during the Beijing Olympics in 2008 showed off the impressive talent, motivation, and organizational ability that are transforming China into a world leader.

The growth of the economies of India and China is one of the most far-reaching recent developments. According to a United Nations University study, "innovation capability has been the critical driving force for economic development in China and India."[10] As the study explains, "The main focus of their reforms has been to link the science sector with the business sector and to provide incentives for innovation activities."[11]

By 2010, the Chinese were able to draw up long-range plans that would place their nation at the forefront of the green movement. They were producing the cheapest solar panels, developing huge wind farms, and manufacturing efficient electric cars. With three thousand years of history behind them, including centuries of economic dominance, most Chinese can take the long view. When the American Secretary of State, Henry Kissinger, in 1972, asked Zhou Enlai what he thought the significance of the French Revolution was, he replied, "It's too early to tell."[12]

Vietnam Shifts to a Market Economy

China's decision in the 1980s to embrace market capitalism, along with the fall of the Soviet Union in 1989, convinced the Vietnamese leaders that they should also consider changing their economic policies. In 1986, the government approved several fundamental economic reforms that have helped the country establishing a quasi-market economy. The government permitted private ownership of industries and land. It also encouraged foreign investment and opened new oil fields. Gradually this former communist nation has also joined the global economy. From 2000 to 2005, its growth rate averaged seven percent, making Vietnam one of the fastest growing economies in the world. As of 2009, Vietnam had one of the world's most trade-oriented economies. The nation has been thoroughly integrated into the world market economy. In a 2009 Vietnamese study of the person its youth most admired, more young people chose Bill Gates than Ho Chi Minh, the father of their nation.[13]

Indonesia's Reforms Create More National Unity

By the 1990s, Indonesia was experiencing significant economic growth, increased industrialization, and improvements in health, education, and living standards. Driven by large oil exports, Indonesia's growth rate had risen to about five percent by 1995.

However, life in Suharto's Indonesia was not all positive. Like other dictators, Suharto rewarded those who supported him and allowed his friends, and especially his son, to accumulate much personal wealth. The growth-oriented economy has destroyed significant portions of the country's rain forest, and basic human rights such as freedom of expression have been drastically curtailed.

Opposing Suharto's totalitarian rule was a strong movement for Muslim identity. Suharto discouraged this; he believed that Indonesian unity depended on equal rights for Hindus, Buddhist, Christians, and Muslims. But the rise of Muslim identity politics has generally resulted in a more liberal and less dogmatic form of the faith there than in Islamic movements in West Asia and Pakistan.

Since 1998, Indonesia has come closer to instituting genuine elections. During this period, called the "Reformasi" (Reform), there was a concerted attempt to balance all the factions in Indonesian society, especially the growing importance of Islam, the demand for more regional autonomy, and the still-powerful military. In 2001, Indonesia chose Megawati Sukarnoputri to be its first woman president. Although the nation has recently suffered a devastating tsunami, terrorist attacks, and an earthquake, the economy has stabilized and a new democratic constitution has been ratified.

North Korea Expands Its Nuclear Program

At the end of the century, North Korea remained one of the handful of communist states in the world. Kim Il-sung and his son, Kim Jong-il, have maintained one of the most authoritarian governments in the world and at the same time provided almost no benefits for their citizens. The people of North Korea have experienced famines and food shortages and have not been provided with even the barest of necessities.

During the Clinton administration, the U.S. found out that North Korea was developing nuclear materials for a bomb. Negotiators worked with the North Korean government to find a way to end its nuclear program. In his last months of office, President Clinton had his suitcase packed, ready go to North Korea to sign an agreement that would have ended its nuclear development in return for U.S. economic aid and help in building peaceful nuclear facilities.

With the election of George W. Bush, those diplomatic initiatives were replaced by an effort to use American power to spread democracy in the world. As a result, sanctions were instituted against North Korea. After Kim Jong-il authorized nuclear development and the country fired several test rockets over Japan, the Bush administration in the late 1990s resumed talks with North Korea, but as of 2010, this small isolated nation has continued to develop and test nuclear weapons and rockets. The United States has encouraged China to take a more active role in convincing Korean leaders to abandon their quest for nuclear weapons, and South Korea has made many overtures to its neighbor. But despite international disapproval, South Korea has not changed its policies.

THE QUEST FOR STABLE REGIMES IN AFRICA, LATIN AMERICA, AND WEST ASIA

Setting the Stage

After 1989, in the aftermath of the Cold War, the United States and other European nations encouraged democracy and economic reforms in various states. Some made democratization a condition for receiving development aid. In addition, political fragmentation and ethnic conflicts complicate economic development in many areas.

However, the political realities of multi-ethnic states have made it difficult for these nations to create multiparty, open systems. Opposition parties have often used violent protests to gain political power. Strong leaders then maintained that establishing stability was a higher value than democracy.

The United Nations Human Development Report of 2004, which evaluated 175 countries on such criteria as life expectancy, education, and per capita income, ranked 25 African nations lowest of the nations of the world.[14] Most of the new nations in Africa have also had difficulty achieving democratic rule. Ghana and Sierra Leone are exceptions: both have become working democracies.

Trade Agreements with Latin America

Latin American nations began opening their borders to globalization in the 1990s, and several have enjoyed a new prosperity. The more robust economies in the 1990s were averaging an annual GDP growth of over five percent. This growth helped to reduce poverty and create higher-paying jobs.

Countries like Brazil began to welcome foreign investment that in past centuries they had seen as North American exploitation of their resources. These investments have financed the opening of the rain forest to mining and large-scale farming. The ecological costs of these practices are enormous and will have lasting effects on both Brazil and the world's climate. The United States took the lead in organizing a North American free trade zone and later a similar arrangement with Central America.

During the 1960s and 1970s, many Latin American nations, especially Brazil, Argentina, and Mexico, borrowed large sums of money from international lenders. By the 1980s these nations owed huge international debts that amounted to up to fifty-five percent of their GDP. Moreover, many still relied on exporting large supplies of oil, tropical fruits, and minerals rather than on indigenous industrial development.

At the 2009 World Economic Forum on Latin America, world leaders pointed to the need for vastly improved educational standards as the key to future economic development. President Óscar Arias Sánchez of Costa Rica spoke of the small number of Latin American teenagers who go on to higher education and warned, "If we don't educate people, it will be very difficult to have progress."[15]

In the early 1990s, President George H. W. Bush tried to redirect United States policy away from supporting dictators and exploiting the nations south of the U.S. border. Early in his presidency he met with his Mexican and Canadian counterparts to work on a proposal that would promote free trade among the three nations.

Under President Clinton's leadership and after vigorous debates, the three nations signed the North American Free Trade Agreement (NAFTA) in 1994. NAFTA called for eliminating tariffs on more than half of U.S. imports from Mexico and more than one-third of U.S. exports to Mexico. Most U.S.–Canada trade was already duty free, but the treaty promised the elimination of almost all U.S.–Mexico tariffs within ten years of its implementation. A few tariffs on U.S. agricultural exports were to be phased out in fifteen years.

After NAFTA went into effect, vocal critics in all three nations attacked the treaty because they believed it would help big business at the expense of labor and small farmers. Some Canadians charged that NAFTA led to foreign investors taking over Canadian companies. American labor unions consistently argued that NAFTA has cost the United States nearly four million manufacturing jobs. Mexico claimed that the $10 billion the U.S. uses to subsidize U.S. farmers, which is more than Mexico's entire agricultural budget, has nearly destroyed Mexico's corn production.

On the positive side, under NAFTA Mexico's exports had increased by $292 billion by 2008. However, the agreements have not led to full employment in Mexico. About half a million Mexicans fled to the United States each year during the first decade of the twenty-first century.[16]

The End of Apartheid in South Africa

Perhaps the most impressive nonviolent political achievement after India's independence in 1947 was the peaceful end of apartheid and the triumph of democracy in South Africa.

That story began in 1907, when the British defeated the Zulu-led coalition of African ethnic groups and also Dutch Protestant settlers known as Boers, and took control of areas in southern Africa. In 1910, Cape Colony was unified under British dominion. By 1912, 74 percent of the population was composed of black Africans. About three-fourths of the population was black and only about 14 percent were white Dutch and English settlers. The rest of the population was made up largely of South Asians and mixed races. Britain granted independence to South Africa and its white minority government in 1934. This decision left the majority black population in a totally subjugated political system. They fought for equality over the next several decades.

In the 1940s the Afrikaner National Party took power and introduced the policy of *apartheid* in order to legally control the majority black population. In the 1950s several new apartheid laws were passed that further strengthened the rigid segregation policy. The new laws kept the majority black population subjugated and totally segregated from the white minority. Under apartheid, black Africans were required to carry passbooks, their travel was restricted, most performed menial jobs, and they had to use segregated public facilities.

In a further effort to divide the population, the government created African "homelands," which resembled Native American reservations rather than the safe and prosperous havens the government claimed they were. Life in these homelands was harsh: there were few basic public facilities or opportunities for jobs or investment, and no chance for upward mobility.

As early as 1912, black Africans had formed the African National

Congress (ANC). Its goal was to unite black South Africans in an effort to end the white minority's oppressive rule. Even though the white government tried to control the ANC's activities, its power and influence grew as more and more black Africans chafed under the oppressive and illegitimate apartheid system. The nationalist movement grew even stronger after white oppression intensified and violent attacks on peaceful demonstrations increased in the 1960s.

By this time Nelson Mandela, a young, charismatic black South African who was born in 1918, had emerged as the leader of the nationalist movement. In 1964, the government arrested Mandela and sentenced him to life in prison. During his long imprisonment, Mandela studied Gandhi's nonviolent resistance philosophy and other nationalist struggles, and he became a symbol of the anti-apartheid movement. Despite his long years in jail, he retained his human gentleness and seemingly bore no hatred toward his oppressors.

Steve Biko (1946–1977) was another important nationalist leader. He founded the Black Peoples' Convention, a coalition of black consciousness groups that worked for social uplift. Biko also helped organize guerrilla groups to fight against apartheid. In 1976 he organized major antigovernment protests. He was imprisoned in 1977 for his role in these uprisings and that same year, after being tortured, he died of brain injuries.

After an increasing number of protests, marches, and open resistance against the government, coupled with international sanctions against South Africa, in 1994 Nelson Mandela was released from jail and the African National Congress gained power. The years of enforced separation between black and white South Africans and the resettlement of many black South Africans on "reservations" ended. In the first free and open election South Africa had ever held, Mandela was elected president of South Africa. Since then, the African National Congress has continued to lead the country.

Archbishop Desmond Tutu (b. 1931), another outstanding South African leader, has played a significant role in creating South African democracy. After the fall of white rule, Tutu led the effort to organize the Truth and Reconciliation Commission. Hundreds of witnesses testified about their experiences under apartheid at these hearings. Unlike a war crimes tribunal, this commission did not punish anyone but tried instead to create empathy and understanding between the black majority and white minority. These tribunals, where the perpetrators of horrible crimes and their victims confronted each other, have become a model for how to deal constructively with human rights violations. Bishop Tutu was awarded the Nobel Peace Prize in 1984.

Nelson Mandela and F. W. de Klerk

In 1999, South Africa held its second free election and Thabo Mbeki, Mandela's chosen deputy, won an overwhelming victory. In 2003, Mbeki led the ANC to a two-thirds majority in parliament for the first time. However, after many investigations over alleged corruption, in 2008 Mbeki resigned. Part of the opposition to him came from his consistent denial of his country's growing HIV/AIDS crisis, which sparked both local and international criticism.

Despite the difficulties of transferring oppressive white rule into a genuine democratic system, South Africans are now living together as they build a functioning democracy and meet the demands of the global economy. Few people in 1980 would have predicted the end of apartheid and an integrated South African society.

Progress in Building Stable African States

By 2008, Africa was home to 53 independent, sovereign nations. Technically, most of them were republics governed by a president. However, many of these have actually been led by poorly educated military officers with no governing experience. Many of these rulers sought personal gain and often tried to turn one ethnic group against another in an effort to increase their own power.

From 1960 to 1985 there were seventy coups and thirteen assassinations of sitting presidents in Africa. Even in the more successful African states, one-party rule has been common. Ghana, Ivory Coast, Senegal, Guinea, Mali, Niger, Benin, and Togo have all been gov-

erned by strongmen backed by the military. Few nations have managed to achieve anything close to a genuine democratic system. One
early leader in the Central African Republic, following Napoleon's
example, even crowned himself emperor. In Ghana, Nkruma began
his rule as a promising democrat, but he soon became an autocratic
ruler who demanded total obedience from his subjects. The Democratic Republic of Congo is an especially tragic case. Rape has been
used as an instrument of war, and fathers and husbands are often
forced to watch their wives and mothers raped repeatedly.

Some of the new African states produced outstanding leaders such
as Julius Nyerere in Tanzania, Jomo Kenyatta in Kenya, and Nelson
Mandela in South Africa. However, most nations have had difficulty
creating a viable middle class and prospering economically despite
their rich natural resources. Pervasive illiteracy, government corrup-

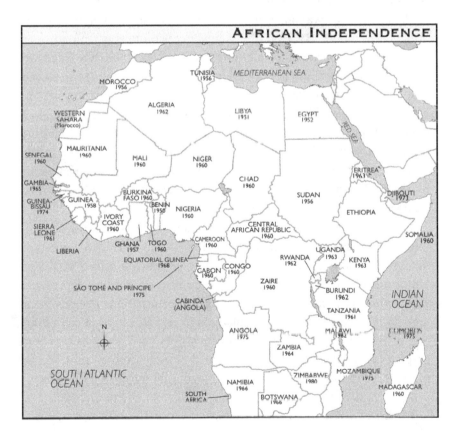

tion and mismanagement, and frequent ethnic wars have inhibited development and the creation of stable, representative governments.

Kenya is somewhat typical of the huge challenges that many African states have faced as they worked to move from single-party rule or military dictatorships to a more democratic system during the first decades of independence. Daniel Moi succeeded Kenyatta in 1978. After years of his one-party rule, President Moi installed a complicated voting system that again restricted democratic rights, and in 1987 was again elected president. He then jailed Kenneth Matiba, one of his most vocal opponents.

Despite his dictatorial rule, Moi did carry out a number of reforms. By the end of the 1980s, he attempted to restrict the export of ivory and he appointed the archaeologist, Richard Leakey, as director of wildlife. Leakey, well known for his important archaeological finds, was successful in limiting the exploitation of Kenya's large animals.

President Moi was also an avid anti-communist, which won him American support. By 1991 the Kenyan constitution permitted opposition political parties to function. However, political violence was still common. Defenders of President Moi argued that "Moi may be one of the most corrupt leaders in the world, but he has kept Kenya peaceful." Throughout the 1990s, the World Bank and the International Monetary Fund pressed Kenya to make basic economic reforms. However, Moi was able to forestall any real efforts at reform by saying that no white men should be allowed to govern Kenya and by manipulating the vote and rigging the elections. In 1998, a terrorist bomber blew up the U.S. embassy in Nairobi.

In 2002, Mwai Kibaki became president of Kenya, and he instituted several economic and political reforms. He instituted a pro-business policy and offered free primary education to all children. Unfortunately, he failed to keep his promise of inviting representatives from the many ethnic and religious groups into his governing tent, and the corruption that he pledged to end still persisted. In 2004, one of the worst droughts in Kenyan history took the lives of forty percent of Kenya's cattle and threatened more than three million people with starvation.[17] Despite Kibaki's continuing problems, Kenya's economic growth rate reached a respectable six percent in 2006.

More recently, there have been many positive developments in

Africa. In Ghana and South Africa, democratic governments seem to be solidly in place, and Nigeria has been moving in that direction. The International Criminal Court has been allowed to prosecute cases against the recruitment of child soldiers in the Republic of the Congo. In Zimbabwe in 2009, when Morgan Tsvangirai accepted a role in the government, Robert Mugabe's one-man rule seemed to be giving way to a more representative system.

Most of the new nations in Africa have had difficulty achieving both democratic rule and economic growth. By 2009, Botswana was the most successful democratic nation in Africa, and it also enjoyed the highest rate of economic growth. Admittedly, Botswana has one of the richest diamond mines in the world, but many other nations with plentiful resources have not enjoyed such prosperity.

Providing adequate health care throughout Africa has been a continuing challenge. Doctors have inadequate facilities and little medicine. Hospitals can provide few services and are often staffed by men and women with little or no training except what they get on the job. In addition, since the 1980s the HIV/AIDS epidemic has been ravaging much of the continent. A 2008 United Nations report stated, "Sub-Saharan Africa is more heavily affected by HIV/AIDS than any other region of the world."[18] But there are hopeful developments. Some nations are solving the perennial problem of malaria that has in the past claimed about 900,000 lives annually in Africa.[19] There are now some excellent educational and medical programs to control HIV/AIDS.

One encouraging indicator is that foreign investment in Africa increased from $7 billion in 2002 to $53 billion in 2008. During that same period, economic growth in the whole African continent averaged around five percent.[20] Under the Obama administration, the United States began to urge African nations to diversify their economies and move away from their dependence on exporting oil, in part because the search for alternate energy sources means the demand for oil may decrease.

The 2008 Freedom Index evaluation of civil liberties and political rights in Africa south of the Sahara found that only about 11 out of 53 African countries are free.[21] Despite formidable obstacles, most of the new nations have developed into stable states and some have achieved robust economic growth. Many observers thought that the 2004 election in Nigeria, Africa's largest country, was deeply flawed. In Uganda the president changed the country's constitution so he could stay in power, while in Ethiopia government forces killed about 200 opposition supporters after the 2005 vote. But there has been a trend toward more democratic rule in several states, especially in the Mugabe-controlled Zimbabwe. Moreover, there have been indications of economic growth and efforts at establishing decent standards of living in these nations.

The formerly colonized African nations began their independence with many challenges. Referred to as "Third World Nations," most of them were very poor when they became independent. Despite their generally low economic status and their large ethnic minorities, by the beginning of the twenty-first century, most of the formerly colonized nations were viable nation-states with sovereign central governments, and a growing number of them were moving toward more democratic political systems. A large number were also developing vibrant economies and finding a place in the global economic system.

The Struggle for Peace in West Asia

The West Asian nations have not been able to create substantial economic growth. The majority of these nations are still exporting natural resources, such as oil and rare metals, as the basis of their economies. Israel is one of the few West Asian nations that has a democracy. It has successfully industrialized and, despite periods of high inflation and with generous American economic and military aid, built a sound economic base with skilled workers that can compete in the global economy. Except in increasingly democratic Turkey and occasional elected governments in Lebanon, authoritarian rulers govern most of the other states in the region, and they have relatively little citizen participation. Most of these nations, whether oil-rich or poor in resources, have largely failed to industrialize or to build a large, cosmopolitan middle class.

The struggle between Israel and the Palestinians has posed a major challenge for all the nations in the region. Most of them regard Israel as an American client state whose existence depends on substantial aid from the United States. At the same time, the United States has sought close relations with the Arab states, especially Saudi Arabia, its main supplier of oil.

After Israel's dramatic victory in the Six-Day War, the United Nations Security Council, on November 22, 1967, adopted Resolution 242. It called for a withdrawal of all Israeli forces and occupation from the West Bank; termination of all claims of territories outside Israel; the disestablishment of military zones; and establishing a UN special representative to oversee the process. The resolution was adopted unanimously and remains the touchstone of most negotiations between Israel and Palestinian representatives.

However, soon after the 1967 war, Israelis began to build settlements in the West Bank. In most cases they took land without com-

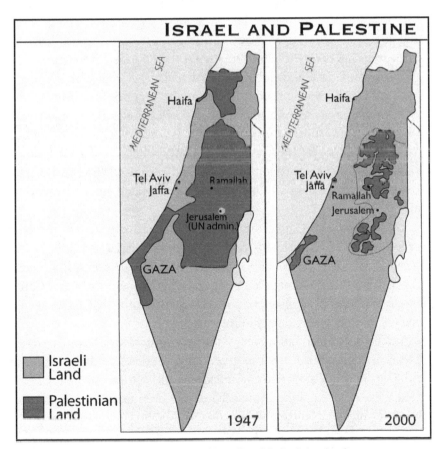

Shifting boundaries of Israeli and Palestinian land

pensating the owners. By 2010, Israelis controlled over half of the choicest land in the West Bank, and has built a highway system to protect the settlements. Israel also took forty percent of the land in Gaza. Palestinians have found it difficult to farm because the Israeli farmers control most of the water and Palestinian farmers are on a strict water ration. The Israeli government established a large number of check points in the occupied West Bank that cost Palestinians going to work or visiting relatives hours of extra travel time. The Israeli police and army also reserve the right to search any house or person living in the Palestinian West Bank.

On October 6, 1973, a third Arab-Israeli war broke out when a joint Egyptian-Syrian attack, with the aid of Jordan and Iraq, was launched during both the Jewish high holiday of Yom Kippur and the Muslim month of Ramadan. The Arab and Egyptian forces did better, and in a U.N.- negotiated peace agreement, Israel gave back some of the land it had taken in 1967. Otherwise, the boundaries remain essentially the same as at the end of the 1967 war.

In 1977, the new Likud Party won the election and Menachem Begin became prime minister. The Likud Party was far more conservative than the long-ruling Liberal Party. More orthodox religious parties also became more powerful. They believe that Israel should claim the ancient homeland that God had promised the Jews. Under Begin, Israel dramatically increased and extended its settlements in the West Bank.

Under President Carter, the United States actively tried to promote peace between Palestinians and Israelis. In the 1978 Camp David Agreement, Egypt got back Sinai, but Israel still controlled Gaza. Egypt gave full diplomatic recognition to Israel, and President Carter stated that Prime Minister Begin had assured him that Israel would end the West Bank settlement program.

Since the Carter initiatives, American presidents have generally backed Israel and the US has given Israel about $3 billion a year in aid. During this time Israel continued to build settlements in the occupied West Bank, and the United States has been unwilling to pressure Israel to stop the settlements.

The Palestine Liberation Organization, which was the coordinating council for Palestinian organizations, was founded during the first

Arab summit meeting in 1964. The PLO is composed of various guerrilla groups and political factions, and is dominated by Al-Fatah, the largest group. Yasir Arafat, Al-Fatah's leader, was chairman of the PLO from 1968 until his death in 2004.

Initially, the PLO was committed to the dissolution of Israel, mainly through the use of armed force. Since its founding, the organization has sponsored innumerable guerrilla raids on Israeli civilian and military targets. The Jordanian government, which was increasingly feeling threatened by the over 400,000 Palestinian refugees living in Jordan, asked the PLO to leave in 1970. In response, the organization moved to Lebanon. In 1974, the PLO received U.N. recognition. The other Arab nations saw the exiled PLO as the basis for a future Palestinian state, made up of land regained from Israel along the west bank of the Jordan River. In 1976, the Arab League granted the PLO full membership.

As of 2010, despite many attempts by many outside nations to broker a peace, relations between Palestinians and Israelis remained tense and hostile. The Norwegians and the Clinton Administration came close to negotiating a general peace between the parties, but having almost gained support of both Israel and the PLO, the peace talks ended in failure.

Although they are poorly armed, Palestinians have staged several *intifadas* (shaking off, uprising), which rely mainly on marches and youngsters throwing stones. Moreover, thousands of Palestinians remain in Israel, although most of their homes were confiscated and their civil rights restricted. In 2007, out of a total population of 5,757,900, there were 2,057,800 Palestinians living in Israel. By 1992 there were 109,000 Israeli settlers in the West Bank and by 2006 there were 267,000. As of 2010, the Israelis were continuing to build settlements in the West Bank.

Among the Palestinian population in Palestine, there are a large number of educated men and women who have the training and skills to aid their country's economic growth. However, because of the almost total lack of business opportunities, financial capital, or freedom of movement because of the Israeli occupation, these people have been unable to help their country reach a settlement and develop economically.

An Israeli wall separating
Israeli and Palestinian land

Over the years several attempts to resolve this tragic problem have failed. The two-state solution would mean creating a Palestinian state and requiring Israel to withdraw all its settlements in the West Bank and Gaza. But the proposed Palestinian state would be very small and lack many resources, and Israel would not allow it to have any armed forces. As of 2010, Israel was continuing to construct a high cement wall that divides Israeli and Palestinian land by cutting through the West Bank. In addition, the United States has given Israel its unwavering support. In 2010, after increasing pressure and diplomatic assistance from the United States, the Israeli government and the Palestinian Authority agreed to resume direct negotiations. However, a lasting agreement acceptable to both sides remained a distant hope.

In addition to the Arab-Israeli conflict, oil has also dominated the policies and histories of several newly independent West Asian nations. Dictators with strong military backing ruled both Iraq and Iran. The Saud family, with strong American support, governed Saudi Arabia, one of the most conservative monarchies in the world. The oil-rich Emirates were also largely ruled by a single party and relied on oil to finance their impressive building projects. Even Egypt and Jordan, states without oil reserves, were both led by individual rulers backed by the military.

With the creation of the Organization of Petrol Exporting Countries (OPEC) in 1960, the oil-rich nations working together were able to exert more control over their economies. By the 1970s, OPEC could control oil prices and bargain as a single unit with oil consuming nations.

In 1973, in response to U.S. support of Israel in its war against Egypt, Syria, and their Arab allies, the OPEC nations announced an oil embargo that increased oil prices by 400 percent. Since that time, OPEC has maintained a stranglehold on the industrial nations that depend on oil imports. Moreover, profits from their rich oil reserves have made it possible for the West Asian oil-producing nations to hire Asian workers rather than industrialize and modernize their states.

As a result, the people in the upper classes of these underdeveloped societies have enjoyed the good life by selling this sought-after natural resource. Meanwhile, the workers and farmers have lagged far behind in every aspect of life. Moreover, the overdependence on oil revenues meant that few of the West Asian states have developed viable economies that would enable them to compete in the global system.

New Democratic Movements

In January and February 2011, hundreds of thousands of citizens filled the streets of several authoritarian-controlled nations across North Africa and West Asia. The size and passion of these peoples' demonstrations surprised observers throughout the world.

The protests began in Tunisia when a government official beat and humiliated a street vendor; this event set off massive protests that led to the ouster of the dictator, Zine El Abidine Ben Ali. The protest movement in Tunisia, which soon spread to Egypt, Yemen, and Algeria, was fueled by a common anger provoked by high unemployment, rising food prices, and the lack of freedom of speech, freedom of the press, and a political voice.

The people of Egypt carried out a dramatic, nonviolent movement, which led to the overthrow of their dictatorial president, Hosni Mubarak. Among the keys to the success of the uprising was the Egyptian army's decision not to attack the protesters and the protesters' widespread use of new social media like Facebook and Twitter, which enabled them to communicate instantly, without censorship, and beyond their borders.

Finally, on February 11, after unrelenting pressure from increasing numbers of demonstrators, Mubarak resigned, and the army temporarily took over the government. Inspired by what the Egyptians had accomplished, the people of other nations in the region also began demanding real democratic reforms. Most serious observers agreed that these popular uprisings would significantly change the political landscape.

SCENE FOUR

WORLD POLITICS IN THE AGE OF AMERICAN PREEMINENCE

Setting the Stage

With the fall of the Berlin Wall and the breakup of the Soviet Union, the world entered a new age of international relations as world diplomacy took on a host of new players. Fifteen new nations were carved out of the former Soviet Union and seven former Soviet satellites regained their independence, East Germany reunified with West Germany. There were now 193 sovereign states that varied in size from Iceland, with a little over 300,000 people, to China's and India's billion-plus populations.

With the demise of the Soviet Union, the United States was the world's only remaining superpower. In 1999, the eminent political scientist Samuel P. Huntington wrote, "The United States, of course, is the sole state with preeminence in every domain of power—economic, military, diplomatic, ideological, technological, and cultural—with the reach and capabilities to promote its interests in virtually every part of the world."[22]

But by 2010, China was seriously challenging America's preeminence as the world's most productive economy, having trillions of dollars in reserve as well as holding a large share of the United States debt. At the same time China was reluctant to take an important role in diplomacy and it was perhaps content to watch the wealth, prominence, and security of the United States diminish.

Is the United States an Empire?

According to the 2003 Defense Department Report, the United States had 702 overseas bases in about 130 countries and another 6,000 bases in the United States and its territories.[23] To staff these bases, the U.S. has stationed about 153,288 military personnel with about an equal number of dependents. Additionally, 34,000 American civilians and approximately 44,446 foreign civilians work at these bases.[24]

Since 1990, the United States has waged war in Iraq, Somalia, Yugoslavia, Iraq (twice), and Afghanistan.

Several major scholars[25] have written extensively on the "American Empire." In his analysis, Paul Kennedy examined some of the major empires such as Britain and France. He cautioned that:

> If . . . too large a portion of the state's resources is diverted from wealth creation and allocated instead to military purposes, then that is likely to lead to a weakening of national power over the longer term. In the same way, if a state overextends itself strategically—by, say, the conquest of extensive territories or the waging of costly wars—it runs the risk that the potential benefits from external expansion may be outweighed by the great expense of it all—a dilemma which becomes acute if the nation concerned has entered a period of relative economic decline.[26]

Whether or not the United States is actually an "empire" remains a debatable question, but it was clear after 1990 that the United States had the most military and economic power. Moreover, many nations not only saw the United States as the dominant world power but also regarded it as a major threat to world peace. A Pew Research Center poll conducted in 2006 found that, "Despite growing concern over Iran's nuclear ambitions, the US presence in Iraq is cited at least as often as Iran—and in many countries much more often—as a danger to world peace."[27]

Vladimir Putin, the Russian president, a strong believer in Russian nationalism, reasoned that powerful states like his own should maintain a sphere of influence around their borders in order to protect their national interests and maintain international stability. At the same time, George W. Bush and his advisors aggressively championed spreading American influence and power around the world.

When the U.S. supported expanding NATO to include many of the former Soviet Satellites, the Russians objected, fearing this was an attempt to rekindle the Cold War. U.S. plans to install missiles in Europe also caused Russian–United States relations to cool considerably.

In his first year as president, Barack Obama began to reinstitute the political realism that had been the core of U.S. policy since the end of World War II. The goal is to understand the vital interests of other nations and accept the limitations of nation-building. The U.S. also made diplomatic overtures to the Arab nations, North Korea, Russia, and Iran. President Obama has also tried to reduce the tensions between the U.S. and Russia, including stopping plans to install U.S. missiles in Europe and signing a new nuclear arms reduction treaty.

In the first decade of the twenty-first century, an increasing number of U.S. citizens began to consider the enormous expense of America's military involvement around the world. The huge increase in the United States debt, the high cost and lack of success in bringing stability to Somalia, Iraq, and Afghanistan, and the growing economic power of the European Union, India, and China were causing many Americans inside and outside of government to question the value of being the dominant military power.

The U.S. and Iran

After the end of World War I, Iran was ruled by shahs and the country was becoming a secular society. Women were not allowed to wear veils and religious influence in politics was discouraged. The Shah supported the rise of a middle class and many peasant farmers began moving to the large cities in search of jobs. The last shah, Mohammad Reza Pahlavi, used some of the country's rich oil reserves to finance the building of impressive public monuments and to equip the army with modern weapons.

The United States believed Iran was one of the important pro-American front-line states encircling the Soviet Union. As a result, it generously supported the shah. However, when Ayatollah Khomeini, who had been in exile in France, returned home in 1979, Iran's secular, pro-American government suddenly collapsed. After successfully leading a revolution that ended the shah's rule, Khomeini rapidly gained control of the ruling elite. He soon became the "supreme leader" and turned Iran into a theocratic state. Khomeini ruled over a parliamentary system that looked similar to European models, but was actually totally subject to his authority.

Women's lives probably changed the most under the new regime.

Whereas the shah had ordered his police to remove women's head-scarves and veils, the ayatollah's police arrested women who were not dressed in orthodox Muslim clothing. New controls over their activities and relationships with men were also imposed. The ruling elite set up local committees to enforce his ideals of public morality and to regulate entertainment and social life. For example, one mid-dle-class man who was taking his maid to shop for food was arrested and forced to marry the maid with whom he had "inappropriately" been seen in public.[28]

The Iranian revolution also dramatically changed Iran's relation-ship with the United States. Instead of being a close American ally, Iran became hostile toward the United States. Khomeini's policies and beliefs were also anti modern. Like others in the new orthodox Islamic groups, he thought western culture was materialistic, immoral, and contrary to Islamic teachings. The Khomeini led revo-lution also attempted to ban western music, clothing, and films from their increasingly puritanical culture.

Between 1980 and 1988, Iraq and Iran waged a brutal war against one another. Traditional Sunni Iraqis' hostility toward Iran's Shiite community, ethnic differences between Arabs (Iraq) and Persians (Iran), and the intense hostility between the secular Saddam Hussein and the deeply religious Ayatollah Khomeini were among the factors that propelled the two Muslim nations into open warfare. Saddam Hussein, the Iraqi dictator, believed that with the modern weapons the Soviet Union supplied his army and the intelligence the United States provided him, Iraq would sweep to an easy victory.

Iraq greatly underestimated the Iranians' willingness to fight a pro-tracted war. The ayatollahs and governing Muslim councils in Iran recalled well-trained officers who had been members of the shah's effective armed forces. In addition, the Iranian air force had modern American planes.

During the first months of fighting, the Iraqi forces successfully invaded Iranian territory but they were soon driven back. After seven years of fighting, which included Saddam Hussein's use of poison gas against the Iranians, the two sides battled to a draw. As a result of the war, 300,000 Iranians died and more than 500,000 were wounded. About 240,000 Iraqis died and an estimated 375,000 were wounded.[29]

Although Iran has held several elections since 1979, it had not become a real democracy as of 2010. The ruling ayatollahs gradually allowed more democratic participation, and in the 1980s and 90s they permitted semi-free elections. The 2009 election that pitted the sitting president Ahmadinejad against a genuine reformer, Mir Hossein Mousavi, challenged the legitimacy of the ayatollahs' system of control.

When Ahmadinejad's victory was announced shortly after the voting ended, hundreds of thousands of Mousavi supporters took to the streets to protest what they thought was a rigged election. After several days of pitched battles between the protestors and the army and police, the demonstrations were forcibly put down and the questionably elected Ahmadinejad took office. Even so, the 2009 protests suggested that the movement toward democracy in Iran was growing.

Western powers led by the United States have repeatedly attempted to stop Iran from making nuclear weapons. Despite boycotts and threats of reprisal, the Iranian leaders continue to expand their nuclear program, which they insist is for peaceful purposes only. Under the Obama administration, initiatives for negotiations moved forward while Iran continued to develop nuclear bomb capacity.

U.S. Involvement in Iraq

Iraq, a new state Britain created after World War I, is composed of three large and distinct ethnic groups: the Kurds in the north; the Shiite Muslim majority; and a large number of Sunni Muslims. After World War II, several harsh, secular Ba'ath Party dictators ruled Iraq. Saddam Hussein, a Sunni who played a key role in the Ba'athist coup, relied on his army and secret police to remain in power from 1979 until the United States overthrew him in 2003.

After the U.S. broke off relations with Ayatollah Khomeini's government in Iran, the United States tried to improve relations with Iraq. However, that effort ended when Saddam Hussein decided to invade Kuwait in 1990. Although Saddam believed that the U.S. had sent him strong signals that the United States would not intervene, President George H. W. Bush sent a half million soldiers to dislodge the Iraqi forces from Kuwait. The United States victory was quick and decisive and the American forces withdrew.

Following their removal, the Shiite Muslim militias that had resisted the American invasion, probably with U.S. encouragement, attempted a revolt against Saddam Hussein. However, the expected American support was not forthcoming and the Iraqi military's superior airpower and better-equipped forces brutally put down the Shiite uprising and kept Saddam in power. In response, the United States established military bases in Saudi Arabia and Kuwait, and insisted on its right to build bases in the other Gulf states, including Bahrain, Qatar, Oman, and the United Arab Emirates.

The conflict with Iraq dramatically demonstrated both the importance of oil and America's willingness to act as the world's "policeman." Many were disappointed that the Bush administration had failed to remove Saddam Hussein. A group of militant American policy experts, known as neoconservatives, warned President Clinton of what they perceived as increasing threats to American power and urged him to install a friendly democratic government in Iraq.

The Clinton administration ignored these conservative demands, but George W. Bush, who was elected president in 2000, and his close advisors, including both Vice President Dick Cheney and Secretary of Defense Donald Rumsfeld, strongly supported an Iraq invasion. After the September 11, 2001, terrorist attacks on the World Trade Center in New York and the Pentagon in Virginia, the Bush administration falsely claimed that Iraq was a haven for terrorists and was about to produce nuclear weapons. President George W. Bush launched an all-out invasion of Iraq that led to a rapid defeat of the Iraqi armies and the U.S. occupation of Baghdad. On May 1, 2003, only two months after the invasion, President Bush stood on the deck of an aircraft carrier and declared "Mission accomplished."

Actually, the war was just beginning. Al Qaeda militants were soon attacking American forces and placing improvised explosive devices (IEDs) in highly populated areas and along highways. At the same time, Sunni and Shiite paramilitary groups began attacking American and British forces.

All during the fighting, the United States was trying to help establish a legitimate Iraqi government. In 2006, with Nouri al-Maliki as prime minister, the Iraqis elected a new parliament that approved a thirty-six-member cabinet. When some stability was finally established by 2009, the U.S. forces began to withdraw, although the United States continued to assist the new government.

The United States had also responded to the September 11 terrorist attacks by sending a modest military force to Afghanistan to destroy Al Qaeda bases there. They were also aiming to capture Mullah Omar, the leader of the Taliban, who controlled Al Qaeda forces, and Osama bin Laden, a young Saudi, who had planned the 9/11 attacks. While initially successful in defeating the Taliban, the U.S. reduced its forces because by then it was involved fighting Iraq. Meanwhile, the Taliban regained its strength and Osama bin Laden eluded capture; he and his followers have established a strong Taliban presence in western Pakistan. From that base, the Taliban began to mount new attacks on American forces in Afghanistan. The Taliban's increasing power in Afghanistan and Western Pakistan became a growing concern, especially because Pakistan has approximately fifty nuclear bombs.

The U.S. in Afghanistan and Pakistan

Despite the increasing use of democratic means to deal with economic and social inequalities, democracy has not fared well in areas where there is ethnic and religious strife. When suicide bombers, who are willing to die in order to forward their cause, set off explosives in public places, the peaceful, democratic transfer of power is often impossible.

When Pakistan was created in 1947, this new state was home to millions of Pashtuns who felt close to fellow Pashtuns living in Afghanistan. The British had drawn the Durand Line, separating Afghanistan from what is now Pakistan, in 1894 as a way of dividing the large Pashtun population. The British had left the Pashtuns living in what is now Pakistan's Northwest Frontier region and in so-called "tribal areas" to govern themselves.

This unusual arrangement worked until 1979 when the Soviets decided to invade Afghanistan in order to support the Marxist government then in power. In response, thousands of Afghans, joined by Muslim volunteers from around the world, formed the Mujahideen and fought against the Soviet occupation. The Afghan Mujahideen resistance was supported and financed by volunteer Muslim groups from Saudi Arabia, Pakistan, Somalia, and several other Muslim nations. Osama bin Laden, a young Saudi, emerged as an important leader of the Mujahideen and a generous financial supporter as well.

During the Soviet-Afghan War from 1979 to 1988, the American CIA channeled more than a billion dollars through Pakistan to the Mujahideen and also supplied them with modern weapons. Meanwhile, the Pakistani government was the chief conduit for American aid and for contributions from other Muslim nations to the Mujahideen. By 1988, the Soviet invasion and occupation was totally defeated, a major factor in the later downfall of the Soviet system.

By 1992, most of Afghanistan was relatively peaceful. However, the thousands of Muslim volunteers who had gone there to fight the Soviets remained in the country, while the United States withdrew from active participation in Afghan affairs. Some of these "foreign" volunteers, under the leadership of Osama bin Laden, formed Al Qaeda (the base), a terrorist organization that resented American bases in or near Muslim holy sites.

Into this power vacuum stepped Mohammad Zia ul-Haq, Pakistan's dictator from 1977 until his death in 1988, and then the democratically elected Benazir Bhutto, who was prime minister from 1989 to 1996. They both used the militant Muslim volunteers, including the Afghans and their foreign counterparts like Osama bin Laden, to form the Taliban (students), a militant Islamic group that began to destabilize Afghanistan. In the 1990s, while Bhutto was Prime Minster, the Pakistani government and army actively supported the Taliban with generous financial and military assistance, much of which came from United States aid.

The Taliban welcomed Al Qaeda, which began planning terrorist attacks against states that they thought threatening Islam and especially against the United States, whom they saw building military bases in Saudi Arabia, the heart of historic Islam. This cozy relationship between Pakistan and the Taliban was strained after 2001.

On September 11 of that year, members of Al Qaeda attacked the World Trade Center and the Pentagon, and sent another hijacked plane toward a Washington target. (Thanks to the resistance of the brave passengers of United Flight 93, that plane crashed in Pennsylvania before it could reach its target.) In response, the United States launched a war against the Taliban by invading Afghanistan. However, after quickly driving the Taliban out of northern Afghanistan, a mainly non-Pashtun area, the U.S. did not succeed in capturing Osama bin Laden, the leader of Al Qaeda.

Even though American military forces had Osama bin Laden cornered in the eastern region of Afghanistan in 2003, he was allowed to escape into Pakistan, where he continued to direct Al Qaeda activities. From 2001 to 2008, the US sent more than $10 billion in aid to Pakistan. Some of that aid went to the Taliban in western Pakistan. As the Taliban grew stronger, the United States began to pressure the Pakistani government to take steps against it.

Under intense pressure from the United States, the Pakistani government joined the struggle against the Taliban in Western Pakistan. In 2009, it began sending its army into the nearly autonomous western Pashtun areas to fight the Taliban. By this time the Taliban had gained control over large areas in the region and were using Pakistani bases to support the Taliban in Afghanistan.

As of 2010, Afghanistan was increasingly controlled by a renewed Taliban resurgence. Despite the presence of a large American and NATO force in the country, the American-led forces Alliance seemed unable to stop the Taliban's growing influence. Meanwhile, with a weak Pakistani prime minister and an army divided over whether to attack the Taliban or assign most of its forces against India, Pakistan seemed paralyzed. With strong United States support in 2009, the Pakistani army finally launched a major offensive in South Waziristan, the Taliban stronghold in Pakistan. By the end of 2009, the Pakistani army, with U.S. assistance, had greatly reduced the Taliban control in their western provinces, but the area was far from stable, and Taliban forces in Western Pakistan were still launching attacks against Americans in Afghanistan. The increasing instability in Pakistan became even more problematic when a massive flood of the Indus River in 2010 displaced a fifth of the population.

Maintaining World Power Challenges
U.S. Economic Realities

While many nations experienced economic growth after 1989, the economic realities in the United States were quite different. During the 1990s, as American companies moved their factories to nations like China and Indonesia where lower wages prevailed, manufacturing in the United States rapidly declined. The areas full of deserted steel mills and factories in the U.S. became known as the "rust belt." Workers in the manufacturing centers were hit the hardest. The United States' reliance on imports, especially from China, also continued to undermine American manufacturing. Many workers who lost high-paying manufacturing jobs began competing with younger people for low-paying service jobs.

In 1970, one-fourth of American workers were employed in manufacturing. By 2005, the number of manufacturing jobs had shrunk to about ten percent. In 2000, the value of U.S. manufacturing amounted to $9.9 billion; in 2009 it was only $3.3 billion.

By 2000, only about fourteen percent of American workers were members of unions,[30] and unions had ceased to be the major political force they had been before 1980. The decline in manufacturing jobs as well as the decline in the importance of labor unions meant that many American workers fell out of the middle class. There has also been a steady increase in the already wide gap between the rich and the poor.

To maintain the consumption levels that were possible in the golden years of prosperity between 1945 and 1980, many more American wives entered the labor market to earn a second income. Undoubtedly, the expanding professional opportunities that opened up with the successes of the women's movement were a key factor in the increasing number of women joining the work force. Even with two incomes, many families still ran up large credit card debts. In the 1990s, many also took out second mortgages on their homes so they could buy more goods. By 2000, the savings rate in the United States had shrunk to almost zero.

In the 1990s, many nations had accumulated hundreds of billions of dollars as a result of their favorable balance of trade with the United States. By 2008, the People's Republic of China had accumulated about 3 trillion U.S. dollars. Investment bankers also had billions of dollars that they hoped to invest, and the U.S. Federal Reserve Bank had lowered interest rates to all-time lows. This world glut of money presented a "golden" opportunity for investors.

During the 1990s, the selling price of homes in the U.S., and to a lesser extent in Europe, was soaring. With easy credit and no down payment required, individuals took out second mortgages on their homes to pay for vacations or to buy more things. Many other homeowners bought second houses, kept them for a year, and then resold them at a huge profit. In Florida and California particularly, this real estate boom fueled robust economic growth.

The easy credit coupled with the housing boom led the financial industry to introduce new financial instruments that greatly increased the amount of credit available to consumers. The banks that created home mortgages began to collect the mortgages in bundles, something like clumps of asparagus. Then they sliced up each bundle, so that each slice was made up of parts of lots of mortgages. They sold the bundles of mortgages to investment bankers. The investment bankers, using the bundles of mortgages as security, were able to borrow up to thirty times the amount that the "securitized" bundles of mortgages were worth.

Investors reasoned that because each bundle was made up of hundreds of different individual mortgages, it was highly unlikely that a few or even a majority of the mortgages in any bundle would default. As a result, their investments were thought to be secure. While the mortgages seemed to represent actual real estate, in fact, they were turned into paper financial instruments—not actual wealth, but the basis for extending more credit.

The financial wizards had based their plan on sophisticated computer models that few could understand, and almost all of these transactions were beyond government regulation. No wonder an average person did not realize that the elaborate pyramid did not represent real houses and yards, but depended on the ability of the individual mortgage holder to make his or her payments every month. Eager salesmen had sold adjustable mortgages that provided easy payments for the first few months or years, but after that soon rose way beyond the borrower's ability to pay.

Despite the mathematical models that said this could not happen, when the prices of many houses in 2007 began to fall below the amount the owner owed on the mortgage, many owners defaulted on their loans. Some just abandoned their homes. When thousands of homeowners defaulted, the financial house of cards tumbled down in just a few months. The investment banks that had made billions in profits from this scheme, and had rewarded their leaders with hundreds of millions of dollars in bonuses, suddenly found that the mortgage bundles they were using for securities were worthless. To add to the world's financial woes, large insurance companies such as AIG, which had insured these investment banks against loss, were unable to pay off even a fraction of their new debts.

Investment banks around the world had bought billions of dollars of mortgage-based securities; most of these were now worthless. When several of America's largest investment banks teetered on the brink of bankruptcy, the world financial system threatened to collapse with them. For the first time in modern history, Iceland went bankrupt and Ireland nearly did. Banks around the world stopped lending and the global system stalled.

Only the massive intervention of governments stopped the bleeding. The United States government invested trillions of dollars to prop up insurance companies and failing banks. Great Britain and other European countries, except for Germany, also came to the aid of bankers. The crash was the worst financial disaster since the Great Depression of the 1930s and led to massive unemployment and the end of the unregulated global financial system that had grown out of the "Washington Consensus" and the American gospel of the free market.

The effects were worldwide. The PRC found that the demand for its exports had decreased drastically.

Friday, October 25, 1929

Tuesday, September 30, 2008

Wall Street then and now

They slowed their production, causing many factories to close. Millions of unemployed Chinese workers flocked back to their villages, which were already poor. Fortunately, with its dollar surplus, China was able to invest $586 billion in a stimulus package that created jobs in construction and other fields. With the loss of foreign contracts, India's economy also slipped into recession, but because Indian bankers were not deeply involved in the housing market financial transactions, they remained largely free of the meltdown of financial institutions in the United States and Europe.

The worldwide impact of the 2008 financial crisis led many economists to rethink their faith in the free market. Many of the nations involved in this crisis promised to develop new national and international regulations. Several international meetings focused on developing a more coherent system of international financial regulations were convened in 2009 and 2010. From 1980 to 2008, economic leaders of the United States had systematically demolished most of the financial regulations put in place since the New Deal of the 1930s and 40s.

As a result of this near-depression, many governments, especially in Europe and the United States, had learned that vibrant capitalism depends on the deep-rooted mutual trust, honesty, and community bonds that form the context for financial transactions and reasonable regulations. This trust was severely undermined by the 2008 crisis. As Adam Smith had said 200 years earlier, without laws and justice, society "would crumble into atoms" and "a man would enter an assembly of men as he enters a den of lions."[31]

SUMMARY

With the beginning of a new millennium, people around the world were seeking a world order that would allow them to live in peace and stability and earn enough to support their families. However, because various populations had experienced different histories and lived within different cultural systems, they disagreed on the best way to achieve peace and prosperity. The variety of clashing world-views, not only among nations but also between groups and even individual people, often prevented governments from building a consensus and solving their fundamental problems.

Among the many competing ideas was the role of military force in solving problems. Generally, nations that had suffered through devastating wars were often reluctant to look for military solutions to the world's problems. The Chinese, having lived through a violent century during which they has lost more than fifty million lives in war, seemed more willing to invest their energies in building economic superiority instead of expanding their influence by armed aggression.

Europeans, who had endured four and a half centuries of brutal wars, including two world wars that destroyed millions of people and many large cities, came out of World War II more chastened by their war experiences than their American allies. Many seemed to have realized that fighting a war was not the best way to seek peace. Instead, why not work to ensure that factories have the safest and most up-to-date working conditions, or publicly support health systems for all, or champion educational opportunities that expose young people to new, challenging insights that might lead to fulfilling work?

Even many people in the United States, who had never experienced bombings or combat on their own soil or in their cities, began to question the wisdom of warfare. During the recent U.S. wars in Korea, Vietnam, Iraq, and Afghanistan, public enthusiasm was high in the beginning of each war, but dramatically waned as the wars dragged on. Moreover, there was a growing concern among Americans that the trillion dollars invested in the Iraq war and the hundreds of billions in Afghanistan were not worth the mounting public debt and were resulting in diminishing funds for public services and welfare.

ACT SEVEN

Living in the New Global Age

At the beginning of the twenty-first century, anxiety and uncertainty were still major forces in the world. Terrorist threats continued, and large armies seemed powerless to stop young men who were willing die for their cause. News programs regularly reported ethnic violence that led to unimaginable numbers of deaths. Many people were turning to religion as a bulwark against fear, uncertainty, and disappointment because the global economy was not creating the good life they had hoped for, yet globalization seemed to roll on unabated.

The recent sweeping changes in technology, communications, and finance have ushered in a new global age. Business transactions can now be carried on twenty-four hours a day. Millions of dollars can be electronically transferred in seconds to any part of the world. Multinational corporations can close down factories in one country and open them in another where labor costs are cheaper. A musical group anywhere in the world can post their act on the internet and attract fans in Mumbai or Shanghai or Little Rock.

Globalization has brought tectonic shifts in social arrangements. It has enabled some people to become incredibly wealthy; it has driven others into poverty. National leaders realize that educating both men and women holds the key to their growth and prosperity. Uneducated workers, who earlier had found high-paying jobs in manufacturing, have begun to move down the economic ladder. Rapid changes challenge traditional values and religious beliefs. And the backlash against this new cosmopolitan global culture is taking many forms including ethnic identity, religious fundamentalism, and new waves of antigovernment protests. Globalization has also brought many new challenges that all of us will have to face.

SCENE ONE

GLOBALIZATION IS CHANGING OUR LIVES

Setting the Stage

Perhaps the generation born in the 1940s and 50s has lived to witness more rapid changes in the world than any other generation. Its members have seen unprecedented economic growth not only bringing new prosperity and longevity to millions of people, but at the same time plunging millions of others into poverty. In almost all regions, people are living longer than ever before, with access to better health care, more advanced schooling, and more opportunity for jobs. For the first time, more people worldwide live in cities than in rural areas.

As people try to adjust to the flood of new electronic gadgets and new systems of instant communication, new inventions in this field seem to come on the market month after month. The dizzying pace of news from around the world is available on cable networks twenty-four hours a day, and many people can communicate by mobile phones and email to anyone in any part of the world.

However, this maze of new technologies and greater wealth does not immediately translate into a better life for all everyone. Many areas of the world are standing on the sidelines; millions around the world and even within the highly globalized states are not sharing in the increasing wealth of globalization and are worse off than before. As industries move around the world to find cheaper labor for their manufacturing, higher-paid workers in the U.S., once protected by labor unions, have been forced to accept wage cuts and loss of benefits. In addition, people without good education have been falling behind and they often have to take low-paying service jobs. In agricultural sectors around the world, small farmers who could not compete with large-scale agribusinesses have been shunted aside and some have even taken their own lives.

As people argue the relative merits of globalization, nothing seems capable of stopping its spread. The challenge is clear: How can we find better ways to ensure that the benefits of globalization are spread more equally to all?

The Computer Age Enhances Global Communication

Although computers have been used since the 1950s, several recent inventions radically improved their effectiveness. One was the integrated circuit that replaced separate transistors, resistors, capacitors, and all the connecting wiring with a single crystal (or "chip"). Another was Intel's invention of the microprocessor. The 2009 Nobel Prize in physics was awarded to Charles K. Kao, who discovered how to transmit light through fiber optics, and to Willard S. Boyle and George E. Smith, who designed the first digital-imaging sensor.

By 2009, there were 186,000 miles of fiber-optic cables carrying billions of signals from powerful computers all over the world. For the first time, information could be shared immediately almost anywhere. The digital revolution has been applied to such things as cameras, television, the Internet, mobile phones, imaging machines in hospitals, and the Hubble space telescope. X-rays, CT scans, and MRIs allow physicians to glean information about the tiniest details of the human body. Financial transactions are now possible 24 hours a day so people can transfer money electronically and buy and sell stocks and bonds at almost any time.

A sign in a South Indian temple

Easy and inexpensive electronic communication has affected both the research that goes into gathering information and the way news is disseminated. Reporters can file stories and send digital images instantly. An increasing number of consumers are reading their newspapers online, and news organizations can constantly add up-to-date news. Some scholars predict that printed newspapers and books will soon become obsolete.

The Internet has also spawned millions of personal websites and blogs. Whether or not the information people post is accurate, it competes with the results of investigative reporting and information based on scholarly research. Many readers believe that opinions posted on the Internet are as true and reliable as news from other sources. Personal histories have also flourished as millions post their individual stories on their own websites, blogs, and social network sites. IPods hold thousands of musical pieces and works of art and can be found in an increasing number of ears, especially among the young.

Dr. Martin Cooper, considered the inventor of the portable handset telephone, made the first call on a portable mobile phone in April 1973. Telephones, television, films, and most importantly the Internet, which developed in the 1980s, are common even in the poorest nations. By the end of the twentieth century, more of the world's people were in direct contact than ever before. Over 2.5 billion were talking over telephones, with China leading the world with some 805 million users.[1] The internet in 2010 had over 1.9 billion users, with some 825 million in Asia alone.[2]

It is hard to know the long-range effects of the proliferation of cell phones or the seemingly constant contact they enable between parents and children, or of having electronic friends from around the world on social networking sites such as MySpace, Facebook, or Twitter. And what happens when people compete for the most hits or friends on these sites?

It is obvious that innovations in communication are made to order for advertisers. The ability to influence consumer habits with text and images was firmly established by the use of radio and television, which vastly enhanced the growth of the consumer society. By the 1960s, it was not uncommon for television sets in U.S. homes to be left on all day and into the night. By 1970, virtually every home in the United States had at least one television set. Not only were ads aired every few minutes, but the programs themselves stimulated potential consumers to desire the same clothes, makeup, cars, and houses the actors and actresses had. The Internet is another powerful means of creating worldwide consumer demand.

The globalization of communications, supported mainly by the world's youth, has helped shape a global culture. Entertainment and sports figures such as Michael Jordan, David Beckham, Michael Jackson, Madonna, the Beatles, and U2 were known by more people than previous celebrities could have imagined. It may be too early to tell whether our present "Information Age" is bringing people closer together or separating them into small groups that share the same ideas and prejudices.

Even the history you are now studying is undergoing major changes, in part through the multiple perspectives that globalization and instant communication bring. In 1919, American historians developed a historic narrative they called "Western Civilization." This narrative left out most of the world's people, including most women, peasants, workers, and people of color, until they became colonial subjects.

With the end of colonialism, "Western Civ" started to disappear from the curriculum, and a new conception of the past called "World History" began to flourish. Creative world historians such as William McNeill and Marshal Hodgson integrated Asia, Africa, and Muslim civilizations in the story of the human past. World historians now feature "encounters and interactions" among peoples all over the world and welcome all people into the new history.

Innovations and Influences among Artists

Since World War II, the arts have often both reflected and shaped cultural diversity. Experimentation with radically new forms of expression has expanded artistic and moral boundaries. Modernism attempted to offer a sense of order and truth, but could not deliver on this goal in the modern, pluralistic age. By the end of the twentieth century, the arts were part of the postmodern movement, and no single narrative had a monopoly on truth. By the 1990s, the sense that the observer was a key component of both science and the arts, a message foreshadowed by Einstein in 1905, had become a central theme.

Increased international contact and globalization has enriched artistic fields such as architecture, painting, and literature. By the end of the twentieth century, architects, artists, and writers were breaking old boundaries and experimenting with radically new forms and styles, and it was often hard to discern the message a particular artist wanted to convey. Even, or perhaps especially, in the arts, a sense of anxiety permeated the search for the new.

Henry-Russell Hitchcock and Philip Johnson, two U.S. architects, coined the term "International Architecture" for the 1932 exhibition of modern architecture held in New York City. Leading architects of this school included Le Corbusier in France and Walter Gropius in Germany. The internationalists created glass, steel, and concrete buildings with little or no ornamentation. The 1958 Seagram's building in New York City is considered a fine example of this style.

Other outstanding twentieth-century buildings include the Danish architect John Utzon's Sidney Opera House in Australia, which is as much a freestanding sculpture as a building, and Frank Lloyd Wright's Guggenheim Museum in New York City. Wright, much influenced by Japanese art and architecture, also championed blending houses into their natural surroundings.

By the 1980s, postmodern architecture seemed to be replacing modern. Postmodernist architects began to use familiar shapes and details in unexpected, and sometimes amusing, ways. Philip Johnson's AT&T building in New York City, now the Sony Building, which combines many architectural traditions, is one example. However, this new style was found wanting only a decade later. Frank Owen Gehry (b. 1929), one of the world's best-known architects of the later twentieth century, is justly famous for his creative design of titanium-covered buildings that feature gentle curves instead of boxy shapes. His best-known buildings include the Guggenheim Museum in Bilbao, Spain, and the Getty Museum in Los Angeles.

Following World War II, American artists led a movement called Abstract Expressionism that dominated the art field until about 1970. The growing admiration for this movement resulted in New York City replacing Paris as the major center of world art. Rather than trying to represent nature and humans realistically, abstract expressionist artists sought to represent emotions, themes, and color combinations, often on large canvases. They experimented with new materials and innovative ways of seeing, and sometimes used large brushes to drip paint on the canvas or to throw paint at it. Jackson Pollock (1912–1956), Mark Rothko (1903–1970), and Willem de Kooning (1904–1997) are among the best-known American abstract expressionist artists.

In the last decades of the twentieth century, artists were combining many traditional forms. They also began experimenting with "installation art" that might feature reading a play or poem but does not exist after the installation is completed. A startling example of this was the work of the Bulgarian Christo Javocheff and his wife Jeanne. They created large-scale environmental works, including wrapping colorful cloth around the Reichstag in Berlin, Germany, and unwinding a twenty-four-mile-long strip of cloth in a field in California.

Increasing global influences can be seen in music as well. Rhythm and blues gave way to rock and roll, and these musical styles with

An Indian rock band in Madurai, India

African-American roots spread around the world. Elvis Presley, the Supremes, and Michael Jackson exemplified a growing white-black musical synthesis. American jazz has also become an international musical form, borrowing from and influencing composers worldwide.

John Cage (1912–1992), one of the most important twentieth composers, was deeply influenced by Chinese culture. Seeking a guide that would free his work "from human will," in 1951 he discovered the *I Ching*, the ancient Chinese text on divination and chance. From then on, Cage used this text as a guide for his musical compositions. He would ask the *I Ching* a question and then try "imitating nature in its manner of operation." Among the works that he felt came close to his goal are Imaginary Landscape No. 4 for 12 Radios and Music of Changes for Piano.[3]

Literature Crosses National Boundaries

In the wake of World War II, many French writers were attracted to existentialism, a school of thought that emphasized the human actor as a thinking, feeling, and creative subject who alone makes judgments and takes meaningful action. About the same time, a new movement called "the Theater of the Absurd" was offering serious plays, such as Ionesco's *The Rhinoceros*, that presented seemingly meaningless human experiences, and where the oddest and most improbable random acts defined reality.

Since World War II, major writers have continued to infuse modern literature with insights from many areas of the world, and readers have begun to appreciate works by authors in many countries. Indian novels, partly because many of those authors write in English, have had a wide readership. Salman Rushdie's work combines several styles and an engaging sense of fantasy that give his books an exhilarating tone. R. K. Narayan and Arundhati Roy have won worldwide praise. Roy's *The God of Small Things* has sold more than seven million copies worldwide.

The works of the Nigerian writer Chinua Achebe and the Trinidadian author V. S. Naipaul have offered generations of readers a vivid depiction of the impact of colonialism on subject peoples. Aleksandr Solzhenitsyn exposed the harsh life of people imprisoned in the Soviet Siberian gulags. Gao Xingjian has taken millions of readers who live outside of China into the hearts and minds of average Chinese people. The Mexican novelist, Gabriel García Márquez, a Nobel laureate and one of the writers who has experimented with magical realism, achieved worldwide prominence with his *Love in the Time of Cholera*. Naguib Mahfouz has revealed everyday life in Egypt. The Romanian novelist Herta Mueller, who won the 2009 Nobel Prize, describes some of the harsh and brutal experiences of people living in authoritarian states.

Films have also become an international phenomenon. Outstanding films are now as likely to be produced in China, India, or Korea as in the United States. India released about 900 Bollywood films per year in the 1990s, while Hollywood made about 250. Filmmaking is increasing in the Philippines, Iran, South Korea, Taiwan, Japan, Singapore, and Hong Kong. The Chinese language film "Crouching Tiger, Hidden Dragon," a Chinese–Hong Kong–Taiwan–United States co-production, grossed more than $100 million in the United States alone.

Postmodernism Mixes Most Everything Together

It appears that increased globalization has resulted in more tolerance for and acceptance of multiple cultures and lifestyles. As the twentieth century wore on, the growing sympathy for a "live and let live" society, where differences are readily embraced, led to more social movements for equality. Great strides were made in racial equality as well, symbolized by the election in 2008 of Barack Obama, the first African-American president of the United States.

Postmodernism rejects a single narrative and the search for truth and instead focuses on social and political processes. Many in the movement point to power as the factor that tends to define reality. They also are apt to distrust theories and ideologies.

Postmodernism resulted in a proliferation of narratives and approaches to history. Anyone who wanted to create a personal narrative could mix and match items of clothing, art forms, literary techniques, and other creative expressions. Rock and roll music, which has become a major world art form, was open to anyone who took the time to create a group and learn to play the guitar. Many rock music stars came from working-class backgrounds. From England to China and India, youngsters were mixing local variations with their own classical musical traditions.

A Growing Concern for the Environment

Many people who once had believed that industrialization would be the salvation of the world's poor have begun to realize that the effects of industrialization are a mixed blessing. Factories around the world are dumping toxic waste into the water tables and the air. Winds blow polluted air across borders that no army or missile shield can defend. Poisoned waters flow into the oceans, where fish eat waste that includes pollutants such as mercury. When we consume those fish, we absorb some of those pollutants and also release them into the food chain.

Lester Brown's annual survey *The State of the World* reports that at the end of the 20th century, "the most dangerous effects of human activity were apparent in six areas: fresh water, rangelands, oceanic fisheries, forests, biological diversity, and global atmosphere."[4] Brown explains: "While the Agricultural Revolution transformed the earth's surface, the Industrial Revolution is transforming the earth's atmosphere."[5]

The energy humans consumed in 2005 was sixty to ninety thousand times as much as people who lived in the first agricultural age consumed. Oil and coal, both exhaustible carbon sources, took millions of years to be formed. As we have seen, coal was at the heart of the first industrial revolution and its use has continued to increase dramatically. The dramatic increase in its consumption, whether to heat homes, drive machines, or produce electricity, has had consequences no one imagined in 1800. Seventy percent of the world's coal, and ninety-five percent of that in the U.S., is now obtained by open-cast mining, the most environmentally damaging of all methods. Vast pits are made in mountaintops in order to extract the coal. The process is toxic and ruins nearby streams and farmlands.[6]

A 1994 study by the U.S. Energy Information Agency stated:

> Coal is an important source of energy in the United States, and the Nation's reliance on this fossil fuel for electricity generation is growing. The combustion of

> coal, however, adds a significant amount of carbon
> dioxide to the atmosphere per unit of heat energy,
> more than does the combustion of other fossil fuels
> . . . . [Note 1] Coal combustion emits almost twice
> as much carbon dioxide per unit of energy as does
> the combustion of natural gas, whereas the amount
> from crude oil combustion falls between coal and
> natural gas.[7]

The major industrial powers, especially the United States, are the major contributors to global warming and do more to pollute the earth's air and water than people living in less industrialized nations. Although Americans make up only five percent of the world's population, they consume thirty percent of the world's energy, while all the nations in the "third world" consume only about ten percent of the world's energy. The average American consumes twice as much energy as the average European and thirty times that of the average Indian.[8] Most of that energy comes from burning fossil fuels, the major cause of global warming; forty percent of the nation's energy comes from petroleum, twenty-three percent from coal, and twenty-three percent from natural gas.

Much of the poisoning of the earth is the result of agricultural innovations. Before Rachel Carson's influential book, *Silent Spring*, and the worldwide ban on DDT in the 1970s, this deadly insecticide was upsetting the natural balance of nature. However, even after the ban led to a remarkable ecosystem recovery, fertilizers have continued to flow from the land into streams and rivers, where they kill marine life. Historically, small farmers used animal manure as a rich natural fertilizer; now it is often collected as useless waste in huge industrialized pig and chicken farms, and the waste runs into large bodies of water such as the Chesapeake Bay, further destroying valuable wetlands. Moreover, large industries sometimes leak dangerous chemicals or cause accidental explosions that kill thousands of innocent people.

The 1984 Union Carbide leak in Bhopal, India, left thousands of people dead and many blind and ill.[9] The nuclear power plant meltdown in Chernobyl turned thousands of acres of rich agricultural land in Belarus and Ukraine into toxic land, unfit for farming. Airborne radioactive fallout from Chernobyl also claimed many cancer victims in Europe. Major oil spills, such as the Exxon Valdez tanker accident in 1989 and the millions of gallons of oil spilled into the sea during the two Gulf Wars, are among the countless examples of pollution. In 2010 the explosion of a large British Petroleum oil rig, the Deepwater Horizon, in the Gulf of Mexico led to the largest oil spill in history. This disaster's most severe impact was on the area around New Orleans, which was still recovering from Hurricane Katrina's destruction in 2005.

Less dramatic but more devastating causes of environmental destruction continue unabated. New farming methods lead to tons of topsoil being lost each year. The building of dams and levees disturb fish habitats and has led to more intensive flooding than we have seen in centuries. Even relatively small dams prevent salmon from swimming upstream to spawn. Cutting down trees, especially those in the rain forests, prevents them from absorbing carbon dioxide and leaves more of it in the atmosphere as a "greenhouse gas" that contributes to global warming. Higher temperatures are causing deserts, especially in Africa, to expand.

The automobile is one of the greatest ecological threats to the planet. Cars and factories put more than five and a half billion tons of carbon dioxide (CO_2) into the air each year. By 2010, CO_2 levels had reached about 350 parts per million, twice the levels present during the last ice age. By 2150, if nothing is done to change the amounts of CO_2 released into the atmosphere, they will nearly double again to 550–600 parts per million.[10]

Scientists have found that an increase in carbon dioxide in the earth's atmosphere causes a process they call a "greenhouse effect" that increases temperatures. The radical increase in CO_2 is slowly raising temperatures around the world. Unchecked, these rising temperatures will completely melt the polar ice cap by 2015. A 2.5-degree temperature change by 2050 would be the equivalent of the changes since the end of the last ice age. Should Greenland's thick ice sheets also melt completely, the consequence will be an estimated 23-foot rise in the oceans.

Try to imagine a world that is just 6 degrees warmer, which would cause a dramatic rise in sea levels. What would happen to national

A Chinese wind farm

boundaries? What islands and coastal areas would disappear? Picture the Netherlands, much of the southern half of Florida, or much of Manhattan under water and the seas inundating much of Bangladesh and Shanghai.

The Kyoto Treaty in 2005 was an attempt to get a comprehensive international agreement to check global warming by reducing greenhouse gases and controlling increasing carbon dioxide emissions. Although a large majority of nations have ratified the treaty, several nations, including the United States, refused to do so. In 2009, another international climate conference in Copenhagen was held to deal with global warming. Governmental representatives from 170 countries attended. Attending representatives from NGOs, journalists, political activists, and others interested in the problem totaled around 8,000, attesting to the rising public consciousness of this threat to the word but only a mild general statement of concern resulted. As of 2010, there have been no significant international agreements to cut greenhouse gases or to control increasing CO_2 emissions.

Globalization and Health

It has become abundantly clear that the way we treat our physical environment directly and indirectly affects our health. However, in spite of the growing number of environmental threats, the vast improvements in medical science and the growth of government-financed health care have contributed greatly to people's health in the industrialized nations.

The life expectancy of the people living in contemporary industrialized societies is far longer than that of any earlier generation. As of 2009, life expectancy in Japan was 82 years; in the United States, it is about 78 years, while in Zimbabwe a newborn can expect to live only to age 36. Many people can shield themselves from the temperature changes that previously dictated how people dressed and acted. Thermostats connected to oil or gas furnaces keep rooms at an even temperature in winter, air conditioners in houses and cars provide cool comfort on hot days, and humidifiers can maintain the proper level of moisture in the air.

Physicians perform open heart and brain surgeries that would have seemed like science fiction only a few decades ago. Wonder drugs such as the antibiotic penicillin, discovered in 1931, can cure diseases that earlier would have meant certain death. Public health measures include pasteurized milk, purified drinking water, and the ability to monitor air quality, which all contribute to better health and longer life.

New medicines and innovative treatments keep many people free from pain and help them recover from sicknesses and injury. Children have access to inoculations from diseases that historically claimed millions of young lives. Many women give birth in hospitals where sickly newborn infants can receive life-saving treatment. Diseases such as tuberculosis, typhoid fever, yellow fever, and many types of flu that once terrorized the public can now be treated and often prevented.

The influenza epidemic following World War I was one of the worst killers in human history. Between 20 million and 100 million people died. Ten times more Americans died from influenza than died in World War I. Although modern medicines and inoculations have greatly reduced the death rates of world pandemics, many thousands, mostly in the nonindustrialized nations, still die from curable illnesses including diarrhea, food poisoning, and malaria.

In our own day, the spread of Acquired Immune Deficiency Syndrome (HIV/AIDS) has killed nearly 30 million people worldwide and has infected as many as 80 million. Its worst effects have been in Sub-Saharan Africa. Although AIDS has been the most lethal recent worldwide pandemic, other new viruses and germs continue to spread new strains of influenza around the world.

Globalization has made it easier to take immediate steps worldwide to reduce the spread of disease. The United Nations reports that most countries now have centers for disease control that can inform citizens how to avoid contact with these infections and how to treat them. Scientists have also developed vaccines for some of these new strains of influenza. At the same time, bacteria and viruses continue to mutate and develop resistance to existing antibiotics and vaccinations, and globalization has made it easier for germs to travel great distances.

Globalization also affects what food we eat. After World War II, the food industry began to adapt to the new technologies, advertising, chemical discoveries, and changing family habits. Huge farm machinery, including powerful tractors and combines, enabled farmers to plant thousands of acres of land with a single crop such as soybeans, corn, wheat, or barley. Farmers also have access to strong pesticides like DDT and its successors, chemical fertilizers, and weed killers. Farmers in the American Great Plains can plant a large crop of wheat or corn in the spring, spray it with pesticides and then, in the fall, harvest the grain and truck it to the mammoth grain elevators for processing. Unfortunately, some of these pesticides have proven to be very harmful to the environment.

Scientists have also genetically altered seeds in order to significantly increase crop yields. In the 1950s Norman Bourlag and other scientists developed new seeds for wheat and rice that dramatically increased yields. In the 1950s and 60s these new seeds led to the "Green Revolution" and enabled nations such as Mexico and India to become self-sufficient in foods. Hormones injected into animals have resulted in increased milk production and more rapid growth. Scientists have only recently begun warning people about the negative effects those hormones may have on human beings.

In an attempt to regulate the unstable market for food and animal products, many governments subsidize farmers. In France, subsidies help keep small farmers solvent and able to compete. But when governments in industrialized nations subsidize the food their farmers produce, these farmers can easily undersell food grown in countries that do not offer subsidies. In the U.S., large industrial farms have also been driving small farmers out of business. By 2000, only a million U.S. farmers were able to supply all the food the population needs.

Moreover, surplus U.S. crops have helped change eating habits. For example, because corn syrup is now very cheap and abundant, it is widely used in commercial food preparation, especially in the fast-food industry. This has contributed to a rapid rise in obesity in the U.S. An increasing number of Americans lead far more sedentary lives than in earlier generations and relish "fast foods" that they can eat in cars, while working, or "on the run." The increasing number of people eating outside the home is also due in part to the many women who are working outside the home and because many people have more disposable income. Fast foods are a major cause of obesity.

How Does Globalization Challenge and Enrich Values?

The breathtaking advances in such things as medicine, entertainment, communications, and food production have been accompanied by dramatic changes in family organization, especially in the industrialized nations. Changes in family life exemplify fundamental changes in the society at large. Birth control and the desire for fewer children caused birth rates to decrease, but the number of out-of-wedlock teenage pregnancies has risen dramatically. The desire for romantic relationships, although historically an unstable basis for successful marriages, had spread around the world. Films, novels, and television all celebrated the delights of romantic relationships.

Although so-called love marriages have increased, the number of successful marriages has declined. There are more breakups of married and cohabiting couples in the United States than in any other Western country: about half of all marriages now end in divorce.[11] Sri Lanka lies on the other end of the spectrum, with only .15 per thousand marriages or only about a one percent divorce rate.[12] A growing number of unmarried couples live together. As of 2002, about sixteen percent of all couples in Canada who were living together were unmarried, and in Sweden, about fifty percent.

In addition, many couples never marry and an increasing number of individuals live alone. In the United States in the 1990s, 27 million households had only one person. Perhaps the rising value of individualism leads to a greater reliance on legal contracts and lawsuits to settle personal problems rather than on the force of family and community pressures.

Increasing divorce rates, births outside of marriage, and growing numbers of single-parent households have been accompanied by major changes in women's lives. In 1940, about fourteen percent of married women had jobs outside the home. By 1980, half the married women in the United States and Europe worked outside the home and the number was rising. In the first stages of industrialization, women were recruited because factory owners could pay them less than men. However, by the late twentieth century, women were not only closing the unequal pay gap, but were successfully competing in high-level professional careers such as medicine, law, business, and government. In many nations such as India, Sri Lanka, Norway, Ireland, and Germany, women were elected to the highest office in their countries.

As advanced training became a prerequisite for finding good jobs, many more students have sought higher education. In the 1970s, the number of universities in the world doubled. By the 1990s, millions of students were attending European universities as well as higher educational institutions in India, Mexico, the Philippines and several other nations.

In the 1960s, in the heady atmosphere of a worldwide student movement, students challenged the authority of their governments, parents, and university administrators. Many U.S. students sought greater power in school governance and expressed their antipathy to their government's close relationships with capitalists and its waging of the Vietnam War. Young women demanded greater sexual freedom. African-Americans struggled for civil rights and an end to racial prejudice. Across the industrialized countries, college students staged strikes, performed psychodramas, marched while chanting antigovernment slogans, and in some cases, such as at Columbia University in New York, occupied administration offices in an effort to get their demands instituted. Most Latin American nations crushed the protests, while the French and Americans negotiated with their rebelling students, made concessions, and instituted reforms.

For a brief period, it was Chinese students who enjoyed their newfound power the most. Mao Zedong had built his Cultural Revolution in the 1970s almost entirely on the youth, whom he perceived to be more innocent and revolutionary than their parents. We have already noted that in 1989, China's student-led democracy movement attracted thousands of demonstrators to Tiananmen Square, which they controlled for days. However, the Chinese authorities finally broke up the demonstrations by firing on the young people, killing hundreds, arresting others, and dispersing the rest.

Globalization Enhances the Consumer Revolution

By the twentieth century, increasing leisure time and more disposable income for a greater number of people helped stimulate a demand for all kinds of goods. New means of communication were becoming available to average people and mass production meant many goods cost less. When asked why he was paying his auto workers the princely sum of $5 a day, the industrialist Henry Ford replied that he wanted them to be able to buy the cars they were making.

Even those who didn't buy much could imagine owning items from the world's vast treasure trove. Youngsters with little other reading material dreamed of having the items pictured in catalogues, while the ads surrounding the news in newspapers and magazines made readers desire the countless goodies that they imagined "everyone else" must be buying.

Unlike people who had lived though the 1930s depression in Europe and the United States, their children, raised in an era of growing prosperity in the 1940s and 50s, assumed consumerism was a natural right. Despite the uncertainties and fears of the post–World War II era, the United States, Europe, and Japan began a long period of rebuilding and an era of prosperity. In the United States, most of the women who had provided much of the labor force during the war effort left the workplace so that the thirteen million returning soldiers and sailors could have their jobs. Most of the factories in the industrialized world quickly turned to peacetime production of new cars, homes, refrigerators, and all the other conveniences the public had longed for during the war years.

By the 1950s in the industrialized world, shopping had become a way of life. Following World War II, according to one scholar, the United States became the "Consumer Republic." She explained, "I am convinced that Americans after World War II saw their nation as the model for the world of a society committed to mass consumption and what were assumed to be its far-reaching benefits."[13]

The almost unimaginable productivity of the twentieth century held the promise of satisfying everyone's desire for new products. What had earlier been luxury goods for the few soon became necessities for many. Conspicuous consumption was becoming a way of life for many people in the industrialized societies. In fact, many Americans began to think of themselves as consumers. The shift towards "I am what I buy" was even changing the meaning of citizenship from personal political liberty to the right to own things.[14]

The slogan "Do your own thing," which was so popular among young people, often meant "Buy whatever you want now." Instead of delaying getting what you wanted, many young people came to expect instant gratification for their desires, which they were not shy to express. In 1968, "I take my desires for reality, for I believe in the reality of my desires" was scrawled on a Paris wall.[15] Personal and social liberation seemed to go hand in hand.

Ironically, some people worried that the student revolution might undermine the basis of modern capitalism. After all, capitalism depends on postponing fulfilling one's desires in order to save money that you can invest later, whereas young people in the United States were thinking, "Buy now and pay later."[16]

But businessmen quickly adapted their marketing strategies to appeal to these young people. Instead of expecting consumers to save for the future, they gave them credit cards so they wouldn't have to worry about paying for them—until later. Textile and shoe manufacturers retooled to provide jeans and sneakers that they sold at premium prices. Blue jeans, once what poor farmers and cowboys wore, could be found everywhere, and they demonstrated the power of youth to shape world fashion. By the end of the twentieth century, most CDs and music downloads were being sold to young people from fifteen to twenty years old.

With the industrialized economies as their model, people in the emerging nations began to share the dream of a higher standard of living. However, many millions have had little chance to participate in the consumer society. The U.N. Food and Agricultural Organization reported that as of 2006, 854 million people worldwide, or about 12.6 percent of the world's population, did not even have enough to eat. Child labor is common and illiteracy still remains very high. Only about a fourth of school age children go on to secondary school.

Five-sixths of the world's population is unable to benefit from most of the recent medical and technological innovations. Many live in squalid urban slums without running water or clean toilets. Child labor is common and life expectancy ranges from below 35 in the lowest ten nations to more than 80 in Japan and Sweden. One-third of the world's population is forced to live on the equivalent of two dollars or less a day and the lowest billion barely survive on only one dollar a day.

In any discussion of important social, scientific, and technical advances, we must ask how the benefits from these innovations can be shared equally around the world. Perhaps the fact that most of the benefits have gone to the people who live in the industrialized societies helps explain some of the anger, protests, and anti-Western sentiments that many people have. It is to some of these concerns that we now turn.

SCENE TWO

LIVING WITH UNCERTAINTY IN THE NUCLEAR AGE

Setting the Stage

From the beginning of the twentieth century, scientists, psychoanalysts, artists, writers, and philosophers were making discoveries and observations that ate away at people's sense of security. Enlightenment philosophers and scientists such as Newton had argued that once humans found the "truth" about the universe, they would adapt their governments and other social institutions to fit these eternal truths. However, more recent scientists such as Bohr and Heisenberg discovered that even the smallest particles inside atoms move in uncertain ways. Freud and Jung concluded that the human "subconscious" was a whirlpool of free-floating instincts, drives, and motivations that help shape how humans act. Further, artists were ushering in "modernism" and "abstract art," which also seemed to reflect a sense of uncertainty.

The devastation of World War I had left millions disillusioned and seemed to undercut the belief that rational progress was inevitable. During the 1920s, many people in Europe and the United States had focused on living for the moment rather than seeking some utopian dream. The realistic literature written during the Great Depression tended to question the possibility of human beings ever building a harmonious world. W. H. Auden gave voice to this feeling of insecurity in his poem, "The Age of Anxiety":

> He is tired out;
> His last illusions have lost patience
> With the human enterprise.
> The end comes; he
> Joins the majority, the jaw-dropped
> Mildewed mob and is modest at last.[17]

The Nuclear Threat

Perhaps the greatest cause of fear and uncertainty was the atomic bomb that can kill hundreds of millions of people and ruin the environment. As we have noted, in the early years after the first use of atomic weapons, students in the United States were told to duck under their desks and cover their faces in the event of a nuclear attack, as if such actions would make them safe, and television ads instructed families how to dig bomb shelters and even offered lists of food and reading materials they should store away in their shelters, although surviving a nuclear attack was most unlikely.

People reacted to the nuclear threat in many different ways. Some counseled building more bombs and developing rockets that could intercept nuclear warheads. Some joined peace movements in hopes of convincing everyone that having nuclear armaments would eventually result in their use. A few dug bomb shelters. Many feared there was no way to resolve the nuclear threat.

A pervasive fear of nuclear extermination led Britain, the United States, and the Soviet Union to ban the testing of nuclear weapons in the atmosphere, in space, and under water in 1963. Five years later the Soviet Union and the United States introduced a Nuclear Non-Proliferation Treaty (NPT) that was intended to prevent the spread of nuclear weapons to nations that did not already have them. In the years that followed, 137 nations, including Canada and the United States, signed the Non-Proliferation Treaty. Israel, India, Pakistan, and North Korea were among the nations that did not sign this treaty, and since then, they have all developed nuclear weapons.

There have been other efforts to ban the spread of nuclear weapons and to reduce the number of weapons nations already have. The cornerstone of efforts to control nuclear proliferation was the Strategic Arms Limitation Talks (SALT), beginning in 1969. SALT I led in 1972 to the Anti-Ballistic Missile (ABM) Treaty, and was followed by the Helsinki Accords in 1975 that called for mutual cooperation among nations on both sides of the Cold War.

In 1979, SALT II limited U.S. and Soviet ICBMs and strategic bomber-based nuclear forces. The 1991 Strategic Arms Reduction Treaty (START I) required the United States and the Soviet Union to reduce their deployed strategic arsenals to 1,600 delivery vehicles, carrying no more than 6,000 warheads. In 2002, Presidents George W. Bush and Vladimir Putin agreed to hold the United States and Russia to strategic arsenals of 1,700–2,200 warheads each, approximately two-thirds fewer than current levels. This warhead limit was to expire in 2012.[18] After taking office in 2009, President Obama pledged to work with Russia to carry out major nuclear weapons reduction.

Up until 2010 most efforts to reduce the number of atomic weapons have largely failed. According to a report published by the U.S. State Department in April 2009, Russia had 3,909 nuclear warheads, while the US had 5,576 warheads.[19] To make nuclear arms control even more complex, other nations also had stockpiles of nuclear weapons, including France with 700, Israel with 80, China with 180, Pakistan with 70–90, and several others with five or more as of 2010.[20] Only South Africa, out of all the nuclear nations, agreed to dismantle its nuclear project. Several other nations, including Iran, are believed to be developing them. The proliferation of atomic weapons has made the twenty-first century even more vulnerable than when only five nations possessed nuclear weapons. The prospect that a small group of terrorists might obtain a nuclear weapon has intensified the fear of a nuclear nightmare across the world.

Terrorism Spreads

A dramatic increase in the use of terrorism is also contributing to deep seated anxiety worldwide. A number of small but determined individuals and groups have acquired deadly weapons or perfected their bomb-making skills. These groups can severely damage property and kill huge numbers of people. Terrorists also hijack airplanes that they then use as bargaining ploys in getting their demands.

In Germany in the late 1970s, the Red Army Faction, popularly known as the Baader-Meinhof Gang, launched attacks in Germany and Italy. The Baader-Meinhof Gang was largely comprised of upper- and middle-class young people who hated capitalism and wanted to destroy West Germany's political and economic system. On the political right, the New Order in Italy and the Charles Martel Club in France threw bombs in support of authoritarian rule.

In Britain, the Irish Republican Army (IRA) used bombs to try to unify Northern Ireland and the Irish Republic. During their terrorist attacks, thousands of innocent people, including many children, lost their lives.

In the 1980s and 90s, militant Palestinians used terrorist tactics against Israel, including killing Israeli athletes in the 1972 Olympics. In 1983, the group Islamic Jihad claimed responsibility for driving two suicide trucks loaded with bombs into the U.S. Marine barracks in Beirut and killing 299 servicemen. In 1988, Libyan terrorists placed a bomb on Pan American Flight 103, killing all 259 passengers as well as eleven residents of Lockerbie, Scotland.

Perhaps no nation has suffered more terrorism than Sri Lanka. Sri Lankan terrorists were the first to make widespread use of suicide bombers. Most of their attacks have been carried out by the Liberation Tigers of Tamil Eelam (LTTE), also known as the Tamil Tigers. Since the 1980s, these Tamil militants have been fighting for a homeland for ethnic Tamils, who are a large minority in Sri Lanka. Tamil Tiger suicide bombers were responsible for the assassination of Rajiv Gandhi, India's prime minister, in 1991 as well as prominent Sri Lankan leaders, government officials, and political leaders.

In the dispute between India and Pakistan over Kashmir, Pakistan resorted to terrorism. In the 1980s and 90s, Islamic terrorists in the Indian state of Kashmir killed thousands of civilians. In 1985, a terrorist bomb destroyed Air India Flight 182 and killed all on board. As

A terrorist attack in India

of 2006, at least 232 of India's 608 districts have suffered terrorist attacks.[21] In November 2008, Mumbai, India, suffered a major terrorist assault that originated in Pakistan. At that time, at least ten coordinated attacks struck two of Mumbai's largest hotels, a major railway station, and a Jewish Center, killing 173 and wounding 308 people.[22]

The United States experienced terrorism in 1993 when a small group of Islamic terrorists planted a bomb in the basement of the World Trade Center in New York. Fortunately, that attack caused only minor damage. Two years later, Timothy McVeigh and Terry Nichols, members of an American militia that sought to destroy the U.S. government, drove a truck bomb into the Alfred P. Murrah Federal Building in Oklahoma City, killing 168 and wounding 60.

On September 11, 2001, Al Qaeda terrorists hijacked four airliners to attack New York City and Washington, D.C., killing 2,973 people on the planes and on the ground.[23]

The United States reacted to these sudden attacks by striking against the Taliban in Afghanistan in October 2001 and invading Iraq in March 2003. The decision to invade Iraq was based in large part on false claims that Iraq had been involved with the 9/11 attacks and that it was developing nuclear bombs and harboring other terrorists who intended to attack the United States.

In March 2004, three days before general elections in Spain, Al Qaeda terrorists bombed several trains in Madrid, Spain. The attacks killed 191 and wounded 1,800. In 2005, young militant Muslims in London, England, attacked several buses and subway lines. Unsuccessful terrorist attacks against the United States have also been planned in Yemen.

The increasing use of terrorism has posed a dramatic new challenge, especially because military forces have been unable to thwart all of them. Many, but certainly not all, terrorist groups develop in states where the central control is weak. The governments of both Afghanistan and Pakistan have tacit knowledge of terrorist organizations in their countries, but authorities have been unable to arrest them or prevent the attacks.

Religious Revivals and Fundamentalism Offer Certainty

The uncertainty heightened by the nuclear threat and repeated terrorist attacks, and exacerbated by changes brought about by modernity and globalization, has promoted many different responses. Leaders of several religions have questioned the values of modernity and argued that the West's morals and values are too materialistic. The spread of Western popular culture has caused critics to conclude that Western influences are corrupting their young people.[24]

After the hedonism of the 1960s and 70s, a renewed religious fervor developed. Evangelical and Pentecostal Protestants were successful in spreading their beliefs in Eastern Europe and Latin America. Millions of people flocked to traditional religions that offered comfort and security in an uncertain world. The religious resurgence has been particularly strong in the United States. Protestant megachurches integrate the Biblical message with rock and roll music and light shows, and some church complexes also offer haircuts, bowling, family counseling, and sports. Sermons that formerly had warned people not to sin are sometimes replaced by instruction in ways to fulfill one's desires. Many also stress patriotism and treat nationalism like a religious value. Pope Benedict XVI, elected in 2005, has strongly urged his fellow Roman Catholics to turn away from the acids of modernity and return to traditional values that include opposing birth control, homosexuality, and abortion.

Moreover, in the later twentieth and early twenty-first centuries, conservative political parties were also deeply involved in the battles over values. Small but vocal political parties in many nations of the world were preaching racial and national purity and advocating the expulsion of immigrants. These movements have been especially strong in Europe, where as many as fifteen million Muslims were living by 2010.

The reaction against modernity has found expression in political polarization not only in the United States but also in nations such as India and Iran. Civil discussions among members of different political parties have turned into hostile and even hate-filled debates. Extreme religious beliefs have also motivated terrorist attacks. From Al Qaeda's base in Pakistan, its operatives have recruited young Muslims as terrorist volunteers, including as suicide bombers.

Similar religious revivals have swept Muslims in West Asia and Hindus in India. Islamic conservatives have sponsored a general revolt against what they perceived as western hedonism and materialism. Muslim revivalists have been particularly critical of the United States and its revealing clothing styles, high divorce rate, and sex-saturated popular entertainment. Militant Islamists insist that their faith should come before nationalist loyalties, and some have attempted to replace existing laws with more orthodox Muslim practices.

Fundamentalism and militant pieties have developed in every major religion during the twentieth century. The term "fundamentalism" was first used in the United States in 1910 by Protestant groups that insisted on a literal reading of the Bible. By the 1980s, it had become a popular way to describe any religious group that insisted on following orthodox interpretations of its faith and that upheld "traditional" conservative values, especially about proper roles for women. There are fundamentalists in Christianity, Judaism, Islam, Sikhism, Confucianism, and Hinduism.

Fundamentalism represents a critique of the secularization of the modern world, and fundamentalists typically want religion to shape political life and public behavior. Some fundamentalist groups have even been willing to use force to spread their teachings.

Many find the increase in fundamentalism in Hinduism strange, because historically that faith has stressed tolerance and openness. However, by 1980, small Hindu nationalist groups, which had originally formed in the 1920s, had become a major force in Indian politics. In 1992, the Hindutva movement, comprised of militant Hindu fundamentalists, destroyed a Muslim mosque in Ayodhya in central India. They insisted that the mosque had been built on the site of a Hindu temple marking the birthplace of the Hindu god Rama. In 1996 and again in 2004, the BJP, the major Hindu party, won India's general election. Since then, India's Congress Party–led coalition has defeated the BJP several times.

The militant Islamic revival has enjoyed the most support in the West Asian Muslim states. Wahabism was founded by Muhammad Ibn Abd al-Wahhab (1703–1791) in the eighteenth century. Its followers advocate a return to the simple life of the early followers of Muhammad and who disavow anything they deemed a departure from the teachings of the founders of Islam. Believers take a harsh view of anyone within their religion who does not agree with their ideals.

Wahabism became the orthodox form of Islam in Saudi Arabia. The Wahabis helped put the House of Al-Saud on the throne in the 1930s by unifying the rival tribal factions in Arabia. To this day, the Wahabis are closely identified with the Saudi kings and Saudi society. They run the schools, govern the daily lives of the women, and pass judgment on those they think are criminals or have violated Islamic law. In spite of opposition from most mainstream Muslim sects, Wahabism continues to attract followers.

Several other orthodox movements similar to Wahabism have flourished among contemporary Muslims. These movements generally strive to purify Islam of its recent additions. These conservative movements are often called *salafi*, from an Arabic word meaning "precede."[25] Many Muslim countries have Salafi groups. Salafi interpretations of the Qur'an tend to attract young, disenfranchised youth who believe they have been left behind in the increasing globalization and are not sharing equally in the fruits of modernization.

At the same time, Salafi Islam also attracts highly educated groups such as physicians, attorneys, and engineers. Salafi leaders promote what they consider to be the noble ideals of martyrdom, jihad, and sacrifice for Allah. The most militant of the Salafi movements want to recreate a global caliphate governed by Muslim clerics. Osama bin Laden was apparently very attracted by Salafi ideals.

Feisal Abdul Rauf, an Islamic scholar, claims that much of what we identify today as Muslim fundamentalism is really a reaction to perceived attacks against the faith.[26] Karen Armstrong, the well-known religious scholar, adds, "When people feel that their backs are to the wall and they are fighting for survival, they can, very often, turn to violence. So fundamentalism often develops in a kind of symbiotic relationship with a modernity that is felt to be aggressive and intrusive."[27]

In Israel the Gush Emunim, a fundamentalist, fiercely ethnocentric Jewish religious group, was officially organized in 1974 as a reaction to Israel's victory in the Yom Kippur War in October 1973. However, the spiritual inspiration for the new movement came directly from Israel's impressive victory in the Six-Day War in 1967 against the

Palestinians, Egypt, Syria, and Jordan. Leaders of this group declared that God had given Israel its lightning victory in that conflict and had once again rescued his people and demonstrated his might.

Ethnic Nationalism and Genocide

Ethnic nationalism is another, often violent, expression of a group's effort to gain acceptance and legitimacy in the modern world. Ethnic nationalism is usually found when a large ethnic, religious, racial, or culturally defined group is a significant minority in a large state. Ethnic nationalism, as we have seen, has resulted in the modern state becoming the legal embodiment of a specific group's sense of being a unique people. Among the nationalist ingredients are the sense of a common language, culture, and history that serve as the glue of modern identity and help shape the modern world's political history.

Even in the most culturally homogeneous nations such as Japan and France, there have always been minorities that did not share the rest of the country's ethnic and/or religious identity. The Basques in Spain, the Kurds in Turkey and Iran, and the Muslim Bosnians in Yugoslavia are just a few of the many small ethnic groups that have felt estranged in their nation-states.

Within the very large pluralistic nation-states such as the PRC, Russia, and the United States, creating a sense of national unity has been even more problematic. All of these states faced strong challenges in uniting their minorities. This has also been true in some of the colonial states in Africa where the Europeans mixed together several major ethnic groups.

As ethnic nationalism has intensified, it has sometimes led to genocide, "the systematic attempt to destroy a national, ethnic, racial, or religious group totally or in part."[28] Trying to eliminate whole groups has had a very long history. The Romans tried to destroy the Carthaginians. The Spanish in the "New World" massacred whole villages of Native Americans. The Thirty Years' War in Europe was punctuated by massacres of Protestants and Catholics. In the colonization of Africa, modern European armies systematically killed large number of Africans. During World War I, the Turks were responsible for the deaths of thousands of Armenians. But the Nazis' attempt to eliminate the Jewish people is a most shocking example of genocide.

Over the centuries, many European nations have practiced various degrees of anti-Semitism. Pogroms against European Jews were common as people made them scapegoats for such disparate calamities as the Black Plague of the fourteenth century and Germany's defeat in World War I.

Beginning in the 1930s, anti-Semitism reached new heights in Hitler's Germany. From the time the Nazis took power in 1934, they encouraged Germans to turn against Jews. The Nazis removed Jews from public offices, drove them out of business, and organized youth groups to beat them up and seize their property. In 1938, during a well-organized rampage against Jewish shops and homes, Germans were given free rein to smash windows and loot Jewish stores in a violent outburst of anti-Semitism known as "Kristallnacht" (Night of Broken Glass).

During the early years of World War II, as Nazi forces advanced through Europe, Hitler's government ordered the killing of thousands of Jews in Poland, Ukraine, and Russia. Nazi policies also included the systematic extermination of people in mental institutions, Roma

A Nazi death camp

(gypsies), and homosexuals. Not content with the efficiency of massive shootings and burials in open graves, German officials planned the "final solution" for exterminating all Jews, now known as the Holocaust or Sho'ah.

The Holocaust began in earnest in 1942 with the construction of concentration camps at Auschwitz, Bergen-Belsen, Majdanek, and Treblinka. The Germans used large gas chambers and crematoriums in these camps to efficiently kill and dispose of thousands of Jews daily. The plans to exterminate the Jews required massive investments, complex systems of transport, modern technology, and the cooperation of hundreds of thousands of people in Germany and in most of the countries the Germans occupied.

Sadly, many people willingly helped round up Jews and send them to their death in the camps. Romania's Fascist leaders enthusiastically sent 60,000 Jews to their deaths. The Vichy Government in France willingly rounded up Jews and sent about 90,000 to the German-run camps. In the Netherlands, 110,000 Jews were sent to their graves, and in Poland, about three million Jews were killed.[29] Of all the European nations Germany occupied, only Denmark and Bulgaria seriously resisted German demands to turn over Jews so they could be sent to the death camps. Neutral Sweden welcomed Jewish refugees from Norway and Denmark and worked to save them.

Another tragic example of genocide occurred as the Vietnam War spilled over into Cambodia. In 1975, while King Sihanouk was in exile, the Khmer Rouge, a militant communist group assisted by the Soviets and Chinese, took over the country. Under Pol Pot, who ruled Cambodia until his death in 1998, the Khmer Rouge isolated Cambodia from the rest of the world and embarked on a systematic program of persecution and genocide.

Pol Pot closed schools, hospitals, and factories, abolished banking and money, and tried to eliminate religion. The Khmer Rouge confiscated all private property and forced people to leave the cities and go out to live and work in the countryside on collective farms. He hoped to turn Cambodia into a totally agricultural society. These programs uprooted millions.

Pol Pot ordered the execution of any educated person. Often just wearing glasses was enough to get you killed. Most professors, teachers, writers, artists, and leaders were systematically killed. Family members caught communicating with their parents, siblings, or children could be executed. In all, Pol Pot's regime killed between 1.4 and 2.2 million Cambodians out of a population of only around five million.[30]

Ethnic and religious violence also raged in the Philippines and Thailand. Muslims in the Southern Philippines, called Moros, had been fighting against assimilation by the Catholics from the north. They also criticized the government for failing to help develop the south economically. Fifteen of the Philippines' poorest provinces are located in the south, and it also has the country's lowest literacy

Skulls of Cambodians killed during Pol Pot's regime

rate and life expectancy.[31] In southern Thailand, Muslims and Buddhists have fought for years. Six million poor Thai Muslims have also fought for their independence.

One of the most tragic examples of genocide since World War II involved the Tutsi and the Hutu, two major ethnic groups who lived in the former Belgian colonies of Burundi and Rwanda in Africa. In both these states, the Hutu were the largest ethnic group. However, the Tutsi, who comprised only about one-tenth of the population, had most of the power. The Belgian colonialists believed the Tutsi were not indigenous Africans and had white ancestors. The Belgians therefore elevated the Tutsi over the Hutu. In the 1950s, before independence, the Tutsi controlled 43 of the 45 major chiefdoms.[32]

In Rwanda, the Hutu were the majority, and they were ruling in 1962 when Rwanda became independent. Because the Hutu government persecuted and killed Tutsi residents, nearly 500,000 Tutsi fled from the country. In the 1980s, as the population increased, there was a shortage of arable land and increased competition for jobs and scarce resources. The ruling Hutu used this as an excuse to exile several hundred thousand more Tutsi.

By 1990, the approximately 700,000 Tutsi living outside Rwanda had formed the Rwandan Patriotic Front (RPF) that sponsored the Rwandan Patriotic Army. In October 1990, the RPF launched a civil war in Rwanda. Interpreting this invasion as treason, the Hutus indiscriminately murdered hundreds of thousands of Tutsi.

In 1993, a temporary, fragile peace was established that allowed some Tutsi to serve in the Rwandan government. Unfortunately, in 1994, when a plane carrying a Rwandan official crashed, the Tutsi blamed the Hutu, and the civil war turned into a mutual genocide. As a result, over 800,000 were killed; most of them were innocent people.

The ethnic strife between Tutsi and Hutu spread into the neighboring Democratic Republic of the Congo, Africa's third-largest state. The mineral-rich Congo had attracted people from Uganda, Angola, and Zimbabwe who sought access to its diamonds, gold, timber, coltan (a basic component of cell phones, computers, and DVD players) and cassiterite. Making a tragic situation worse, many of the 20,000 peacekeeping forces the United Nations had stationed in the Congo looted and raped, just as other outside groups had done.

The most influential outside group in the Congo was the Tutsi group led by Paul Kagame, the leader of the Rwandan government. When Kagame installed a Tutsi government in Rwanda, two million Hutus fled to the Eastern Congo. In 1995, the Rwandans opened fire on a Hutu refugee camp, killing thousands of Hutu.[33] Kagame then ordered Tutsi forces to go after the Hutu in the Congo. Weak Congo leaders, including Joseph Kabila, who was elected in 2001, have been able to do little to stop these intrusions.

The Rwandan and Ugandan settlers who occupied large areas of the mineral-rich land in eastern Congo benefited from taking Congolese resources for their own economic development. Without a genuine army, the weak Congolese government could do little to protect the country. To make matters worse, a number of warlords with their own private armies were killing, looting, and raping.

From 1998 to 2009, the various ethnic wars in the Congo have taken millions of lives.[34] Moreover, soldiers from several armies, including United Nations forces, have committed systematic rape against hundreds of thousands of innocent Congolese women and some men. In 2008, the United Nations considered the Congo the rape capital of the world.[35]

The Darfur region of Sudan has also experienced tragic ethnic conflict. Darfur, which is about the size of Texas, is home to racially mixed tribes of nomadic camel herders, who identify themselves as Arabs, and a majority of settled farmers who identify themselves as Africans. The Arab nomads want to drive the African farmers off their land. The militant Arabs, led by an organization of armed gunmen called the Janjaweed, have had the support of the Sudanese government, although that government publicly denies it.

The two groups began their armed conflict in 2003 when the Sudan Liberation Army (SLA) rebelled against the government and accused it of oppressing black Africans and backing Arabs. From 2003 to 2010, the Sudanese government has pursued a scorched-earth policy and the Janjaweed have committed genocide against the Sudanese Africans. Besides the massive killings, the Janjaweed have systematically raped African women. The refugee women who must bring water each day from wells near the refugee camps live in constant fear of rape. As of 2009, the Darfur genocide had taken at least 400,000 lives and left 2,500,000 refugees homeless.[36]

The breakup of Yugoslavia in the 1990s also resulted in mass killings. Religious and ethnic conflict between the Serbs and Muslims has periodically irrupted since 1922. Memories of those clashes helped fuel violence among the Catholic Croats, the Serbian Eastern Orthodox Christians, and the Bosnian Muslims in the mining town of Srebrenica in July 1995. While the international community and U.N. peacekeepers looked on, Serb armed forces identified civilian Muslims and murdered thousands of the men, then systematically killed Muslims hiding in the forests.

Following this massacre, the Clinton administration, which had done nothing to stop the Rwandan genocide, urged the United Nations and NATO to establish peacekeeping forces along the boundaries of the newly independent nations that were carved out of the former Yugoslavia largely along ethnic boundary lines.

Ethnic nationalism in the twentieth century has taken many forms.

We have just considered cases that led to violence. In other cases, such as French-speaking Montreal, pluralistic India, and multilingual Switzerland, ethnic competition and the search for identity have resulted in peaceful nations that honor multiculturalism. But even in nations with significant ethnic minorities, the competition for such things as recognition, jobs, places in universities, and representation in government present a constant challenge. Democracies tend to be able to mediate these ethnic disputes when all the ethnic groups have representation and a voice. It is often in the more totalitarian states, such as Iraq under Saddam Hussein, that ethnic groups are controlled by violence.

SCENE THREE

CHALLENGES IN THE GLOBAL AGE

Setting the Stage

In looking back at the long sweep of history, we can see a long line of revolutions and fundamental changes in politics, technologies, ways to produce goods, and in our worldviews and values systems. If we seriously tried to determine whether human history has been more positive or negative, many of us could argue either side. When trying to evaluate past events, we perhaps have to admit that most of the great changes of the past brought many advantages to some and much pain to others. Each of the great changes probably rearranged the winners and losers and many, like the Industrial Revolution, created vast new wealth that can be used in many different ways.

The combination of pluses and minuses is certainly true of globalization, which has brought new abundance to hundreds of millions of people and helped strengthen the growing acceptance of free-market capitalism around the world but has also resulted in greater pain for many, including small farmers, people without marketable skills, and workers in the more industrialized economies. Even the communist systems in China and Russia and India's planned economy joined the free-market system after 1980. By 2000, most regional economies, societies, and cultures were becoming integrated into a complex network of instant communication and rapid exchanges of goods, capital, and ideas.

The global economic system expanded further in 1986 when the People's Republic of China, which had been under the command economy of the Communist Party, joined the globalization movement. Five years later, India, which had had a mixed economy with large sectors controlled by centralized government planning, also welcomed world competition. With the breakup of the Soviet Union in 1989, Russia and most of its former satellite states also began to participate in the global system.

Inequality and Globalization

Undoubtedly, globalization has helped create more wealth and consumerism than existed at any other time in the past. But globalization has also contributed to new economic winners and losers and it is widening the gap between the rich and the poor. The richest one percent of the world's population owns forty percent of the total household wealth, while the bottom half of the world survives with barely one percent of that wealth. In the United States at the end of 2001, ten percent of the population owned seventy-one percent of the wealth, and the top one percent controlled thirty-eight percent. On the other hand, the bottom forty percent owned less than one percent of the nation's wealth.[37]

The growing disparities in national incomes seemed to be a trend throughout the world except in Europe, where the well-established welfare states have evened out the disparity between rich and poor. By the end of the twentieth century, the income gap between the upper twenty percent of the population and the lowest twenty percent was about thirty-three to one. Thirty-one percent of Brazil's citizens lived below the poverty level, while the top twenty percent earned sixty percent of the income. In Finland, at the other end of the distribution scale, the disparity between the richest twenty percent and the lowest fifth was only about four to one.

In the early years of the twenty-first century, the biggest losers seem to have been small farmers and industrial workers. In their rush to manufacture consumer items, countries such as India and China did not modernize their agriculture production. Indian and Chinese farmers are suffering more now because produce grown in the United States undersells their goods. As a result, in the first decade of the twenty-first century, an alarming number of Indian cotton farmers who could not compete against the heavily subsidized American cotton farmers have been committing suicide. Meanwhile, industrial workers in the United States, and to a lesser extent in Europe, saw their real incomes decline because workers around the world were being paid much lower hourly wages.

Exports have become the driving force for many economies. However, in order for the economies of countries such as China and India to continue to expand, Americans and Europeans must buy more of their goods. It seems that the real economic winners in the globalization game are financiers, investment bankers, and speculators. People who run large hedge funds have made billions of dollars by betting for or against national currencies whose values rise and fall as they "float" on the world market.

Advances in the production of new consumer goods have been limited largely to the industrialized nations in Europe and North America. In the nations that have been struggling to industrialize and provide basic necessities for their citizens, the standard of living has remained at a tragically low level. Sadly, most of the twentieth-century discoveries that have extended life expectancy and make life more enjoyable are only available to about 15 percent of the people in the world, and most of them live in the thirty-six industrialized nations.[38] Even in highly developed nations such as the United States, inequality had been growing. In the U.S. "[between 1979 and 2007, average after-tax incomes for the top 1 percent rose by 281 percent . . .—an increase in income of $973,100 per household—compared to increases of 25 percent ($11,200 per household) for the middle fifth of households and 16 percent ($2,400 per household) for the bottom fifth."[39]

Those of us living in industrial countries use more energy, consume more resource, have more wealth to maintain our high standards, and also do more to pollute the earth's air and water, than all the people living in less industrialized nations. The United States is the world's highest consumer of energy. Most of it comes from burning fossil fuels, the major cause of global warming; forty percent of the nation's energy came from petroleum, twenty-three percent from coal, and twenty-three percent from natural gas.

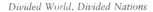

Divided World, Divided Nations

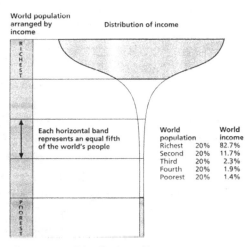

Distribution of income

The Exploitation of Women

In 2009, a Pulitzer Prize–winning newspaper columnist wrote: "In the 19th century, the paramount moral challenge was slavery. In the 20th century, it was totalitarianism. In this century, it is the brutality inflicted on so many women and girls around the globe: sex trafficking, acid attacks, bride burnings and mass rape."[40]

In China and India, "missing women" and the exploitation of young women is particularly acute. In China, the one-child policy, established in 1979, punishes families that have more than one child. Because most Chinese couples want a son, unborn female fetuses are often aborted, and girl babies receive inferior medical care after birth.

One study found that "the imbalance between the sexes is now so distorted [in China] that there are 111 million men in China—more than three times the population of Canada—who will not be able to find a wife."[41] Another study found that 39,000 baby girls died annually in China because parents didn't give them the same medical care and attention that the boys received—and that was just in the first year of life.[42] In 2005, China had 107 males for every 100 females in its overall population (and an even greater disproportion among newborns), and India had 108 males for every 100 females.

Amartya Sen, winner of a Nobel Prize in Economics, revealed that "More than 100 million women are missing." Since women live longer than men, there really should be more women than men in the world. Yet Sen found that in countries where sons are more valued than daughters, women and girls "disappear." Sen concluded that as a result of the poor treatment of girls, about 107 million females were missing from the world.[43]

The severe shortage of women in China has led to kidnapping and slave-trading women. One investigator found: "Since 1990, say official Chinese figures, 64,000 women—8,000 a year on average—have been rescued by authorities from forced 'marriages'. The number who have not been saved can only be guessed at."[44]

In India, as in China, the practices of aborting female fetuses and withholding food and medicines for female babies and girls partly explain India's "missing women." Another explanation is female infanticide. One writer found that, "in rural India, the centuries-old practice of female infanticide can still be considered a wise course of action."[45] Since brides are usually expected to bring a dowry to the husband's family, marrying off a daughter can be very expensive. This partially explains a family's preference for sons.

Unfortunately, in North India "bride burning" has become a major problem since the 1980s. When a wife dies, her widower is free to marry again and get another dowry. Many of the deaths do not appear to have been accidents. However, instead of trying to outlaw dowries, women reformers in India are now trying to reinstate traditional inheritance laws that give the daughter, not her husband, a portion of her family's wealth when she marries.

Increasing Slavery around the World

The International Labor Organization (ILO) estimated that in 2008, there were "12.3 million people in forced labor, bonded labor, forced child labor, and sexual servitude . . . other estimates range from 4 million to 27 million."[46] According to one study, over two million children are sexually exploited every year.[47]

Across Asia, tens of thousands of children are forced into slavery yearly. Many of the estimated 200,000 child slaves in West and Central Africa were sold by their parents or talked into what seemed to be promising jobs by unscrupulous recruiters. Some work on farms with their families as bonded laborers. Agents trick others into servitude as camel jockeys, fisher boys, or beggars. In Burma, the state kidnaps young people and forces them to become soldiers. According to the International Labor Organization, at least 1 million children are prostitutes, with the greatest numbers in Thailand, India, Taiwan, and the Philippines.[48] The U.S. State Department believes Cambodia is a key transit and destination point in this trade.

In 2008, a major American investment bank concluded that "Gender inequality hurts economic growth." The chief economist of the World Bank concluded that "Women are the key to ending hunger in Africa." In addition to being a human tragedy, the enslavement of millions of women and girls is also an impediment to international development. The vast majority of trafficked children, of which there are about 1.2 million per year, are girls. In West and Central Africa, nearly ninety percent of trafficked domestic workers, who are at high risk for sexual abuse, are girls.[49]

Population Growth and Multiculturalism

The population of the world did not reach one billion people until 1825. It then took only another century for the earth to have two billion inhabitants. In 1960, only 35 years later, the world population totaled three billion. By 1975, there were four billion, and by the later 1980s, another billion had been added. In 2009, 6.8 billion people were sharing our planet. Population increases are a major reason that the world's consumption of goods has skyrocketed. Industrialization has made it possible to lower the price of many goods, furthering the demand.

The most rapid increases in population have occurred outside the industrialized countries. In fact, Japan's population has declined and the population of the United States would have decreased without immigration. The population of the industrial societies has been growing older, leaving fewer younger workers to support older retirees.

For the first time, more people live in cities than in the countryside, and the largest cities are outside of Europe and the United States. Megalopolises with more than nine million people included Seoul, Tehran, Karachi, Jakarta, Manila, New Delhi, and Bangkok. Cairo, Mexico City, São Paulo, Shanghai, and Mumbai each has over ten million inhabitants. Meanwhile, Paris London, and New York, until recently the world's largest cities, have been surpassed. Paris has a population of two million in the city with another eight million in its metropolitan area. London has 7.5 million and New York about eight million.

During the nineteenth century, millions of people left Europe for other nations. Between 1890 and 1920, about 27 million Europeans who were searching for work went to the United States, Australia, and other countries. Most of the migrants were poor farmers from Ireland, Italy, Eastern Europe, and Scandinavia. In 1920 about one in seven Americans was foreign born.[50] Many poorer European migrants moved to richer areas in Britain, France, and Germany. Many Europeans also migrated to Latin America.

At the end of World War II, another period of massive migrations occurred. About 12 million migrants, mostly from Bangladesh, Sri Lanka, Pakistan, and the Philippines, sought employment in Japan, Singapore, and Taiwan. Many Indians and Pakistanis migrated to the oil-rich countries in West Asia where they worked as servants and laborers. By 1980, more than half the labor force in Saudi Arabia, Libya, and Kuwait consisted of foreign workers.[51]

Several European states, especially Germany and Italy, which had lost millions of young men in the two world wars, imported "guest workers" to fill factory and service jobs. France and Switzerland also welcomed foreign labor. Over 30 million people migrated to Western Europe between 1945 and 1975.[52] Many of these immigrants came from areas that had been under French, Dutch, or British rule.

By 1980, Germany had more than four million guest workers, mostly Turks and West Asians. In 1950 there were hardly any Muslims in Western Europe, but by 2000, between fifteen and seventeen million Muslims were living there. Of this number, approximately five million lived in France, four million in Germany, and two million in Britain.[53]

Each of the nations that welcomed immigrants had its own policy toward the newcomers. The British government, following its colonial policy, encouraged cultural pluralism and helped develop separate ethnic institutions such as mosques, temples, and language schools.

A mosque in Paris, France

France, on the other hand, following its traditional colonial policy, expected immigrants to act like French people. The French Parliament even banned Muslim girls from wearing head scarves in school. During the first half of the twentieth century, the United States also followed a similar policy of assimilation and the schools and sought to make newcomers part of existing American culture. However, after 1960, the U.S. began to embrace a more multicultural policy that encouraged the various immigrant groups to retain their own cultures. The school curricula reflected this change, even as the new policy was hotly debated in the so-called "culture wars." In the U.S., Muslim girls were free to wear head scarves if they chose to do so. More recently, the French government has been trying to forbid Muslim women from wearing burkas.

Children's names are one indicator of the huge changes that have taken place in the population of Europe. In England, Jack was the most popular boy's name for years. However, in 2007, Muhammad, named after the Muslim prophet, was a close second.[54] In 2007 and 2008, the most common boys' name in Brussels, Belgium, was also Muhammad.[55]

Although the major religions and ideologies, including Christianity, Islam, Buddhism, Liberalism, and Marxism, have all opposed racism and ethnic violence, "primordial loyalties" have played a significant role in the post-1945 world. A primordial loyalty—one's emotional commitment to his or her race, religion, and language—often develops in nations that have two or more ethnic, religious, or linguistic groups.

Daniel Patrick Moynihan, a former United States senator, argued that liberalism and Marxism, the two dominant twentieth-century ideologies, kept many people from appreciating the emotional importance that ethnic loyalties exert.[56] Followers of both those ideologies believe people will ultimately transfer their primordial loyalties from their tribe or religious group to a larger identity, especially if identifying with that new group provides economic advantages. Liberalism, in particular, stresses individualism and does not recognize that group identity often transcends a longing for individual liberty and upward mobility.

Resistance to Globalization and Westernization

In 1993, the *New York Times* identified forty-eight ongoing ethnic wars: nine were in Europe; seven in West Asia; fifteen in Africa; thirteen in Asia; and four in Latin America.[57] In the 1990s, ethnic and religious strife tore Yugoslavia apart and led to the creation of Bosnia and Herzegovina, Croatia, Macedonia, Montenegro, Serbia, and Slovenia. In South Africa, the struggle between the minority ruling whites and subject majority blacks raged for years before white minority rule was overturned.

Colonialism heightened primordial loyalties. The English and Dutch consciously practiced a divide-and-rule strategy that played ethnic groups off against each other, such as Hindus and Muslims in India and different ethnic and language groups in Indonesia. As a result, when many nations gained independence, their populations were involved in emotionally charged ethnic conflicts.

In the 1980s, identity politics became enormously popular and self-identified groups insisted that the world recognize their uniqueness. A large number of these groups formed political parties and gained power. Minorities sought to rewrite school histories that they thought were biased in favor of the dominant group. Controversies over Japanese textbooks caused diplomatic disputes with both China and Korea. Educators in the U.S. rewrote school curricula to encompass material on a variety of ethnic groups, while opponents of multiculturalism mobilized to adopt textbooks that were more nationalistic and patriotic.

The Disney invasion

Some groups resist globalization because they fear it is another name for Westernization. Those with conservative views about the place of women, sexual practices, materialism, and personal freedom fiercely challenge what they see as an effort by the West to impose its values. Many fear that the Internet and its reliance on English is a new form of imperialism. They cite television, films, and popular music as the beachheads of a new invasion that seeks to transform the world into fast-food shops and strip malls. The resistance to globalization has also resulted in violent terrorist attacks and in angry protests at the meetings of the World Trade Organization.

Resistance to globalization as a form of Americanization is also evident. In Iran in 1979, the revolt against Americanization helped Iranians overthrow the shah and install an orthodox Muslim government that was hostile to many features of modern Western culture. In Saudi Arabia, Osama bin Laden championed a violent movement to throw Americans out of the country. As we have seen, anti-American sentiment served as a major motivation for the September 11 attacks.

Many Orthodox Christians and Muslims believed globalization and modernity seriously threatened their beliefs, especially family values and the role of women. Indians regularly march against Coca-Cola for its alleged exploitation of their scarce resources such as fresh drinking water. In other societies people picket McDonald's restaurants and Western films. Some critics of global trade and communication fear that unregulated globalization will result in one homogeneous world culture.

A FINAL CURTAIN CALL

As we end this final volume of *The Human Drama*, we leave the world in the early twenty-first century in the midst of the increasing influence of globalization. This new world, with over 190 nation-states struggling for a place in the new order, grew out of the bloody twentieth century that began with Europe at the pinnacle of world power, in political and economic control of much of Asia and Africa.

The achievement of world power among the European nations and the increasing power of Japan and the United States led to the two most destructive wars in world history and the breakdown of the global trading system. The instability of the world system in this period prompted many to question the idea of progress and the decline of democracy in the face of the new ideologies of Fascism and Communism. The new scientific discoveries of relativity and quantum physics only added to the sense of anxiety.

The era after World War II was a time of perhaps the most accelerated changes in human history. New developments in technology, especially in the field of communications, linked people around the world into a web of instant messaging, in which billions of dollars in wealth could be transferred with the touch of a computer button. The new technologies led to an unprecedented rise in productivity, especially as formerly colonized peoples formed a proliferation of new nations and pursued long delayed industrialization.

Ironically, the surge in the world's wealth did not seem to lead to a better material life for all the world's people. As of 2010, a third of them were forced to live on less than two dollars per day, and hundreds of millions lacked even basic foods. As we end the Human Drama, the widening gap between the rich nations and the poor and between the richest people and the rest is continuing to grow.

None of us knows how this most recent act will continue to unfold or what acts will follow. We do know that globalization has given rise to dramatic economic growth in many nations and has changed the lives of hundreds of millions of people. We also know that globalization has produced large groups of winners and a very large number of losers.

Having highlighted some of the major issues and challenges of the new global order, we hope that you have a clearer idea of how we all got to where we are now. As you looked back on the human drama, we hope you sometimes felt deeply sad about the choices people made. "Why did you make the decision to go to war, when the war accomplished almost nothing?" "How could you have enslaved millions of people just to make profits from sugar and coffee?" "Why have we been so indifferent to the poor?"

We hope that you have thought about the choices people made at the time, and that you are now encouraged, with the options available to you, to try to solve some of the challenges our communities, our countries, and the world community now face in this most complicated of times. The future, like the past, is not predetermined by some outside force; history is a compilation of the choices people make. Therefore, the future will be a reflection of the choices you and others around the world make.

With the growing acceptance that there are no utopian solutions to the challenges, most people carry on their everyday lives attending school, doing their homework, finding work, raising families, and participating in civic affairs, all while becoming increasingly aware that we are each responsible for the survival of our fragile planet. We may also be realizing that the challenges we all face can be solved only through cooperation and sacrifice, especially by those living in the richest nations in the world.

NOTES

Act One

1. Quoted in Walbank et al., *Civilization: Past and Present*, 2:412.
2. Ibid., 2:414.
3. Ibid., 2:440.
4. Steven Mintz, "Learn About World War I," Digital History (2007), http://www.digitalhistory.uh.edu/modules/ww1/index.cfm.
5. John Maynard Keynes, *The Economic Consequences of the Peace*, 211.
6. Walbank et al., *Civilization: Past and Present*, 454.
7. Keynes, *Economic Consequences of the Peace*, 278–79.
8. Jennifer Rosenberg, "Flappers in the Roaring Twenties," About.com: Twentieth Century History, http://history1900s.about.com/od/1920s/a/flappers.htm.
9. Valerie Hansen and Kenneth R. Curtis, *Voyages in World History*, vol. 2 (Boston: Wadsworth Cengage Learning, 2010), 325.
10. Richard Overy, *Russia's War*, 119.
11. Serguey Ivanov, Anatoly Vichnevsky, and Sergei Zakharov, "Population Policy in Russia," chapter 118 in Graziella Caselli, Jacques Vallin, and Guillaume Wunsch, *Demography: Analysis and Synthesis: A Treatise in Population Studies*, 4 vols. (Amsterdam; Boston: Academic Press [an imprint of Elsevier], 2006), 4:426.
12. Robert C. Tucker, *Stalin As Revolutionary, 1879–1929: A Study in History and Personality* (New York: W.W. Norton, 1973), 228.
13. Orest Subtelny, *Ukraine: A History*, 420, 421.
14. Robert Conquest, *The Great Terror: A Reassessment* (New York: Oxford University Press, 1991), 132–38.

Act Two

1. Julian Thomas, quoted in Connie McNeely, *Constructing the Nation-State*, 7.
2. "The Fourteen Points Essential to Peace Set Forth by Mr. Wilson on January 8 Last," *New York Times*, October 9, 1918, 2.
3. William Digby, in *"Prosperous" British India: A Revelation from Official Records* (London: Irwin, 1901), claims that the Industrial Revolution in Britain was funded substantially by wealth obtained from British-ruled India.
4. For various estimates of the number, see Leonard A. Gordon, review of

Paul R. Greenough's *Prosperity and Misery in Modern Bengal: The Famine of 1943–1944*, in *The American Historical Review* 88, no. 4 (Oct. 1983): 1051; Richard Stevenson, *Bengal Tiger and British Lion: An Account of the Bengal Famine of 1943* (iUniverse, 2005), 138–39; and Michael Portillo, "Listen to the Bengal Famine," The Things We Forgot to Remember (BBC Radio 4/Open University, January 7, 2008), http://www.open2.net/thingsweforgot/bengalfamine_programme.html.

5. Rudrangshu Mukherjee, *The Penguin Gandhi Reader* (London: Penguin, 1995), 65, 66.

6. Eric Wolf, *Peasant Wars of the Twentieth Century*, 167.

7. Atul Kohli, "Where Do High Growth Political Economies Come From? The Japanese Lineage of Korea's 'Developmental State,'" *World Development* 22, no. 9 (September 1994): 1273.

8. Malcom E. Yapp, *The Making of the Modern Near East, 1792–1923* (London; New York: Longman, 1987), 290.

9. UK Archive files PRO CAB 27/2, cited in Doreen Ingrams, *Palestine Papers, 1917–1922: Seeds of Conflict* (New York: George Braziller, 1973), 48.

10. Richard W. Bulliet et al., *The Earth and Its Peoples: A Global History*, vol. 2, *Since 1500*, 3rd ed. (Boston: Houghton Mifflin, 2005), 793.

11. Ibid.

12. Marvine Howe, *Turkey Today: A Nation Divided over Islam's Revival*, 76.

13. Gertrude Bell, quoted in Emory C. Bogle, *The Modern Middle East: From Imperialism to Freedom, 1800–1958* (Upper Saddle River, N.J.: Prentice Hall, 1996), 103.

14. Bulliet et al., *The Earth and Its Peoples*, 793.

Act Three

1. Jones and Montgomery, *Civilization Through the Centuries*, 791.

2. James E. McLellan III and Harold Dorn, *Science and Technology in World History: An Introduction*, 348.

3. Calvin Tomkins, *Duchamp: A Biography* (New York: Henry Holt, 1996), 83.

4. Clive Ponting, *Progress and Barbarism: The World in the Twentieth Century,* 131.

5. Jones and Montgomery, *Civilization Through the Centuries*, 738.

6. Thomas O'Brien, "Making the Americas: U.S. Business People and Latin Americans from the Age of Revolutions to the Era of Globalization," *The History Compass* 2 (2004): LA 067, 12.

7. Francois Caron, trans. Barbara Bray, *An Economic History of Modern France*, p. 269.

8. Winston Churchill, *Blood, Sweat, and Tears*, 297.

9. Jones and Montgomery, *Civilization Through the Centuries*, 778.

10. John Ellis, *World War II: A Statistical Survey: The Essential Facts and Figures for All the Combatants* (New York: Facts on File, 1993), 110.

11. "Bloodiest Battle in History Remembered," RT Top Stories, February 2, 2008, http://rt.com/Top_News/2008-02-02/Bloodiest_battle_in_history_remembered.html?fullstory.

12. George Feifer, *Tennozan: The Battle of Okinawa and the Atomic Bomb* (New York: Ticknor & Fields, 1992), 578; Roy E. Appleman et al., *Okinawa: The Last Battle*, 468.

13. Ponting, *World History*, 781.

14. Ponting, *Progress and Barbarism*, 281; World War II Casualties: Human Losses by Country, http://en.wikipedia.org/wiki/World_War_II_casualties#Human_losses_by_country; "How Many American Troops Have Died in War?" History News Network News Archives, http://hnn.us/roundup/comments/44965.html.

15. R. J. Rummel, preface to *Democide: Nazi Genocide and Mass Murder* (New Brunswick, N.J.: Transaction Publishers, 1991).

Act Four

1. Ponting, *World History*, 781.

2. Ibid.

3. Antony Beevor, "'They raped every German female from eight to 80,'" *The Manchester Guardian*, 1 May 2002.

4. Jones and Montgomery, *Civilization Through the Centuries*, 810.

5. Ibid.

6. Charter of the United Nations: Preamble, 1945, http://www.un.org/en/documents/charter/preamble.shtml.

7. Winston S. Churchill, "Iron Curtain Speech," March 5, 1946, excerpted in Modern History Sourcebook, Fordham University, http://www.fordham.edu/halsall/mod/churchill-iron.html.

8. "European Union: Evolution," The Columbia Electronic Encyclopedia, 6th ed., 2007, http://www.infoplease.com/ce6/history/A0858055.html.

9. Allen C. Kelley, "Economic Consequences of Population Change in the Third World," *Journal of Economic Literature* 26, no. 4 (December 1988): 1687.

10. Jawaharlal Nehru, Speech on the Granting of Indian Independence, August 14, 1947, Modern History Sourcebook, http://www.fordham.edu/halsall/mod/1947nehru1.html.

11. "Pakistani Elections 2008: Political History of Pakistan," http://www.elections.com.pk/contents.php?i=4.

12. Ami Isseroff, "The Population of Palestine Prior to 1948," Population of

Ottoman and Mandate Palestine: Statistical and Demographic Considerations, MidEast Web, http://www.mideastweb.org/palpop.htm.

13. Lance Morrow, "The Shoes of Imelda Marcos," *Time*, March 31, 1986, http://www.time.com/time/magazine/article/0,9171,961002,00.html.

Act Five

1. "Great Leap Forward," The Columbia Electronic Encyclopedia (Columbia University Press; Pearson Education, publishing as Infoplease, 2007), http://www.infoplease.com/ce6/history/A0821672.html.

2. Matthew White, "Source List and Detailed Death Tolls for the Twentieth Century Hemoclysm," http://users.erols.com/mwhite28/warstat1.htm.

3. Katrina Vanden Heuvel and Stephen F. Cohen, "Gorbachev on 1989" (cover story), *Nation* 289 (November 16, 2009): 11.

4. David Christian, *Maps of Time: An Introduction to Big History*, 463.

5. Henry Luce, "The American Century," *Life* Magazine, February 17, 1941.

6. Martin Calhoun, "U.S. Military Spending, 1945–1996: Annual Military Spending," Center for Defense Information, 1996, http://www.cdi.org/Issues/milspend.html.

7. Hobsbawm, *The Age of Extremes,* 337.

8. Chalmers Johnson, *Blowback: The Costs and Consequences of American Empire*, 178.

9. Chalmers Johnson, *MITI and the Japanese Miracle*, vii.

10. GeoHive, "Countries with Highest Population for 1950, 2010, and 2050," http://www.geohive.com/earth/population3.aspx, retrieved September 4, 2010.

11. Gisela Bock and Pat Thane, *Maternity and Gender Policies*, excerpted in Hughes and Hughes, *Women in World History*, vol. 2, 157.

Act Six

1. Katrina Vanden Heuvel and Stephen F. Cohen, "Gorbachev on 1989" (cover story), *Nation* 289 (November 16, 2009): 11.

2. Peace Pledge Union, "Bosnia 1995: The Genocide," http://www.ppu.org.uk/genocide/g_bosnia1.html.

3. William Cooper, "Economic Conditions in Mid-1996," in chapter 6, "The Economy," of *Russia: A Country Study*, ed. Glenn E. Curtis (Washington, D.C.: Federal Research Division, Library of Congress, 1998), http://lcweb2.loc.gov/frd/cs/rutoc.html, retrieved 2008-11-26 from http://lcweb2.loc.gov/cgi-bin/query/r?frd/cstdy:@field(DOCID+ru0119).

4. Abstract for Ariel Cohen, "Facing the Russian Rhetoric in Eurasia," Analytical Articles, Central Asia–Caucasus Institute Analyst, http://

www.cacianalyst.org/?q=taxonomy/term/2/0&page=63.

5. "People" and "Economy," European Union, in Central Intelligence Agency, *The World Factbook,* https://www.cia.gov/library/publications/the-world-factbook/geos/ee.html.

6. Richard Burdett, professor of architecture and urbanism at the London School of Economics, quoted in David Barboza, "China Builds Its Dreams, and Some Fear a Bubble," *New York Times*, October 18, 2005, http://www.nytimes.com/2005/10/18/business/worldbusiness/18bubble. html.

7. Rumana Hussain, "China's Next 30 Years: Building the World's Biggest Cities," *Now Public*, December 12, 2008, http://www.nowpublic.com/world/china-s-next-30-years-building-world-s-biggest-cities-1.

8. Nicholas D. Kristof, "A Reassessment of How Many Died In the Military Crackdown in Beijing," *The New York Times,* June 21, 1989, http://www.nytimes.com/1989/06/21/world/a-reassessment-of-how-many-died-in-the-military-crackdown-in-beijing.html.

9. "China's Growing Economy Mints Billionaires," *New York Times*, October 13, 2009, http://www.nytimes.com/2009/10/14/business/global/14rich.html.

10. Peilei Fan, "Innovation Capacity and Economic Development: China and India," United Nations University–World Institute for Development Economics Research, Research Paper No. 2008/31 (March 2008): 1, http://www.wider.unu.edu/publications/working-papers/research-papers/2008/en_GB/rp2008-31/.

11. Ibid., abstract.

12. Quoted in Chalmers Johnson, *Nemesis: The Last Days of the American Republic*, 54.

13. "With Bill Gates as Pin-Up, Vietnamese Rush into E-Business," Sawf News, November 25, 2006, http://www.sawfnews.com/business/28417.aspx.

14. "Third World Countries in Terms of their Human Development," One World—Nations Online: Countries of the Third World, July 24, 2009, http://www.nationsonline.org/oneworld/third_world.htm#Human-Development.

15. "Enhancing Innovation in Business and Social Issues," report from the World Economic Forum on Latin America, April 15–16, 2008, http://www.weforum.org/pdf/SummitReports/LatinAmerica2008/social_issues.htm.

16. Elisabeth Malkin, "Nafta's Promise, Unfulfilled," *New York Times*, March 23, 2009, http://www.nytimes.com/2009/03/24/business/worldbusiness/24peso.html.

17. Wairagala Wakabi, "'Worst drought in a decade' leaves Kenya crippled," *The Lancet* 367, issue 9514 (March 18, 2006): 891–92.

18. UNAIDS, "2008 Report on the Global AIDS Epidemic," http://www. unaids.org/en/KnowledgeCentre/HIVData/GlobalReport/2008/2008_Glo bal_report.asp.

19. Roll Back Malaria, "Malaria in Africa," http://www.rollbackmalaria. org/cmc_upload/0/000/015/370/RBMInfosheet_3.htm.

20. John Simon, quoted in Charles W. Corey, "Africa Is New Frontier of Global Economy," http://www.america.gov/st/econ-english/2008/Octo-ber/20081010111004WCyeroC0.1286432.html.

21. "African Democracy," Burning Our Money blog, July 1, 2008, http:// burningourmoney.blogspot.com/2008/07/african-democracy.html.

22. Samuel P. Huntington, "The Lonely Superpower," *Foreign Affairs* 78, no. 2 (March–April 1999): 36.

23. Chalmers Johnson, "America's Empire of Bases," January 15, 2004, http://www.tomdispatch.com/post/1181/chalmers_johnson_on_garrison-ing_the_planet.

24. Ibid.

25. Andrew J. Bacevich, *American Empire: The Realities and Consequences of U.S. Diplomacy*; Niall Ferguson, *Empire: The Rise and Demise of the British World Order and the Lessons for Global Power*; Paul Kennedy, *The Rise and Fall of the Great Powers: Economic Change and Military Conflict from 1500 to 2000*.

26. Kennedy, *The Rise and Fall of the Great Powers*, xvi.

27. Ewen MacAskill, "US Seen as a Bigger Threat to Peace than Iran, Worldwide Poll Suggests," *The Guardian*, June 15, 2006, http://www. guardian.co.uk/world/2006/jun/15/usa.iran.

28. Conversation with Prof. Farhad Kazemi, New York University, April 1980.

29. "The Iran-Iraq War (1980–1988)," GlobalSecurity.org, http://www.glob-alsecurity.org/military/world/war/iran-iraq.htm.

30. Institute for Women's Policy Research, "The Benefits of Unionization for Workers in the Retail Food Industry," IWPR Publication #C351 (February 2002), 1, http://iwpr.org/pdf/c351.pdf.

31. See Adam Smith, *Moral Sentiments*, book 2, chapter 2, section 3.3 and 4:86.

Act Seven

1. "China Runs to Pick Up the Phone," *Asia Times Online*, September 30, 2006, http://www.atimes.com/atimes/China_Business/HI30Cb01.html.

2. World Internet Usage and Population Statistics (statistics for June 10, 2010), http://www.internetworldstats.com/stats.htm.

3. Richard Kostelanetz, *Conversing with Cage*, 2nd ed. (New York: Rout-ledge, 2003), 67–68.

4. Lester R. Brown, *Eco-Economy: Building an Economy for the Earth* (New York: W.W. Norton, 2001), 11.

5. Ibid., 93.

6. Ponting, *Progress and Barbarism*, 544.

7. B. D. Hong and E. R. Slatick, "Carbon Dioxide Emission Factors for Coal," Energy Information Administration, *Quarterly Coal Report, January–April 1994*, DOE/EIA-0121(94/Q1) (Washington, D.C., August 1994), 1–8, available at http://www.eia.doe.gov/cneaf/coal/quarterly/co2_article/co2.html.

8. Ponting, *Progress and Barbarism*, 292.

9. See Ward Morehouse and M. Arun Subramaniam, *The Bhopal Tragedy: What Really Happened and What It Means for American Workers and Communities at Risk.*

10. Lester Brown, *State of the World*, 1999, quoted in David Christian, *Maps of Time: An Introduction to Big History* (Berkeley, Calif.: University of California Press, 2005), 460.

11. Andrew Cherlin, *The Marriage-Go-Round* (New York: Alfred A. Knopf, 2009), 4.

12. "Divorce Rate (Most Recent) by Country," People Statistics, NationMaster.com, http://www.nationmaster.com/graph/peo_div_rat-people-divorce-rate.

13. Lizabeth Cohen, *A Consumers' Republic: The Politics of Mass Consumption in Postwar America*, 7–8.

14. See Tony Judt, *Ill Fares the Land* (New York: Penguin, 2010), and Lizabeth Cohen, *A Consumers' Republic.*

15. Josh MacPhee, "Street Art and Social Movements," Justseeds blog, February 17, 2009, http://www.justseeds.org/blog/2009/02/street_art_and_social_movement.html.

16. Hobsbawm, *The Age of Extremes: A History of the World, 1914–1991*, 341.

17. W. H. Auden, "The Age of Anxiety," in *Collected Poems*, edited by Edward Mendelson (New York: The Modern Library, 1991), 479.

18. Phillip C. Bleek, "U.S., Russia Sign Treaty Cutting Deployed Nuclear Forces," *Arms Control Today* (June 2002), http://www.armscontrol.org/act/2002_06/sortjune02.

19. "Russia to Keep at Least 1,500 Nuclear Warheads," Russian Information Agency Novosti, October 6, 2009, http://en.rian.ru/russia/200906 10/155218357.html.

20. "Status of World Nuclear Forces," Nuclear Information Project, Federation of American Scientists, http://www.fas.org/programs/ssp/nukes/nuclearweapons/nukestatus.html.

21. "800 Terror Cells Active in Country," *The Times of India*, August 12, 2008, http://timesofindia.indiatimes.com/news/india/800-terror-cells-

active-in-country/articleshow/3356589.cms.

22. Press Information Bureau (Government of India) press release, "HM announces measures to enhance security," December 11, 2008, http://pib. nic.in/release/release.asp?relid=45446.

23. Sean Alfano, "War Casualties Pass 9/11 Death Toll," CBS News, September 22, 2006, http://www.cbsnews.com/stories/2006/09/22/terror/ main2035427.shtml.

24. Karen Armstrong, in "Fundamentalism and the Modern World," A Dialogue with Karen Armstrong, Susannah Heschel, Jim Wallis, and Feisal Abdul Rauf, *Sojourners Magazine* (March–April 2002), http://www. sojo.net/index.cfm?action=magazine.article&issue=soj0203&article=020310.

25. "Salafi Islam," GlobalSecurity.org, http://www.globalsecurity.org/military/intro/islam-salafi.htm; Nuh Ha Mim Keller, "Who or What is a Salafi? Is Their Approach Balid?" (1995), http://www.masud.co.uk/ ISLAM/nuh/salafi.htm.

26. In "Fundamentalism and the Modern World," A Dialogue with Karen Armstrong, Susannah Heschel, Jim Wallis, and Feisal Abdul Rauf.

27. Karen Armstrong, ibid.

28. Ponting, *Progress and Barbarism*, 502.

29. Ibid., 523.

30. Bruce Sharp, "Counting Hell: The Death Toll of the Khmer Rouge Regime in Cambodia," April 2005, http://www.mekong.net/cambodia/ deaths.htm

31. Art Ryan and L. Seachon, "Insurgencies in History: A Blueprint for Future Strategy," Philippine Army, OG5 Digest, October–December 2004, p. 16, http://www.army.mil.ph/OG5_articles/Insegencies.htm.

32. Ponting, *Progress and Barbarism*, 506.

33. Howard W. French, "Kagome's Hidden War in the Congo," *New York Review of Books*, September 4, 2009, 45.

34. Ibid., 44.

35. Jeffrey Gettleman, "Symbol of Unhealed Congo: Male Rape Victims," *New York Times*, August 5, 2009, A-1, http://www.nytimes.com/2009/08 /05/world/africa/05congo.html.

36. DarfurScores.Org, "Genocide in Darfur, Sudan," http://www.darfurscores.org/darfur.

37. Peter Phillips and Project Censored, *Censored 2007:The Top 25 Censored Stories* (New York: Seven Stories Press, 2006), 207.

38. See the UNICEF Report, *Progress For Children: A Child Survival Report Card, Volume 1, 2004* (New York: UNICEF Division of Communication), http://www.unicef.org/publications/index_23557.html.

39. Arloc Sherman and Chad Stone, "Income Gaps Between Very Rich and Everyone Else More than Tripled in Last Three Decades, New Data

Show," Center on Budget and Policy Priorities report, June 25, 2010, http://www.cbpp.org/files/6-25-10inc.pdf.

40. Nicholas D. Kristof and Sheryl WuDunn, "The Women's Crusade," *New York Times Magazine*, August 17, 2009, http://www.nytimes.com /2009/08/23/magazine/23Women-t.html.

41. Sten Johansson and Ola Nygren, "The Missing Girls of China: A New Demographic Account," *Population and Development Review* 17, no. 1 (March 1991): 40–41.

42. Kristof and WuDunn, "The Women's Crusade."

43. Amartya Sen, "More Than 100 Million Women Are Missing," *New York Review of Books* 37, no. 20 (December 20, 1990): 37.

44. Jonathan Manthorpe, "China Battles Slave Trading in Women: Female Infanticide Fuels a Brisk Trade in Wives," *The Vancouver Sun*, January 11, 1999.

45. John-Thor Dahlburg, "Where Killing Baby Girls 'is no big sin,'" *The Los Angeles Times*, February 28, 1994.

46. U.S. Department of State, "Introduction to State Department's Trafficking in Persons Report," June 4, 2008, http://www.america.gov/st/text-trans-english/2008/June/20080604114725eaifas0.7835047.html.

47. Minga: Teens Fighting Sexual Exploitation, http://mingagroup.org/theissue/.

48. Alex Perry and Mae Sai, "The Shame," cover story, *Time Asia* special issue on child slavery, June 21, 1993, http://www.time.com/time/asia/features/slavery/cover3.html.

49. Robyn Dixon, "Africa's Bitter Cycle of Child Slavery," *Los Angeles Times*, July 12, 2009.

50. Ponting, *Progress and Barbarism*, 47.

51. Ibid., 49.

52. Ibid., 48.

53. Joel S. Fetzer and J. Christopher Soper, *Muslims and the State in Britain, France, and Germany* (Cambridge: Cambridge University Press, 2005), 36.

54. Helen Nugent and Nadia Menuhin, "Muhammad is No 2 in Boy's Names," *The Sunday Times* (London), June 6, 2007, http://www.times-online.co.uk/tol/news/uk/article1890354.ece.

55. Adrian Michaels, "Muslim Europe: The Demographic Time Bomb Transforming Our Continent," *The Telegraph* (UK), August 8, 2009, http://www.telegraph.co.uk/news/worldnews/europe/5994047/Muslim-Europe-the-demographic-time-bomb-transforming-our-continent.html; DPA, "Mohamed the Most Popular Baby Name in Brussels in 2007," Earth Times, September 17, 2008, http://www.earthtimes.org/articles /news/232401,mohamed-the-most-popular-baby-name-in-brussels-in-2007.html; Esther, "Belgium: Mohamed Most Popular Name in Brus-

sels, Antwerp," Islam in Europe blog, November 24, 2009, http://
islamineurope.blogspot.com/2009/11/belgium-mohamed-most-popular-
name-in.html.

56. David Binder and Barbara Crossette, "As Ethnic Wars Multiply, U.S.
Strives for a Policy," *New York Times*, February 7, 1993, http://www.
nytimes.com/1993/02/07/world/as-ethnic-wars-multiply-us-strives-for-a-
policy.html.

57. Ibid.

SELECTED BIBLIOGRAPHY

Adas, Michael. "'High' Imperialism and the 'New' History." In *Islamic & European Expansion: The Forging of a Global Order*, ed. Michael Adas for the American Historical Association. Philadelphia: Temple University Press, 1993.

Adshead, S. A. M. *China in World History*. 3rd ed. New York: St. Martin's Press, 2000.

Anderson, Benedict. *Imagined Communities: Reflections on the Origin and Spread of Nationalism*. 2nd rev. and extended ed., London and New York: Verso, 1991.

Appleman, Roy E., James M. Burns, Russell A. Gugeler, and John Stevens. *Okinawa: The Last Battle*. Vol. 2, part 11, of *United States Army in World War II: The War in the Pacific*. Washington, D.C.: U.S. Government Printing Office, 1948.

Bacevich, Andrew J. *American Empire: The Realities and Consequences of U.S. Diplomacy*. Cambridge, Mass.: Harvard University Press, 2002.

Beard, Charles. *The Industrial Revolution*. New York: Charles Scribner's Sons, 1919.

Bell, Gertrude, quoted in Emory C. Bogle, *The Modern Middle East: From Imperialism to Freedom, 1800–1958*. Englewood, N.J.: Prentice Hall, 1996.

Bolívar, Simón. *El Libertador: Writings of Simón Bolívar*. Trans. Frederick H. Fornoff. Ed. with an introduction and notes by David Bushnell. New York: Oxford University Press, 2003.

Bowden, Witt. "The Rise of the Great Manufacturers in England, 1760–1790." Ph.D. thesis, University of Pennsylvania, 1919.

Bryan, Patrick E. *The Haitian Revolution and Its Effects*. Kingston, Jamaica; Exeter, N.H.: Heinemann, 1984.

Bryson, Bill. *A Short History of Nearly Everything*. New York: Broadway Books, 2003.

Bulliet, Richard W., ed. *The Columbia History of the 20th Century*. New York: Columbia University Press, 1998.

Burke, Edmund, III, and Kenneth Pomeranz. *The Environment and World History*. Berkeley, Calif.: University of California Press, 2009.

Calvin, John. *The Necessity of Reforming the Church*, 1543. Translated by Henry Beveridge, 1843. Dallas: Protestant Heritage Press, 1995.

Caron, François, trans. Barbara Bray. *An Economic History of Modern France*. New York: Columbia University Press, 1979.

Chandra, Bipan. *Modern India*. New Delhi: National Council of Educational Research and Training, 1971.

Chatterjee, Partha. *The Nation and Its Fragments: Colonial and Postcolonial Histories*. Princeton, N.J.: Princeton University Press, 1993.

Chaudhuri, K. N. *Trade and Civilisation in the Indian Ocean: An Economic History from the Rise of Islam to 1750*. Cambridge; New York: Cambridge University Press, 1985.

Christian, David. *Maps of Time: An Introduction to Big History*. Berkeley, Calif.: University of California Press, 2005.

Churchill, Winston. *Blood, Sweat, and Tears*. New York: G.P. Putnam's Sons, 1941.

Cohen, Lizabeth. *A Consumers' Republic: The Politics of Mass Consumption in Postwar America*. New York: Knopf, 2003.

Coles, Paul. *The Ottoman Impact on Europe*. London: Thames and Hudson, 1968.

Cooke, Mervyn. *Britten and the Far East: Asian Influences in the Music of Benjamin Britten*. Woodbridge, England: Boydell and Brewer Publishers, 1998.

Crafts, N. F. R. "British Economic Growth, 1700–1831: A Review of the Evidence." *Economic History Review* 36, no. 2 (May 1983): 177–99.

Dalrymple, William. "The Venetian Treasure Hunt." *The New York Review of Books* 54, no. 12 (July 19, 2007): 29–31.

De Blij, Harm J., and Peter O. Muller. *Geography: Realms, Regions, and Concepts*. 8th ed. New York: John Wiley & Sons, 1997.

Dekkerr, Eduard Dawes (Multatuli). *Max Havelaar*, quoted in William D. Bowman, Frank M. Chiteji, and J. Megan Greene, *Imperialism in the Modern World: Sources and Interpretations*. Upper Saddle River, N.J.: Pearson Prentice Hall, 2007.

Dickens, Charles. *Hard Times*. London: Penguin Classics, 1995.

Digby, William. *"Prosperous" British India: A Revelation from Official Records*. London: T. F. Unwin, 1901.

Diop, David. "Africa." In *A Book of African Verse*, ed. John O. Reed and Clive Wake. London: Heinemann, 1967.

Elkins, Caroline. *Imperial Reckoning: The Untold Story of Britain's Gulag in Kenya*. New York: Henry Holt & Co., 2005.

Embree, Ainslee, ed. *The Hindu Tradition*. New York: Columbia University Press, 1972.

Fairbank, John K., Edwin O. Reischauer, and Albert M. Craig. *East Asia: The Modern Transformation*. Boston: Houghton Mifflin Company, 1965.

Feifer, George. *Tennozan: The Battle of Okinawa and the Atomic Bomb*. Boston: Houghton Mifflin, 1992.

Ferguson, Niall. *Empire: The Rise and Demise of the British World Order and the Lessons for Global Power*. London: Penguin Books, 2002.

Fernández-Armesto, Felipe. *The World: A History.* Upper Saddle River, N.J.: Pearson/Prentice Hall, 2007.

Flynn, Dennis O., Lionel Frost, and A. J. H. Latham, ed. *Pacific Centuries: Pacific and Pacific Rim History since the Sixteenth Century.* London: Routledge; New York: Questia Media America, 1999.

Frank, Andre Gunder. *ReOrient: Global Economy in the Asian Age.* Berkeley, Calif.: University of California Press, 1998.

Frank, Andre Gunder, and Barry K. Gills. *The World System: Five Hundred Years or Five Thousand?* New York: Routledge, 1993.

Garraty, John A., and Peter Gay, eds. *The Columbia History of the World.* New York: Harper & Row, 1981.

Gately, Iain. *Tobacco: A Cultural History of How an Exotic Plant Seduced Civilization.* New York: Grove Press, 2001.

Guha, Naresh. *W. B. Yeats: An Indian Approach.* Calcutta: Jadavpur University, 1968.

Headrick, Daniel. *The Tools of Empire: Technology and European Imperialism in the Nineteenth Century.* New York: Oxford University Press, 1981.

Hobsbawm, Eric. *The Age of Extremes: A History of the World, 1914–1991.* New York: Vintage Books, 1994.

Hourani, Albert. "The Ottoman Background of the Modern Middle East." In Kemal H. Karpat, ed., *The Ottoman State and Its Place in World History.* Leiden: Brill, 1974.

Howe, Marvine. *Turkey Today: A Nation Divided over Islam's Revival.* Boulder, Colo.: Westview Press, 2000.

Hsü, Immanuel C. Y. *The Rise of Modern China,* 5th ed. New York: Oxford University Press, 1995.

Huff, Toby E. *The Rise of Early Modern Science: Islam, China, and the West.* Cambridge: Cambridge University Press, 1995.

Hughes, Sarah S., and Brady Hughes. *Women in World History,* vol. 2, *Readings from 1500 to the Present.* Armonk, N.Y., and London: M. E. Sharpe, 1997.

Itzkowitz, Norman. *Ottoman Empire and Islamic Tradition.* Chicago: University of Chicago Press, 1980.

Johnson, Chalmers. *Blowback: The Costs and Consequences of American Empire.* New York: Henry Holt and Company, 2000.

_____. *Japan: Who Governs? The Rise of the Developmental State.* New York: Norton, 1995.

_____. *MITI and the Japanese Miracle: The Growth of Industrial Policy, 1925–1975.* Stanford, Calif.: Stanford University Press, 1982.

_____. *Nemesis: The Last Days of the American Republic.* New York: Henry Holt and Company, 2006.

Jones, Wilbur Devereux, and Horace Montgomery. *Civilization Through the*

Centuries. Boston: Ginn and Company, 1960.

Kelley, Allen C. "Economic Consequences of Population Change in the Third World," *Journal of Economic Literature* 26, no. 4 (December 1988): 1685–1728.

Kennedy, Paul. *The Rise and Fall of the Great Powers: Economic Change and Military Conflict from 1500 to 2000*. 1st ed. New York: Random House, 1987.

Keynes, John Maynard. *The Economic Consequences of the Peace*. London: Macmillan and Co., 1919.

Kohn, Hans. *The Idea of Nationalism: A Study of Its Origins and Background*. New York: MacMillan Co., 1944.

Marcus, Alan I. *Building Western Civilization: From the Advent of Writing to the Age of Steam*. New York: Harcourt Brace College Publishers, 1998.

Marks, Robert B. *The Origins of the Modern World: A Global and Ecological Narrative*. Lanham, Md.: Rowman & Littlefield, 2002.

McClellan, James E., III, and Harold Dorn. *Science and Technology in World History: An Introduction*. Baltimore: Johns Hopkins University Press, 1999.

McNeely, Connie. *Constructing the Nation-State: International Organization and Prescriptive Action*. Hove, East Sussex, England: Greenwood Publishing Group, 1994.

McNeill, J. R., and William H. McNeill. *The Human Web: A Bird's-Eye View of World History*. New York: W.W. Norton, 2003.

McNeill, William. *The Age of Gunpowder Empires, 1450–1800*. Washington, D.C.: American Historical Association, 1989.

Metcalf, Barbara Daly, and Thomas R. Metcalf. *A Concise History of India*. New York: Cambridge University Press, 2002.

Mill, James. *History of British India*, vol. 2. London: James Madden & Co., 1840.

Morehouse, Ward, and M. Arun Subramaniam. *The Bhopal Tragedy: What Really Happened and What It Means for American Workers and Communities at Risk*. New York: Council on International and Public Affairs, 1986.

Naylor, Philip Chiviges. *France and Algeria: A History of Decolonization and Transformation*. Gainesville: University Press of Florida, 2000.

Nehru, Jawaharlal. *Glimpses of World History*. Bombay: Asia Publishing House, 1962.

Overy, Richard. *Russia's War*. London: Penguin Press, 1998.

Parthasarathi, Prasannan. "Rethinking Wages and Competitiveness in the Eighteenth Century: Britain and South India." *Past and Present* 158 (Feb. 1998): 79–109.

Pearson, Robert P., and Leon Clark. *Through Middle Eastern Eyes*. New York: Center for International Training and Education, 1993.

Persons, Stow. *American Minds: A History of Ideas.* New York: Holt, 1958.

Pomeranz, Kenneth. *The Great Divergence: China, Europe, and the Making of the Modern World Economy.* Princeton, N.J.: Princeton University Press, 2000.

Pomeranz, Kenneth, and Steven Topik. *The World that Trade Created: Society, Culture and the World Economy, 1400 to the Present.* Armonk, N.Y.: M. E. Sharpe, 1999.

Ponting, Clive. *Progress and Barbarism: The World in the Twentieth Century.* London: Chatto & Windus, 1998.

_____. *World History: A New Perspective.* London: Chatto & Windus, 2000.

Reischauer, Edwin O., and John K. Fairbank. *East Asia: The Great Tradition.* Boston: Houghton Mifflin Company, 1960.

Rietbergen, Peter. *Europe: A Cultural History.* London: Routledge, 1998.

Robinson, Francis, ed. *The Cambridge Illustrated History of the Islamic World.* Cambridge, England: Cambridge University Press, 1996.

Robinson, James Harvey. *Readings in European History,* vol. 2. Boston: Ginn & Company, 1906.

Runciman, Steven. *A History of the Crusades,* vol. 3: *The Kingdom of Acre.* Cambridge: Cambridge University Press, 1954.

Shapin, Steven. *The Scientific Revolution.* Chicago: University of Chicago Press, 1996.

Smith, Adam. *An Inquiry into the Nature and Causes of Wealth of Nations,* ed. R. H. Campbell and A. S. Skinner. London: Clarendon Press, 1976.

_____. *The Theory of Moral Sentiments,* ed. D. D. Raphael and A. L. Macfie. New York: Clarendon Press, 1976.

Stearns, Peter N. *The Industrial Revolution in World History.* Boulder, Colo.: Westview Press, 2007.

Stromberg, Roland N. *European Intellectual History Since 1789.* 4th ed. Englewood Cliffs, N.J.: Prentice-Hall, Inc., 1986.

Subtelny, Orest. *Ukraine: A History.* 3rd ed. Toronto: University of Toronto Press, 2000.

Thompson, E. P. "Time, Work-Discipline and Industrial Capitalism." Chapter 6 of *Customs in Common* (London: Penguin Books, 1993). Available at http://libcom.org/library/time-work-discipline-industrial-capitalism-e-p-thompson.

Tilly, Charles. *Coercion, Capital, and European States, AD 990–1992.* Cambridge, Mass., and Oxford, England: Blackwell, 1992.

Tomkins, Calvin. *Duchamp: A Biography.* New York: Henry Holt, 1996.

Trocki, Carl. *Opium, Empire and the Global Economy: A Study of the Asian Opium Trade, 1750–1950.* London: Routledge, 1999.

Tytler, Sarah. *Marie Antoinette.* Boston: G.P. Putnam's Sons, 1883.

Vernède, R. V. *British Life in India.* Delhi: Oxford University Press, 1995.

Vernoff, Edward, and Peter J. Seybolt. *Through Chinese Eyes: Tradition, Revolution, and Transformation*. 3rd ed. New York: Center for International Training and Education, 2007.

Walbank, T. Walter, Alastair M. Taylor, and George Barr Carson, Jr. *Civilization: Past and Present*, vol. 2. Chicago: Scott, Foresman and Company, 1965.

Wichmann, Siegfried. *Japonisme: The Japanese Influence on Western Art since 1858*. New York: Thames and Hudson, 1999.

Wolf, Eric. *Peasant Wars of the Twentieth Century*. Norman, Okla.: University of Oklahoma Press, 1969.

SOURCES OF ILLUSTRATIONS

Act Five

Act Six

Act Seven

INDEX

CPSIA information can be obtained
at www.ICGtesting.com
Printed in the USA
FSHW01n1210280818
51626FS